# SCIENCE AND
# RELIGION

W. A. Sumner

The Book Guild Ltd

First published in Great Britain in 2020 by
The Book Guild Ltd
9 Priory Business Park
Wistow Road, Kibworth
Leicestershire, LE8 0RX
Freephone: 0800 999 2982
www.bookguild.co.uk
Email: info@bookguild.co.uk
Twitter: @bookguild

Typeset in Times

Printed and bound in Great Britain by CPI Group (UK) Ltd, Croydon, CR0 4YY


ISBN 9781913551537


British Library Cataloguing in Publication Data.
A catalogue record for this book is available from the British Library.

MIX
Paper from
responsible sources
FSC® C013604

## About the author

W A Sumner studied theology at Hull Univeristy and acheieved an M Litt from Oxford University. He has spent many years as a teacher and preacher in schools and churches. He is a reader of the Diocese of Birmingham and is also a hospital chaplain.

The front cover of *Science and Religion* was designed by Katie Colclough, the granddaughter of W. A. Sumner.

—

## Acknowledgements

Alan Bates, Julian Philips, Patricia Bates, Peter Kaye, Roger Shiers, John Wyatt and Andrew Pincent.

# Contents

# *Preface*

I was challenged only recently, by a gentleman of sound Methodist conviction, to write a book on Science and Religion. I accepted the challenge, knowing that this would not be an easy matter, but worthwhile nevertheless. A lot has been written on this subject, and I do not claim to have read every single book on the matter. Some of the productions are so difficult that one wonders how the average member of the public would manage to cope with it. Other productions seem to me to trivialise the matter. My aim has been to write something that is comprehendible for the average reader, without making it too high-flown or too simplistic. I want you to see whether or not I have succeeded.

The main problem has been that Science is constantly changing in its pronouncements. Anything that I state as a new discovery today may easily be out-of-date by tomorrow. The same is less true with Religion. Religionists tend to adhere to their convictions in a more consistent manner. Even so, Theology has gone through various changes over the years. New ideas do appear from the theologians, but not with same rapidity as from the Scientists.

I am aware that there are people with some kind of twisted conscience over the issue of Science and Religion. There is the feeling that one ought to take heed of modern advances in Science. The phrase 'it is scientifically proved' is often thrown around, as if this were some kind of magic wand to convince us all. In a way, Science, for many people, has become the 'god' of this age. I would venture to say that this is some kind of idolatry, and can so easily become some kind of modernistic fundamentalism. What I have found, on researching this book, is that certainties are somewhat few and far between. Of theories there is an abundance, and also opinions about which arguments rage. Let us not allow Science to become the high powered dogmatism that many people seem to see it as.

The same situation, only to a lesser extent, applies in the world of religion. Of arguments there are a multitude, leaving one bewildered as to what to believe. Essentially, religion is a matter of faith and personal conviction, and mercifully, in this country at least, there is the freedom to consider matters for oneself and not be forced into some kind of doctrinal set thinking.

I have noticed that literature on this subject has centred on disagreements between Evolutionists and Christians of a certain persuasion, namely, the Fundamentalists. This book will attempt to reach beyond this. There are religionists who see the interpretation of the Bible in very different terms and also other religions with their entire array of philosophy. It will be interesting to see that in some respects, scientific discoveries sometimes happen to tie in with the thoughts of ancient philosophic-religious pundits. That does not mean that I am a syncretist, but I do say that one should take into account what other religions are saying, even if one does not accept what they say.

I am hoping that for those who find themselves feeling guilty about the clash between Genesis 1-2 and the Theory of Evolution, there will some helpful remarks in this book. I believe that this clash is entirely unnecessary. In so many other respects, the sciences, in all their diversity, are strongly supportive of religious faith. Vice versa, a thorough respect for God and his Creation is an excellent starting point for anyone embarking on scientific analysis. The two matters are not in opposition, and anyone reading this book will see why I am saying this.

# Foreword

## by Mr. John Wyatt

I confess to being the "gentleman of sound Methodist conviction" who challenged Bill Sumner to write a book about Science and Religion.

I have known Bill, a retired teacher and preacher, for a long time. He is often to be seen riding his bicycle around Bromsgrove and always offers a cheery "hello!" He is a very talented musician and for several years has accompanied our annual carol singing at coffee and mince pie sessions in the Methodist Church coffee shop. This is where I have got to know him more intimately. Whilst he always has a quip which will put one on one's mettle, he is a most thoughtful and challenging man with whom to engage in conversation.

I have delved into Bill's previous books. The subjects were deep and I found the reading of them a demanding task. However, these books led me to realise that Bill, with his challenging and incisive approach, was the author who could tackle a subject that has intrigued, challenged and inspired me throughout my life. That is, the relationship, the contrasts, and confusions and yet the mutuality of thought between Science and Religion.

This book is the result. The book must have taken many hours of research and yet it discloses that Bill, as I have, has been thinking about this subject for many years and these thoughts did not need research. Bill brings to the pages the product both of his research and his lifetime of experience. He presents his own theories. He challenges generally accepted concepts. Bill's Christian beliefs shine through in every chapter. He constantly refers back to Christianity such as when he likens, in today's world, removing or eliminating a bad gene to, in yesterday's world, Jesus of Nazareth casting out demons. But it is not only Christianity. Bill also draws on many world religions other than Christianity and indeed sometimes draws on his personal theological ideas.

The early chapters on "Evolution and Genesis 1-2", "The Quantum World", and "Biochemistry and religion" set a tone which clearly demonstrates that Bill's thinking is not at all dogmatic and the reader can follow his thought process without in any way losing sight of the fact that there is another point of view to everything.

The middle chapters, "The Mega World and the Big Bang" and "Life on the other planets?" are a fascinating exposition of the theories and facts of space exploration, with occasional reference to such dramas as Star Wars and Star Trek. This brings us back down to earth.

**Chapter 20, a very topical interjection regarding Covid 19, is an up to date example (August 2020) of how religious faith and a crisis which involves medical science, can offer mutual insights.**

Bill's concluding remarks reinforce his desire that we should not be too dogmatic or authoritative, and that we should always be prepared to give some thought at least to alternative views. This book will make a perfect subject for group discussion and debate about very complex matters.

What jumps out of every chapter and hits me is Bill's solid, certain and constant Christian faith. It is the faith of a man who clearly believes that Religion, especially Christianity, and Science more often than not, support each other.

# 1

## *Set in our ways*

There is some kind of impression in people's minds, that Science and Religion are somehow incompatible. One is expected to opt for the one or the other. This, of course, is complete nonsense, and this book will attempt to show that there is no clash between Science and Religion. The clash only occurs in the minds of those who wish to imagine there is some sort of chasm between the two.

In my experience of dealing with religionists and scientists, I have found it impossible to predict what the attitude of either categories will be on these matters. I have come across hard line religionists who want nothing to do with Science, and vice versa, hard line scientists who cannot cope with religion. But it is nowhere near as simple or straightforward as that. I have met scientists who are heavily involved with religion, and even some who are outright Bible fundamentalists. Also I have seen religionists who have a great respect for scientific investigation but do not take all of its findings as the Gospel Truth. I have also met scientists who have a moderate approach to religion, without necessarily making a strong attachment to any kind of faith. As we can see from this, the whole matter is a lot more complicated than many people perhaps imagine. The reason why, may be explored in the next few paragraphs.

Over the years, traditionally speaking, religious commitment has been involved with dogmas which have been offered as the final truth. This does not mean that all religionists have the same doctrine; far from it. Within the Christian orbit, one can see that there have been deep chasms of contrary thought. One wonders why they cannot sort it out and agree on various matters! Many Christians have hard and fast ideas and if they are challenged, find that quite upsetting. To put it in modern jargon, they cannot cope with their 'comfort zone' being disturbed. It becomes even more complicated when inter-faith disagreements come to the surface. However, strange as it may seem, the scientists have the same problem. There is no complete consensus amongst them on many matters. Admittedly, there are major areas of agreement on basic matters stemming from the main areas of Science, ie. Chemistry, Physics and Biology. However, beyond that, arguments rage on all kinds of matters. As with the religionists, one wonders, at times, as to whom to believe! I would suggest that it is a mistake to take either strand of thought too literally, and certainly not take every detail of their claims as established fact in a dogmatic frame of mind. We need to think things through and not allow ourselves to be brainwashed.

What are the essentials of religion, when it comes down to the basics of theology? I would say that it is impossible to view this world and the universe, without asking that fundamental question, "What is it all about? What is its purpose? What is its destiny? And how do I relate to all these matters?" Virtually every religion has some kind of starting point with a myth of some kind,(1) relating to the origin of all things, the universe, this world, and the human race. For some, it is the one God, the original Creator and for others it is a plurality of gods. It is very unusual to come across a theological system that just imagines that the physical world, or universe, just occurred all by itself, out of nothing. One exception could be the Communist system of thought which has attached itself to atheism. However, atheism is not necessarily a component of extreme Socialism. We also find that the Marxist frame of mind still has a form of myth concerning the nature and destiny of mankind. The other exception could be seen in the Buddhist system of thought, with their idea that there was never any beginning for all things. Everything is assumed to have been going on eternally, with no start or finish. Even so, they still spend a lot of time contemplating gods, spirits, principles and other unseen factors, and how they relate to humanity. Normally, people are left with that profound question about how did all things come into existence, the start, the beginning, the primeval impulse, however one wishes to phrase it. This is where belief, faith, lack of faith, a sense of failure or unworthiness enters the picture. That is fundamental to virtually every religion, and that includes Buddhism. We cannot avoid evaluating ourselves in relation to this world and the rest of the universe.

What are the essentials of Science? These remarks apply equally to any form of scientific enquiry, whether it be the physical sciences or the so-called social sciences. Unfortunately, for many people Science has been seen as speculation, guesswork, invention and sometimes sheer fantasy. But the true scientific method is as follows. One looks at some kind of feature in the natural world, one devises experiments with the aim of trying to explain it, not so much in terms of spiritual influences, but in terms of observable physical factors. Having analysed a given matter, one hopes to devise some kind of 'law' and further than that, to put the findings to some kind of practical use. This we call, Technology; inventing new processes which will be useful in everyday life. Unfortunately, not all new discoveries have been helpful in everyday life; some have been distinctly harmful! With these interesting findings, which may or may not be reliable, and we must be prepared to admit, sometimes actually wrong, there is always the urge to seek some kind of meaning or moral implication in these discoveries. A very simple and crude example of this would be as follows (an example someone served up to me once); observation of how animals behave in their mating patterns shows that choosing a new mate every time is perfectly natural and acceptable. The moral implication in this is that 'marriage' in the traditional sense, is unnecessary, and we can fornicate away to our hearts' content with a clear conscience! Is this valid? Firstly, a more thorough knowledge of animal behaviour would reveal that some species do mate for life, which means that the first assumption is faulty, to say the least. Secondly, are we really animals? We see the basic evolutionary assumption that we are supposed to be descended from monkeys!(2) Thirdly, the thought of social and moral chaos is a real threat to the stability of whole communities and nations. However, whole moral and procedural assumptions are regularly made from scientific findings which are not necessarily completely reliable.

This is where Religion and Science share an important human trait; that of trying to see some kind of significance or meaning above and beyond pure observations of the natural world, or indeed of human nature. The religionist tries to see things in terms of influence from some kind of spiritual entity, normally not observable; the scientist tries to see things as functioning according to some kind of 'lawcode' which is again not observable but is nevertheless some kind of unseen reality. From that generalisations can be made about human destiny and worth. One could say that in doing so, the scientists are going beyond their remit. These two approaches do not necessarily contradict each other; matters are simply being understood on two different levels. Both levels can be equally valid and complement each other. Science and Religion are essentially aiming for the answer to the same questions; the difference is that the method of approach is different. They are tackling the same questions but on two different levels of truth.(3)

The search for meaning is an important factor in human nature. It is very unusual to find someone who has absolutely no impression of life and the physical world having any kind of purpose or meaning. That, of course, is the true atheism, that of seeing no significance in life at all. If, however, one has an impression that all things must have had a beginning somewhere in the remote past, it must raise the question of what was going on before that beginning. If there was nothing happening before the start, it does raise up that old quotation from Shakespeare, 'nothing comes of nothing.' If one has no impression of a pre-existent spiritual force, or deity, then it is a real problem which is insoluble for the human mind. If however, one does have an impression of God, it is not easy to visualise the physical world being produced out of nothing, but a lot easier than trying to do without God. It is interesting that in modern atomic theory, it is claimed that all physical things are built up with atoms, the tiniest building blocks of life.(4) But when we come to analyse an atom, we are told that it is only a matter of tiny electrical impulses, a nucleus with electrons circulating round. From this, the atoms combine with other atoms to form molecules and then on to larger structures which give us all the physical features of life. But essentially, there is nothing in an atom but tiny electric charges, plus and minus. To put it another way, something does come from nothing. Still to this day, with all our clever knowledge, we do not know how this comes about. The theist can easily explain it as the creative genius of God; the scientist who tries to leave God out of the picture, is left with a deep conundrum.

If we accept that there must have been a beginning for all things, by force of logic, we have to contemplate the end of all things. It is a fair generalisation to say that if anything has a beginning, it must also have an end, at least, that is how our minds work. The Buddhists seem to be the only theorists who have the impression that there never was a beginning and therefore there never will be an end. The world, and life itself, has been going on eternally and will continue so. However, most other religions have a mythology which includes a creation myth but also some kind of finishing scenario, or some kind of eschatology. It is interesting that the scientists also have the same impression. They are full of speculatory information about the beginning, which is just as much a piece of guesswork as the religious myths are. But they go further and are full of cheerful prognostications about the end of the world, with a sort of calculated eschatology which is highly frightening, just as much as the Apocalypse. Strangely, the two approaches to explaining all matters, have the same basic framework with regard to cosmic history. This is another example of Science and Religion saying basically the same thing.

When considering human history, we see much the same pattern of thought in both areas. This is more obvious with the so-called historical religions, namely Judaism, Christianity and Islam and their derivatives. The course of history, culminating in the active intervention of the creator God, is an important part of their theology. Mankind starts with a golden age of simplicity and closeness to Nature, but progressively mutates to increasingly complicated scenarios. Some would say it is deterioration; others would say it is improvement and refinement. When we consider the scientific view of this, it is much the same, with that impression of evolution, and the assumption that mankind will graduate to something more wonderful in times to come.(5) Other scientists think the opposite is true.(6) It would be fair to say that many of the Eastern religions are less orientated on historical progression. Even so, this frame of mind is not completely absent from their thinking; it is just rather less emphasised. Also there is the impression that this physical world is just an illusion, and the real world is the world of the spirit. Paradoxically, this might link in with atomic theory as described above.

One might, with justification, say that all this is emotionalism. Religion certainly has got a strong involvement with emotion, although not completely and absolutely. Others would say that science is above and beyond emotionalism, but that is a very shaky generalisation. It is far more honest to say that all of us, of whatever inclination, are emotional creatures. It is a part of our make-up and cannot be avoided. If Freud and Jung are to be given any credit, and it would be fair to say there is some substance in their theorizing, we are basically founded on instincts (in the 'id') and our conduct is tempered by something called 'conscience' (in the 'super-ego').(7) Both of these function on the basis of emotion, and that applies to each and every one of us. A theist would almost certainly say that human nature, being what it is, is shaped on emotion by the Creator. One could go further and say that essentially we are irrational,

5

that our lives are shaped not on pure simple logic, but on whims and fancies. How many people would deny that?

The tension between pure rationality and emotion was exemplified by that iconic TV series, Star Trek. Mr. Spock was included in the team on the spaceship for the simple reason that pure cold logic was needed to prevent the earthlings, such as Captain Kirk, from making panicky, irrational decisions when faced with any crisis. One might say that that was a good idea. However, we discover later in the series that Spock is not entirely free from emotion, since he falls in love! The conclusion reached eventually is that one is not completely human unless one has a modicum of emotion, blended in with common sense. One could go further and say that to be human is to function on the basis of love (or in some cases, hate!)

This is a personal view, but is almost certainly shared by many others; that to look at the sky at night and admire the wonder of it all, one can hardly fail to display some kind of emotion. It is fantastic and demands a response on the lines of 'where or what is the Creator of all this?' The same can be said of a full experience of this planet with all its intricate systems and the beauty of Nature. It demands a positive explanation. I say it is not good enough to attempt to explain it all as just some sort of coincidence, a series of mistakes, some sort of blindness blundering along.(8) That view, for me, is totally absurd, but then there are those who do claim to think like that. One might assume that the scientist experimenting with his test tube, might be free from emotion. I would qualify that by saying that the eyes with which he peers down the tube, are already loaded with emotion. He only sees what he thinks he ought to see, and there is a strong tendency to ignore anything that he might not expect to see.

I did an experiment once with copper sulphate, an easy experiment for anyone to try, in which one can see the crystals actually forming. All you need is a moderate microscope and a bit of patience (which is again a form of emotion!). It is an amazing sight to see the crystals actually forming, even if one cannot actually see the atoms and molecules arranging themselves into those beautiful rhombic shapes. I cannot avoid asking myself, what is the energy, the force that makes this happen? What a beautiful sight and the shapes are consistent! Of course, one can talk in terms of electrical impulses plus and minus, that cause the crystalisation to occur, but that does not really answer the question. I say it is impossible to witness these things without some kind of emotional response.

To those who think that emotion can be avoided when attempting to analyse the physical world, I would pose the question; why bother to analyse it at all if there is nothing to be learnt from it? The fact that you are fascinated with it and have the urge to analyse, is also basically emotional.

Emotion is the foundation for every opinion in the world. This applies to politics, religion, philosophy and all kinds of permutations that flow from these basic areas. There is a lot of truth in Mr. Gilbert's amusing line from Iolanthe;

"Every little boy and girl that's born alive, is either a little Liberal or a Conservative."

How true! Admittedly this was coined before the Labour Party began to gain much sway, but the basics of it are still valid. Most of us are a strange mixture of old-fashioned and trendy, hard-line and easy going. This is certainly an aspect of emotionalism, and cannot be avoided. What it means is that we are born with some sort of tendency in our minds and from that come our opinions on all these matters. One can say that whims and fancies shape our lives; very true. We proceed with a basic fancy in our heads and then continue to find reasons to back up our fancies. We believe what we like the sound of. The other side of this is that very few people are entirely consistent with these ideas as they proceed through life. Most people are a peculiar sort of amalgam of one opinion or another. We have Christian Socialists, Christian Conservatives, atheistic believers, agnostics, hard line religionists and easy going, relaxed believers. Even the religions that claim unity of thought and dogma cannot avoid a variety of attitudes amongst their adherents. The same is true with the scientific world. The scientists do not 'all sing from the same hymn sheet', to borrow a teasing metaphor! It is very much a matter of what one has a predilection to assume in the first place. The main issue is to ask ourselves, are we free to think what we feel inclined to think, or are we to be brainwashed for the benefit of some kind of campaign? Even worse, are we to be persecuted for opting for the 'wrong' opinion?

It would be fair to say that many of the religionists, traditionally, have indulged in over-dogmatism and brainwashing. This would apply not just to the Roman Catholics, but also to many a Protestant denomination. One could say that this tendency, which, fair to say, does have its value in some instances, is much reduced in modern times. Even so, there are some religions that still do indulge in the heavy doctrine approach, in spite of the general tendency to liberalisation in the modern world. But it would also be fair to say that many of the scientists also indulge in heavy indoctrination, not least the ones who have decided that atheism is the absolute truth. Strange to relate, when challenged and argued against, they often fail to see that they are just as strongly opinionated as any traditional religionist! Admittedly this does not apply to every scientist. There are many who maintain an open mind, and this is wise, since we have scientific doctrines overturned by new evidence, often enough, in our own times.

I would maintain that an open mind is essential in these matters; the ability to discuss and learn from what others are saying, without going into a panic. That does not mean we have to be swept away by every new idea that crops up; we can give each idea a certain amount of consideration and compare it with what others say. But it is important to allow our basic emotions to have their say. If not, we are not really playing fair with our humanity. Let us admit that we are basically emotional; when we see something beautiful, let us admire it; when we see something horrible or frightening, let us abhor it; when we view the wonders of Nature, let us admire it. Scientist or religionist; we all should share that basic impulse, and it is folly to attempt to deny it.

Much has been said about the so-called 'God-gap'. What this means, if I understand it correctly, is that as scientific knowledge increases, so that vague area which is taken to be the work of God, is shrinking. To take a very crude example, it was believed, in ancient times that thunder and lightning were the angry expression of a god of some description. Thor, in Norse mythology, was believed to be thumping around with his hammer. There are still traces of this idea current today, for when someone is asked, 'What causes it to rain?' the answer one gets is 'Because the clouds are bumping together.'

Now that we have a more complete understanding of static electricity and the adiabatic (9)lapse rate, we can now explain thunder, lightning and rain in terms of physics and changes in temperature. Some would see that as the 'God-gap' being reduced. The same pattern applies to many of the scientific advances in the modern world. There are some scientists who would claim that eventually, when we manage to explain every natural phenomenon, the God-gap will disappear altogether.

Nothing could be further from the truth. In fact, this idea is now being seen as incredibly naive. The truth is, that the more we investigate the natural world, the more we realise there is to be discovered and given an explanation. This is particularly true in the field of astro-physics and in quantum mechanics. (10) The fact is that the more we probe outwards into deep space, the more we realise there is to be discovered. The field of investigation is not shrinking; it is expanding at a rate that we cannot keep pace with. Even with our knowledge of our own solar system, all our pre-conceived ideas about our neighbouring planets regularly have to be revised and in some cases scrapped altogether. We hardly know anything about the distant planets such as Saturn, Uranus and Neptune, and our assumptions about Pluto have had to be thought out again in recent years. If that is so, how much more true will it be regarding other solar systems and heavenly bodies many millions of light years away?

The God-gap, if there is such a thing, is expanding all the time. It is certainly not reducing.

The concept of a God-gap betrays a failure to understand the basic realities about God. The problem is that for many centuries, people have assumed that God is an aged gentleman sitting on a chair in the sky. They will take this concept literally and never stop to consider that it is just metaphor and imagery, verging on idolatry. I am now assuming the existence of God, not in some (11) kind of physical sense, but as an eternal spirit. The Christian understanding of God is that he is not a part of his Creation, but is above and beyond, and yet, he is in and through all of the created world or universe. Obviously, the Pantheists would say that he is actually in all of the created material, but that is only one aspect of a deep and wonderful paradox. Being in and through everything, he is also completely other than the created world. Any sort of talk about a God-gap is nonsensical. It makes no difference whether we understand how things work in the physical world, or not, as the case may be. Gaps or no gaps, God is in and through all things, whether it be a thunderstorm or a beautiful sunset or a fierce animal. It makes no difference what the chemical or physical aspects of things are; it is that eternal spirit that makes everything happen and sustains the entire universe. Of course, if one does not believe that, one is left with the awkward question of what does actually keep everything going. It may appear, superficially, that the universe functions on the basis of chaos, but the more the scientists delve into these matters, the more we realise that it functions according to 'laws'. If we have laws, that implies a 'lawmaker'; laws do not just occur all by themselves. The assumption that there are laws of nature, is a tacit

9

admission that there is a God who frames them. In a way, God is self-evident even to those who try to deny him.

We can see from this, that the relationship between religion and science is far from straightforward. It is very complex, and anybody who tries to see it in black and white terms, is not being realistic. This book will attempt to show just how complex it is.

**Chapter 1 Footnotes**

1. I am using the word 'myth' in the correct sense. For a full treatment of Myth, refer to my book on the subject of *Myth, Legend and Symbolism*.
2. The question of Evolution and Darwin's theory is discussed in chapter 3.
3. Chapter 13 explores different levels of truth.
4. The Quantum world is discussed in chapter 4.
5. Chapter 5 is devoted to Biochemistry in relation to Theology.
6. An example of which is Teilhard De Chardin, an optimistic evolutionist.
7. Dr. John Sandford takes the opposite opinion.
8. Richard Dawkins is a well known example.
9. The adiabatic lapse rate is the rate at which atmospheric temperature decreases with increasing altitude in conditions of thermal equilibrium.
10. Astro-physics are discussed in chapter 6.
11. Chapter 12 discusses 'proofs' for the existence of God.

# 2

## *A Question of Scale*

One of the most important discoveries in recent times has been the factor of scale. On the face of it, this only indirectly involves religion; more acutely it relates to mythology. We shall come to that later. Firstly let us investigate the matter of scale.

One of the major discoveries in modern times has been the awareness of the vastness of outer space. Since we have developed radio telescopes (1) which can probe many millions of light years out into the depths of the universe, it has become clear that enormous distances exist reaching out to somewhere, or possibly nowhere. No one can determine whether the universe actually comes to an end or just goes on eternally. It is clearly beyond the capacity of the human mind to cope with such distances. Just the concept of a light year, which means the distance light can travel in one earth year, if difficult enough. This universe is now known to contain not just millions of stars, but billions, and counting. Each star is likely to have its own solar system, in some sort of arrangement not unlike our own Solar System.

Coming to within range of our own distances, we have been aware of our own Solar System for a long time (see end of chapter for a diagram). Ever since Copernicus decided that the Sun was the centre of it and all the planets circulated round it, in the same direction, we have had what could be called a 'modern' view of our nearest neighbours. That does not mean that we know all about them; far from it. We are still finding out new facts about the other planets almost every day. It would seem fair to say that we have sent probes to all the other planets in the Solar System, but even so, our understanding of how these planets behave is still vestigial. Even if they all circulate round the Sun in the same direction, it would be wrong to say each one's orbit is exactly circular, or even elliptical. They seem to circulate according to criteria that we do not fully understand, as yet. What we have to appreciate is that other stars (suns) millions of light years away, also have their own solar systems. The existence of 'exo-planets' has only recently been claimed. No one has actually seen one of them as yet; it all depends on indirect evidence. But the temptation is strong to assume that if one planet in the Solar System has something which can be termed 'life' on it, so too ought other planets elsewhere. The trouble is, that Alpha Centauri, or nearest star, with its supposed solar system, would take about 30 years to reach, assuming the kind of speeds which we can attain today. (2)

However, the general picture, as far as we can observe from Earth, is that the universe functions on some kind of circular motion. The satellites, such as the Moon, circulate round their planets, in a regular motion. Then the planets circulate round a central 'bonfire' or star. There is some kind of awareness that the whole arrangement is according to some sort of balancing situation. This is working according to some kind of influence of gravity, interacting between the planets and the Sun. One could venture to say that the whole thing is very finely balanced, although demonstrating this would be a serious challenge.

Circular motion is certainly a major factor with regard to the Earth as it spins on its axis. It keeps on spinning at the same rate for the simple reason that there is nothing there to stop it. One could view the Earth as a gigantic gyroscope. The difference is that a model gyroscope does slow down gradually, since there is the atmosphere surrounding it, as opposed to a vacuum. Again, this factor of spinning involves the question of balance. If we observe the galaxies in outer space, we also observe circular motion; the galaxies are spinning or rotating, albeit very slowly.

Looking at the other end of the scale, in miniature, we have become aware of how tiny life can be. Only recently, we have discovered that all physical matter is composed of tiny components called atoms. An atom consists of a nucleus which contains protons and neutrons, and there are electrons which circulate round at very high speed. The protons are positively charged and the electrons negatively charged. So the essential basic building blocks of life are tiny electrical charges acting in a balancing arrangement, and the other ones, the electrons, circulating in a kind of orbit. To look at a diagram of an atom reminds one of the Solar System, except to say that the electrons do not circulate on the same plane as the planets do. The simplest and lightest atom is a hydrogen atom and the most complex and heaviest would be Uranium with seven shells. (3)

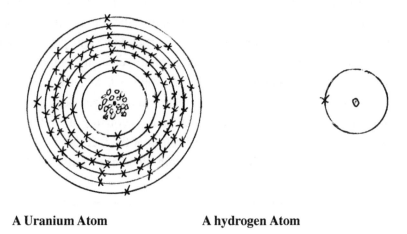

**A Uranium Atom**          **A hydrogen Atom**

Going on from there, some atoms have a degree of instability which means that they are attracted to other atoms to form ions or molecules. In this way, all the physical materials of life are formed, whether it be of the hardest rocks and metals, or the softest of liquids and gases. It is quite a challenge to accept that every physical thing is made up of tiny electrical impulses, in the middle of which is essentially, 'nothing'!

We notice, however, that circular motion is the essence of the whole picture, whether it be on a macro scale or a micro scale. Also the factor of balance is a vital element in the whole stability of creation. Is there a religion whose philosophy centres on circular motion? What about Hinduism and Buddhism?

Circularity is not just confined to matters so far raised. We notice that in this physical world, there are various 'cycles' in operation. The easiest one to see is the water cycle. Water evaporates up into the sky, forms clouds, then starts to rain, trickles down into the rivers and then out to sea. The Sun evaporates it up again. This has been going on for millions of years, but it means that the world's water has been going in circular motion perpetually. In addition to that, the ocean currents make the water circulate to all parts of the globe. There are many other cycles; the carbon cycle, the nitrogen cycle and various others. Everything would appear to function on some kind of circularity, yes, even human life itself; what about History repeating itself?

If taken to its logical conclusion, again, the Hindus and Buddhists could be right on the subject of reincarnation. (4)

Returning to the question of scale, since Dalton's discovery of atoms and their constitution, we are now faced with claims about even tinier factors. (5) Such things as quarks, gluons, gravitons, particles and anti-particles. One wonders how deeply we can speculate on the tiniest elements in the physical world. It reminds us of that old saying, "and bigger fleas have lesser fleas upon their backs to bite them, and lesser fleas have lesser fleas and so ad infinitum." In other words, where will it all end? Theorising about these tiny entities is all the rage at the moment, regardless of the fact that we have not actually seen any of them. There is a certain element of faith involved in accepting such claims!

However, the same is true at the other end of the scale, the macro side of things. We have become aware of larger and larger entities out in space, such as black holes, and enormous galaxies, much larger than our Milky Way. One can pose the question, where will it all end?

Another factor is the so-called Big Bang. It is claimed that the Universe started about 13 and a half billion (earth) years ago, from a tiny speck which exploded and scattered material in all directions. It is claimed that the Universe is still expanding at the rate of about 72 kilometres a second. This figure is, by the way, subject to dispute and uncertainty. This must pose the question, that if the universe is expanding at such an enormous rate, where will it ever end? Will it go on for eternity, or will there be some kind of boundary line into which it will crash, and perhaps go into reverse? This does raise the question of eternity, or infinite progression. It applies to the tiny things as well as the enormous things. The conclusion must be that everyone or everything, has a place on some kind of eternal scale.

The Big Bang, an idea that was suggested in the early 20th century, (6) has now become more or less accepted doctrine in scientific circles. At first, those who were set in their ways, failed to take it seriously. No one was actually there to witness this alleged explosion, and proving its existence is pure speculation. The reasoning is that since the universe is alleged to be expanding, there must have been a time when everything was compressed into a tiny blob of something. This is all very theoretical and speculatory, but even so, people take it as some sort of Gospel Truth. The very thought about what was happening before this alleged Big Bang, seems to send them into nervous convulsions. One wonders why?

It is now time to compare this with what was generally assumed by the ancients. It was generally thought that the earth was flat, with four corners and three levels. This explains the importance of the figure seven in (western) mythological thinking. The top layer was the home of the gods (or if you were a Hebrew, just one God); the middle layer was the playground of mankind; the lower level was the home of devils, lost souls and irredeemably wicked people. It was believed that there were pillars holding the whole structure together, even though no one had ever seen these pillars. They may have been understood as figurative. Also, it was assumed, that since the sky was blue, there must be an ocean up there (called the Firmament) (7), and that explained how the rain sometimes trickled down on to the earth layer. Of course, we now know that the blue of the sky is an optical illusion, and that outer space is actually black. The idea that the earth is flat, is also an illusion, as was realised at the Renaissance and onwards. There is some evidence that some thinkers in the Graeco-Roman world had worked out that the world was round, but they must have been regarded as cranks. It was also assumed that the world was stationary, and that all the planets and stars (including the Sun) circulated around it. This too, as we have now proved, is another illusion, but an understandable one, since there is no indication to us that the world is spinning at a rate of thousands of miles every day. (8) This all raises the question of how we can be deceived by our own observations. Practically all ancient mythologies assumed something like this, although there were slight variations on this general impression. If the ancients could suffer under some kind of mirage, what makes us think we are free from illusions today, even if we have all kinds of scientific gadgets?

The importance of mythological thinking for religious belief cannot be underestimated. Assuming that the world has three layers, is important on a spiritual level. It tells us of God being on a level above and beyond mankind, and the evil forces also on a level below us. So life is a sort of testing ground, to determine whether we go up or down at the moment of death. (9) Just because we are now aware that the world is spherical and there is no shelf up in the sky, does not mean that we have to lose faith. Some have done, but that is because they fail to understand the spiritual importance of the three tiers. Good and evil are still with us, regardless of geographical locations. Human nature is still caught in the tussle between right and wrong. (10). The Biblical writers can hardly be blamed for couching it in literal terms tied up with the impression of a three-tiered universe. We, however, do not have to take

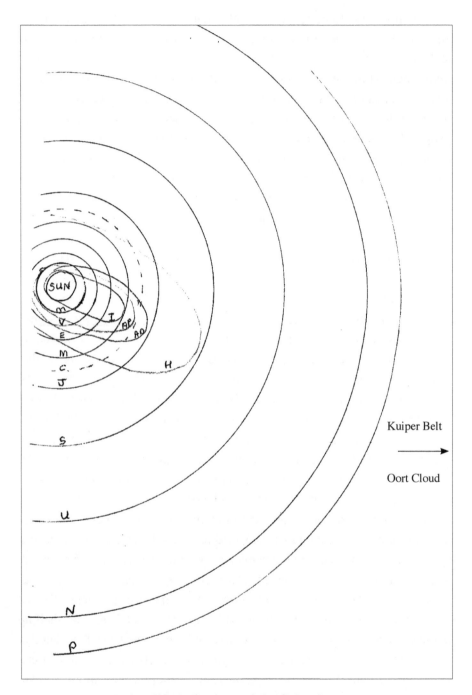

**A simplified diagram of the Solar System**
This shows that the Solar System is a lot more complicated than
we had ever realised before.

| Planet | Distance from the Sun | Orbital time |
|--------|----------------------|--------------|
| M - Mercury | 57.9 mkm | 88 days |
| V - Venus | 105.2 mkm | 225 days |
| E - Earth | 149.6 mkm | 365.5 days |
| I - Icarus | | 2.6 years |
| M- Mars | 227.9 mkm | 687 days |
| Ap - Apollo | | 1.8 years |
| C - Ceres (the Main Belt) | 414 mkm | |
| Ad - Adonis | | 2.6 years |
| J - Jupiter | 778.4 mkm | 11.6 years |
| H - Hidalgo | | 13.7 years |
| S - Saturn | 1.43 bkm | 29.46 years |
| U - Uranus | 2.87 bkm | 84 years |
| N - Neptune | 4.5 bkm | 144.8 years |
| P - Pluto | 5.9 bkm | 247.9 years |
| K - Kuiper Belt | 12 bkm | |
| O - Oort Cloud | 1.6 light years | |

their world view literally. We can take it figuratively and see the theological importance of it, without getting tied up with geographical factors.

However, the interesting question must now be raised; if ancient man can function under some kind of mirage about the created world, how do we know we in our modern world are not working under another collections of mirages? It is all very well to talk of 'proof' and 'evidence', but what do you mean by proof and what do you class as valid evidence? It is relatively easy to make statements about this world, and our neighbouring planets, but even then, some of it is speculative and constantly being changed. We can send probes out to land on places like Mars and obtain data, even if this is a very expensive business. When it comes to probing into deep space and all those claimed factors going on out there, how do we know this is not some sort of delusion, or self-induced mirage? The only way to settle it is to send out a probe and that becomes a massively expensive excercise.

It would be wonderful to construct a modern mythology which included the Big Bang and all kinds of claims about how the stars and the planets were formed. Some scientists do indulge in this kind of scenario. Can this really be called 'science'; speculation, more like. They may claim to have all kinds of evidence, but what do you class as evidence? One might go further and construct an entire theological system of thought based on modern claims about the Universe. The Big Bang could be God snapping his fingers! The black hole could be Hell itself? Heaven might be slightly more difficult to locate, but it has to be somewhere, since practically everyone still assumes there is a heaven waiting for us. Am I being cynical? But this is how mythologies of one kind or another come into being.

What I will say is that one's spiritual and theological horizons do not have to be tied to some kind of geographical understanding of the world, or the universe. An awareness of God does not have to include a throne up in the sky, or anywhere else. When we say that 'God is on the throne', it is metaphorical for him being in charge of everything, the ultimate authority. (11)

But the thing in common between ancient thought and modern thought, is that somewhere in the remote past, there must have been a beginning for all things. None of us, scientists or religionists, can contemplate there having been no start to all things. From the scientific point of view, the Big Bang (assumedly) is the physical explanation for all things; from the theological point of view, which includes the mythological, the spiritual start of all things is the activity of the great Creator, the one who instigated the Big Bang (if there was one). Seen like this, there is no reason for a clash between religion and science. Essentially they are saying the same thing, but in a different mode. (12)

#### Footnotes

1. An example of this would be Joddrell Bank, and also the Hubble telescope.
2. Concorde, flying at Mach 2, was able to keep up with the sunset.
3. Uranium is the heaviest natural atom, atomic number 92. However, hybrid atoms have been made, such as Lawrencium, atomic number 103, with 7 shells, and the heaviest of all is now Ununoctium.
4. This issue, that of Karma, will be discussed in chapter 17.
5. The quantum world, with sub-atomic entities will be discussed in chapter 4.
6. Proposed by Georges Lemaitre in the 1920's.
7. See Genesis chapter 1:7.
8. Since it is spinning at an even rate, it gives the impression of being static.
9. When Uri Gargarin circled the earth in his space ship, he looked out and remarked that he could not see God anywhere. Allan Shepherd, however, declared that he could see God everywhere. It is all a matter of interpretation and what one expects to see.
10. The classic religion and mythology which typifies this tussle was (and still is) Zoroastrianism.
11. See Daniel 7:9 ".. thrones were placed and one that was ancient of days took his seat..."
12. See chapter 13 for different levels of truth.

# 3

## *Evolution and Genesis 1-2*

This issue has been a major cause of upset between religionists and scientists over the last century and a half. It has been the cause of much loss of faith and has stimulated an outburst of atheism in the modern world. There was never any need for this and it is only in recent times that people have begun to realise that this issue is more of a problem to those who worry about these things, than is really necessary. The problem is that the first two chapters of Genesis have been taken literally, and at face value, for many centuries, and now people are taking the Theory of Evolution at face value. I maintain that there is no need for this conflict, and for several reasons.

If one were to think that Evolution is a theory devised by Charles Darwin, this is an inaccurate idea. We can trace ideas about Evolution in the ancient world, even back to the ancient Egyptian Book of the Dead, (1) and the Greek philosophers. The idea resurfaced in recent times because the palaeontologists began to dig up remains of animals, in fossil form, that seemed to bear no resemblance to animals now seen on earth. A French scientist called Lamarck, early in the 19th century, believed that there was something called Evolution, and nearer to the time of Darwin, someone called Wallace was preparing to publish something on that subject. It was Darwin, who managed to popularise this theory, and so he still carries the credit with his publication, The Origin of Species. The point is that Evolution is not just Darwin's own bright idea. It was in the ether in the 19th century. Over the next one hundred and fifty years, it has become more or less standard doctrine in scientific circles, and many people take it as a proven fact. Some, possibly most, scientists are quite dogmatic about it. If one dares to question it, one is regarded as a crank, or more likely a Bible Fundamentalist!

However, there has always been a sizeable tranch of opinion that has opposed Evolution. This would be mainly the fundamentalists, but not entirely. There are others, on what can be claimed as quite rational grounds, that question this theory. After all, it is only a theory; not a fact. (2) Whether it can ever be proved conclusively, one way or the other, would be an interesting question. There is no doubt that Evolution has had a heavy influence on politics, educational policy and scientific investigation itself, over the last century and a half. Often this influence has not been for the benefit of mankind. Sometimes it has resulted in outright cruelty. As stated in the first chapter, I am always suspicious of dogmatisms, especially when people lose patience with those who question them. I have seen scientific dogmatisms come and go; suddenly, the accepted doctrine is disproved and out of fashion. Can we expect Evolution to fall from favour in the coming years? One wonders.

Let us begin with an appraisal of Genesis 1-2. This is two accounts by different writers; we can tell that by the difference in literary style. That in itself does not invalidate the message being offered in the passages. Both of them need to be understood as mythological realisation. I know the fundamentalists will condemn me eternally for saying this, but if we try to take these passages totally at face value, as some kind of historical account, or even a biological text book, we are going to miss the point. Also we shall have to ignore some of the contradictions inherent in the passages. Just seeing the material as mythological, does not imply that it is nonsense; on the contrary, mythology is an essential element in human nature, and tells us much about the basics of the human mind. Virtually every religion or system of thought in the world, is based on some kind of mythological framework, and many of them closely resemble Genesis. Just because Genesis can be seen as mythological, does not mean it is meaningless. It has a lot to say about the human condition, over and above purely scientific and sociological realities.

What is Genesis chapter one saying? It is stressing that there was a time when there was nothing, but out of that came something, caused by the Spirit of God. From that, Creation comes in clearly defined stages, termed as 'days'. The six days of creation have been taken literally by those who do not understand the Hebrew mentality. Nouns involving time, such as days, weeks, years are used, in other parts of the Old Testament, in a different way compared with our precise thinking.(3) Often they are substituted. It is senseless to take them totally at face value in some kind of strictly literal sense. What the passage is saying is that creation occurs in an orderly fashion, cumulatively and in rational order. At the end of each 'day' it is noted that the work is 'very good'. We see the importance of this in the following chapters of Genesis. It is saying, in effect, that there is nothing wrong with God's wonderful work, but it was the disobedience of human kind that rendered it less than wonderful. So we come to the seventh day, which is entitled the Sabbath, the day of rest. This too is important as a social and moral guide, not forgetting the health implications. As we see later in the Bible, it is not just humanity that needs to take rest, but all of Creation, the crops, the animals, in fact everything must regain its strength. So the seven day cycle is important for us all, even if we are not Jewish, and this system of work and rest has come to dominate the whole world. The fact that different religions take a day of rest on other days of the week, is irrelevant.

What is chapter two saying? This is focussed not so much on the process of Creation, but on the appearance of mankind and the animal kingdom. Practically every myth in the world has something to say about the origins of the human race. The first man and his wife are often named.(4) What is not outlined, in other myths, is where it all went wrong. Some myths manage to lay the blame on other factors, but the Bible lays the blame squarely on the temptation and the Fall of mankind; they simply could not follow one simple instruction. It is no accident that this account is followed by the first murder, Cain and Abel, and going on, we see the deterioration in behaviour. What is stressed, before and after the Fall, is the closeness of the humans to the eternal God. They know about God, intuitively, even when they know they are ashamed of themselves. One could say that this is still true for us all, even if some of us claim to be atheists; it is some kind of instinct in the human soul. But we are left with the realisation, which is common to us all, of whatever myth we accept, that this world has got something wrong with it; it ought to be some sort of Paradise, but it is not.

One has to wonder how these passages, juxtaposed in this way, came to be written. It is no doubt that they are both the work of a theological genius. When we consider that this material must have been written in the Iron Age, or possibly even in the Bronze Age, we have to marvel at the literary genius of it. When we compare it with other writings from the Ancient World, the only thing that comes near to it is the philosophisings of the Greek philosophers. Could it have been Moses himself who wrote, or at least, assembled this material? Who knows; but it must have required someone of that spiritual insight and stature to produce such passages. We have to recall that this was very much a pre-scientific age, and certainly a pre-sociological age, which means that it is no use trying to expect 'Moses' to produce a closely worded scientific textbook or a sociological tract on the matter. He was a child of his age, just as we are. Even so, the profound thoughts we find in the passage have had a massive influence right down the centuries, firstly on Jesus himself, then on the teachings of the Church, and even with loss of faith in the modern world, still a strong background influence. Let us not underestimate early Genesis, even if it is mythological.

We now need to say something about Evolution. Why did this matter come to the fore in the last two centuries? The reason is that palaeontologists had been unearthing skeletons and fossils of creatures that were clearly not to be found on earth at the present time. There was an increasing awareness that the age of the earth was not something in the region of 6,000 years, but going back much further in time. As research progressed, the estimation of the earth's age had slipped back to about 13.5 million years, but the time span in which 'life' as we know it, is thought to go back to pre-Cambrian times, namely something like 500 to 600 hundred million years. While it is true that there are still some people who are of the opinion that the world is only about 6,000 years old, presumably because this is based on a literal assessment of the Bible, most people are prepared to accept that it is much older than that. Quite how the scientists manage to arrive at these massive figures is not totally clear, but I think we have to accept that the world is considerably older than 6,000 years. (5)

Taking a brief look at dating methods, there are various methods at work nowadays. Carbon 14, a method which relies on the decay of radio activity, is useful for dating anything up to about 5.5 thousand years old. It only works on wood, bone and shell, and anything derived from these, such as fabric. There are those who feel that it is accurate for anything within historical times, but going further back, the method becomes increasingly inaccurate. It is worth noting now that some of our earliest remains relevant to humanity, are reckoned to go back about 6 to 7 million years, in other words, well beyond the reach of carbon 14 calculation. Someone like Gristhorpe Man, who is reckoned to be about 4,000 BC, could just be in the range of carbon 14, but Cheddar Man, at 10,000 years old, will be well out of range. (6)

We now take a brief look at dendro-chronology. This is a method based on the tree rings of the Bristlecone pine. This too is an ingenious method, but will only work on anything composed of wood, and going back about 5,000 years. It does not really help with remains beyond that, and certainly not with fossils.

Another method is radiometric dating, which does reach back thousands of years, well into the era of fossilization. However, the problem here is that it will only work on igneous rocks. Anything sedimentary or metamorphic is dependent on finding something igneous in conjunction with it. Much, if not all our fossil material is found in sedimentary layers, such as limestone in its various types. This means that dating fossils is always a matter of inference and surmise. (7)

Even with this impression of dating, by various methods, it is still a fair assessment that the world is a lot older than 6,000 years. We have become accustomed to seeing the geological ages in a useful scheme going from Cambrian times (about 540 million years ago) down to the present.

How is this scheme devised? It is all a matter of layers. If we look at a liquorice allsort, we see the same effect. We start with the Cambrian, the oldest rocks and move up through the Ordovician, Devonian, Permian, Triassic, Cretaceous, and Pleistocene, which is the newest kind of rock. What makes these separate stages? It is thought, with some good reason, that at the end of each of these ages, there was some form of 'extinction', by which we mean that there was some kind of massive disaster which wiped out most of life on this planet, but not quite all. It looks very much as if 'life' had to more or less start all over again, except that some creatures managed to survive into a new era. The crocodile is one such example, but there are others. What caused these 'extinctions'? It is thought that there may have been some kind of collision with a meteor which caused a world wide alteration in temperatures, pollution and loss of sunlight. The end-Permian disaster is the easiest to evidence, but scientists speculate that there were others, and moreover in some kind of regular sequence. By this we mean that about every 65 million years, there came the end of an era.(8)

How much credit do we give this scheme? Anyone can see that there are several layers of sedimentary rocks, with a layer of clay separating them. This pattern can be seen in many parts of the world, not just in Britain, and even if the sedimentary layers vary greatly in their thickness, as indeed does the clay, it does give the impression of eras, which contain the remains of different creatures in fossil form. It is not at all clear why creatures in one layer can be markedly different from creatures in another layer. At the same time, we are aware of some creatures persisting from Cambrian times right down to the present. This is quite an enigma.

It would be tempting to see the extinctions, in a regular kind of pattern, as analogous to the six days of Creation as in Genesis, and indeed much of philosophical thinking in later Judaism and also in Greek thinking, was concerned with the mentality of eras or 'eons'. This would not be an easy equation, as there is no consensus on how many eras there have been. The palaeontologists themselves do not entirely agree on their number.

When we come to consider the pattern of thought involved in Evolution, we are confronted with a somewhat different scheme. Darwin, and his followers, had the idea that 'life' started as very simple organisms and gradually developed ('evolved' is the magic word) into more complex structures and eventually giving us modern man and all the animals that we see today. A schematic diagram resembling a tree is often produced, with a sort of continuous flow from elementary to highly complex. Darwin was opposed to the idea of 'extinctions'. However, the extinction theory, which was not well accepted in the early years of evolutionary thought, has managed to gain much more credibility in the 20th century. It is not the exact opposite of Evolution, and does not actually directly contradict the evolutionists, but it does cast a very different light on the matter. We are left with the awkward question of why some creatures, the crocodile being one of them, have managed to survive from Cambrian times, with hardly any alteration their make-up. Why did they not evolve into something else? There is the example of the coelacanth, which was thought to have gone into extinction 300 million years ago, and yet in recent times, several have been fished up in the Indian Ocean. In addition, we have become aware of some creatures which suddenly appear in the fossil record with no apparent 'parent', by which I mean, there is no creature recorded as being something they could have evolved from.

This would indicate that the whole matter of life on this earth is not just a simple, easy progression from basic forms of life to complicated or highly evolved. The whole matter is much more complicated and as yet, beyond our means to explain in full. The scientists are prepared to admit that even now, we are only in possession of about one percent of the available fossil evidence. If we were to recover a more comprehensive selection of fossil material, the picture might seem somewhat different; possibly even totally different. It is so easy to make massive claims and generalisations when only a fragment of the evidence is available. In addition to this, we must remember that dating these findings is not always as conclusive as one might like to think.

Every time a new discovery is made, especially with regard to 'humanoid' remains, there is the urge to rewrite all the textbooks, and rethink the whole matter. Dogmatisms on these matters are not really very appropriate; I am always suspicious of dogmatic claims from scientists.

Taking a closer look at the assumed evolution of the human race, it is the normal assumption that early man descended from something like a monkey. That is the Darwinian, world tree, view of things. But is it as simple as that?

The human race is a comparatively new feature of life on this planet. Humanoids or hominins, as the experts term these remains, can be traced back to about six to seven million years ago. The oldest known remains are Sahelanthropus Tchadensis of the late Miocene period. He lived in Chad, Central Africa and is claimed to be bipedal. The term 'bipedal' seems to be some kind of 'litmus paper' criterion for determining human life, as opposed to animal. We can list about 32 examples of early humans, coming down to such examples as Cheddar Man (10,000 years old), (9) Oetzi, the ice mummy found in the Alps and Gristhorpe Man from North Yorkshire (4,000 years). These last three are of particular interest as they are complete, anatomically, and show hardly any difference from humans today. Going back to the early material, it is very unusual to find a complete skeleton, whether bone or fossil. Most of our finds are fragments, which have the appearance of being deliberately dismembered. This may be because of some kind of burial ritual or sacrificial practice. What we also note is that the remains are very widely spaced, geographically. We find remains in China, Georgia, the Caucasus, parts of Europe, for instance, as well as many parts of Africa. Also, historically they are widely spread. There is no obvious or demonstrable connection between them. Looking at Neanderthal Man, whose remains first appeared in Germany, the heavy bone structure is unlike other humanoid examples. It looks as though the human race might have appeared in different areas, as separate entities, not growing out of one another.

It would be wonderful if DNA testing could assure us of how humanity started, say, in Central Africa and developed in some kind of 'tree' arrangement throughout the known world. The difficulty is, that DNA degrades with time and exposure to other matter. It was difficult enough to take a sample from Cheddar Man, ie, to find a part of his anatomy that was likely to be the least degraded (the inner ear), but other remains, which usually are fragmentary, stretch back to 7 million years, or so it is claimed. One wonders how or why these claims about dating can be so confident.

We see, in textbooks, how it is imagined that the early humanoids were thought to be short and with faces rather like a monkey. Then we see a (supposed) sequence of them getting taller, with an increasingly human face, and a larger cranium. This is all very reassuring for the Evolutionists! (10) But the trouble is, that we have short people nowadays, and some with small heads, and some with faces not unlike a monkey. This may sound politically wrong, but it is true!

The latest sensational discovery was a cave in South Africa, called the Rising Star Cave, in which 2,000 fragments of human remains were found, and 30 individuals could be pieced together. It was claimed that the material would date from about 1.9 million years ago, but evidence for this dating was not given on the programme. Two new species of mankind were claimed to be found; Australopithecus Sediba and Homo Neladi. Both were claimed to have humanoid and monkey features. It was not attempted to show whether these two strains were biologically related or not. What this might indicate, is that there were various strains of humanity appearing in the Miocene period, some of which have gone into extinction (such as the Neanderthals) and some have prevailed into the 21st century. The programme makers were honest enough to admit that all our preconceived ideas might have to be reconsidered, textbooks rewritten, but they could not quite bring themselves to jettison the concept of Evolution itself. What we need to take on board, is that new discoveries are likely to turn up at any time, and put a large question mark against just about any of our precious doctrines on the subject. Again, I say, dogmatism on these matters is not particularly wise. Another thing that it might make us reconsider, is that the idea of mankind coming from only one source, ie. some kind of 'Garden of Eden', some kind of first man and first woman, is also rather difficult to dogmatise over. However, time will tell, as more evidence comes to light.

It was noticeable that on that programme, that everything was to be interpreted in terms of Evolution. If we are to view everything through 'evolution-tinted' spectacles, the conclusions are almost certainly going to appear to support Evolution. It is some kind of circular argument. What would be healthy would be a different set of criteria with which to view all these remains. The results might then be quite interesting.

It is also worth mentioning that chimpanzee remains, so far, have not been as old as humanoid remains. It might be a shocking thing to say, but what if the monkeys are a degraded form of humanity, as opposed to the other way round? Generalisations made on sketchy fossil evidence are easy to make but may also turn out to be completely wrong. An honest scientist will admit the fossil evidence is scarce, to say the least, not continuous and not obviously connected. It seems we still have a lot to learn.

I conclude by saying that we can take both the theological and the scientific view of the origin of the world without becoming over dogmatic. The theological view, as seen in Genesis and the rest of the Bible is fair enough as a basis for three major world religions. What we see in Genesis does not have to affect the theories of the scientists. The scientific view of the origins of life can be taken cautiously. There is no complete agreement amongst the scientists; arguments rage. Even so, we can still appreciate the wonders of Creation, even if we do not have a full explanation for everything. Whether one accepts the Evolutionary approach to these matters, or not, does not have to affect one's understanding of God as the ultimate source of all life, and mankind as he continues to make a mess of this world.

**Footnotes**

1. The Egyptian Book of the Dead. E.A.Wallis Budge, an excellent rendition.
2. One such scientist who argues against Evolution is Michael Behe, in his book, *Science and Evidence for Design in the Universe.*
3. See Daniel and other apocalyptic literature for the way adverbs for time are used.
4. In Norse mythology, Ask and Embla are the first man and woman.
5. The Jewish calendar is based on this calculation.
6. A complete table of early human remains is found on page 337 of my book, *Myth, Legend and Symbolism.*
7. *See chapter on Archaeology (16) for more dating methods.*
8. See Niles Eldridge, Extinction and Evolution, page 13.
9. Gristhorpe Man is preserved in a special museum in Scarborough.
10. See Niles Eldridge, Extinction and Evolution.

# 4

## *The Quantum World*

This concerns the sub-microscopic world of atoms and their inner workings. It is only within recent times that physicists have concerned themselves with this question. Even though the Greek philosophers suggested that there were such things as atoms, it has only been within our own times that delving into such matters has become possible. The problem was that we did not have sufficiently powerful microscopes in order to observe the behaviour and structure of molecules, but now, it seems, we have the ability to distinguish an atom, and even an electron. (1) Even so, so much of this field of study is theoretical and speculative; all the same, many of the findings of the physicists would seem to be with reasonable foundation. The reasons for saying this will emerge later. I have to point out that it is not easy to express in reasonably comprehendible terms, the basics of quantum mechanics. Suffice it to say, that delving into the very essence of reality at the subatomic level, does have implications for religious belief and theology. It is worth noting that many of the pundits in this area are believers and others are not.

The chief names involved with this area of research are as follows; Planck, Bohr, Comte, Heisenberg, Böhm, Schrödinger, Pauli, De Broglie, and most significant of all, Einstein himself. It is interesting to note that all through most of the twentieth century, these theoretical physicists were engaged in endless arguments, many of which are still not satisfactorily settled. In the early days, there were still some who denied the actual existence of atoms; this however seems now to have subsided. Everybody accepts that there are such things as atoms, but how they function and how we analyse them is still not an easy matter.

One of the difficulties that were found with dealing with the quantum world, was that the thought-motifs which we use in the normal world, are simply not appropriate when dealing with the inner workings of atoms. Everyone seemed to approach the matter with the assumptions of the 'macro-world'. As Pauli put it, "we must not bind atoms in the chain of our prejudices..." Even so, metaphors derived from macro-life kept coming into the picture. Such phrases as 'great snorky dragon', and 'God does not play dice' (Einstein), and even 'angels dancing on the point of a needle' keep appearing. It became obvious that the micro world of quantum physics behaves in ways which we do not understand and find beyond us to analyse.

What do we mean by an atom, and quantum physics? The simplest and lightest atom is the hydrogen atom. It has a nucleus consisting of 1 Proton and a single 'shell' with one electron circulating around at massive speed. The Proton is positively charged and the electron is negatively charged. This means that the atom is in balance with itself. There are other isotopes of hydrogen, which involve the inclusion of one or two neutrons; these affect the weight of the atom, but hydrogen in any of its permutations, is the lightest of the building blocks of life. Going on from there, atoms appear with increasing numbers of 'shells' with larger numbers of electrons circulating and the nucleus containing more neutrons and protons. Eventually we arrive at the largest atoms such as Uranium, which is the heaviest natural atom, but there heavier ones which are hybrid, or artificial ones, such as Francium and Lawrencium. These would appear to have 7 'shells'. These become increasingly unstable and emit radio active rays, such as alpha, beta and gamma rays. All these atoms can be viewed in the Periodic Table, which has been expanding all through the twentieth century, as more elements have been discovered. This whole field of knowledge is termed 'quantum mechanics'. We are encouraged to believe that all physical things, from the lightest of gases to the heaviest of metals and rocks, are some kind of composition of this array of atoms. Does this require a leap of faith?

It is slightly less of a stretch of imagination to understand how atoms form into larger formations which can be observed and analysed. There is ionic bonding. Take for instance an atom of sodium and of chlorine; they combine to form an ion and from there sodium chloride crystals form. This is our familiar table salt, tiny crystals of two basic elements. It is all held together by tiny electrical impulses, plus and minus. There is also covalent bonding; the most familiar of these would be water; a combination of one oxygen atom and two hydrogen atoms. $H_2O$. Most of our soft solids, liquids and gases are based on covalent bonding, but we must remember that a diamond which is pure carbon, is bonded covalently in such a way as to form the hardest known substance. There is also metallic bonding, an example of this would be pure gold, but all metals and alloys, bond in much the same way, even if the electronic forces behave in slightly different ways. This is putting the formation of molecules at its simplest; of course, the whole thing becomes much more complicated, as any student of chemistry will admit.

Strangely, the great pundits of the twentieth century seemed to focus on the hydrogen atom, with perhaps some attention to helium, which is the next lightest. At the same time, attention was being paid to the question of whether the atom could be 'split'. This was achieved in 1932 by Cockcroft and Walton (at Cambridge), by managing to break apart the nucleus of an atom. This process centred around Uranium 235, and by 1939, nuclear research had made it possible to construct an atom bomb. This is where the story slides into politics and war strategy.

But the main focus of twentieth century physicists was the dilemma over light itself; whether it consisted of wave motion or particle motion. Isaac Newton had decided it was wave motion, and this had become the accepted doctrine down to the turn of the century. We notice how an accepted doctrine derived from a genius can actually distort future enquiries! It was Einstein that claimed that light consisted of tiny particles, as opposed to wave motion. This difference of opinion went on through the twentieth century and is still a matter of contention, in spite of all the clever gadgetry that has been devised to decide the matter. It was either- or; these clever people hardly ever seemed to see that both propositions were true in their own way. They were looking at a profound paradox but hardly anyone managed to see it. Part of the problem was that they were trying to judge the quantum world by the criteria of the macro-world; this does not work. There is a different kind of logic at work in the sub-atomic world.

To investigate this dilemma over wave or particle motion of light, the classic experiment, which was devised by Einstein, was to have a 'light box'. This idea was tried with all kinds of permutations. A light source was trained on a screen that had two slits in it, and behind that was a photographic plate. As the light shone through the slits, various effects could be obtained. The patterns that resulted were fascinating and were supposed to indicate whether it was wave or particle motion. The experiment became increasingly complicated and fanciful, with beamsplitters, movable mirrors, prisms and calcite crystals. Fascinating patterns were obtained on the photographic plate, but one would have to admit that the results did not convincingly settle the argument.

However, one intriguing aspect of this was as follows. The light particles (assumedly) now became termed as 'light quanta' or 'photons', according to Einstein . When one of the slits in the screen was closed off, the effect was very interesting. The photons seemed to 'know' that one slit was closed and reacted accordingly. This came to be known as the 'thought' experiment. But the implications in this could be far-reaching. Does it imply that a tiny entity like a photon can have (2) some kind of intelligence? Does it have the ability to make decisions? The implications in this could be mind-boggling; at the very least, we are trying to peer into a completely different micro-world that functions in ways that we do not understand, as yet.

Another aspect of this reinforces this suspicion. Heisenberg was one of those that (3) attempted to delve into the inner workings of the atom. We recall that atoms have 'shells' or energy levels upon which electrons move around at colossal speeds. He noted that electrons are capable of 'jumping' from one shell to another, emitting a flash. This is done so rapidly that the word 'jump' is not appropriate. They have been termed 'spectral lines'. The movement is instantaneous. It is not necessarily from one shell to the one adjacent; it might be to another one further over. What causes this to happen? Does an electron make a decision or is there some other logic to it? This again is all very mysterious and still to this day, not properly explained; will it ever be?

Bohr, the Danish pundit based in Copenhagen, was fixated on quantum mechanics, and many other experts were in general agreement with him. Einstein, however, felt that although most of it was sound, it was not the total answer to all those awkward questions. One could say that Einstein's work was left unfinished, as a challenge to some genius in the future. He had the(4) inspiration that there could be a unified field theory which could integrate the electromagnetic spectrum with the theory of general relativity. A few words on these matters might be helpful.

The electromagnetic spectrum as described by Maxwell, concerns how light is split into a rainbow, into different colours. What we see in the rainbow are the visible variations on light, but beyond purple, is ultraviolet light and beyond red, is infrared light. These cannot be seen with the human eye, but are nevertheless very useful for all kinds of processes. There are infra-red cameras and ultra-violet lamps.

The theory of general relativity is much more difficult to grasp. Essentially, Einstein believed that the photon (the light particle) actually has some kind of weight. In other words, there is something actually lighter than hydrogen! If it has weight, it must then be subject to the force of gravity. In other words, light can be 'bent' or distorted in the presence of some kind of body exerting a force of gravity. Such entities would be Jupiter or the Sun. To evidence this, there was an occasion on which experts trooped off to West Africa to witness the passage of Mercury against the (5) Sun. Their observations gave strong confirmation that the gravitational force of the Sun did influence the light coming from that area. Light is warped by gravity.

For many years, Einstein was regarded as a heretic amongst the physicists. Now he is acknowledged as one of the greatest geniuses of all time. What does this tell us? That the rank outsider, the heretic, the one with a crazy idea, can turn out to be the greatest genius! A warning can be taken from this; the Nazi's automatically decided that because Einstein was Jewish, he therefore could not possibly be right. Einstein, providentially was in America when the Holocaust unfolded, and therefore escaped liquidation. However, he knew that the Germans were working on an atomic weapon and so warned Roosevelt. That explains the Manhattan project and the American atom bomb. This just shows how prejudice can actually backfire on one. But now, we are all still living with the legacy of Hiroshima and Nagasaki. Who knows what that will lead to?

If one were to wonder, do we really understand the sub-atomic world of quantum physics, an honest scientist might admit that we do not. The word 'superposition' is used; it is a politically correct word which is used to avoid having say 'we do not understand'. Part of the trouble is that physicists continue to use the thought-forms and vocabulary associated with the wave-motion idea. Clearly, there is a lot more to it that just Newtonian doctrines and phrases. It was Heisenberg who tried to abandon any claim that was unobservable. He focussed only on things that were observable. This was laudable but nevertheless had it shortcomings. As Einstein pointed out, observation is a complex process. As we observe things, our preconceived ideas (theories) tend to force an interpretation on such things that we have never encountered before. It was Heisenberg who admitted that it is the theory that determines what we can or cannot observe. This may seem a very strange remark, but there were those experts who admitted that the act of observing actually interfered with the workings of the sub-atomic world. This may seem a very odd admission, but at least they were honest enough to admit that for all their peerings into that world, they still could not really comprehend it. It is a world that appears to function according to a different system of logic.

It was thought originally that an atom was indivisible, indeed that is what the word 'atom' means. But by 1932, Chadwick discovered the neutron, and the fact that the atom can be split. So the atom has protons, (positive charge), neutrons (no charge) and electrons (negative charge). By 1969, protons and neutrons were discovered to be made up of smaller particles called Quarks. Now, we are told there are six types of quark, termed 'flavours'. (We notice again the quantum world being described in terms of the macro world). The flavours are; up, down, strange, charmed, bottom, and top. Each flavour comes in three colours; red, green and blue, (but not a colour in the sense we use it). So it is not just atoms that are divisible, but protons and neutrons. Each proton and neutron is made up of 3 quarks, one of each colour; a proton had 2 'ups' and 1 'down'; a neutron has 2 'downs' and 1 'up'. Going on from there, each of these particles has a property called 'spin'; it functions like a top or a gyroscope. But the spin does not have a clearly defined axis. There are four kinds of spin. (6)

Spin 0, is a dot, which appears the same from any direction.

Spin 1 is like an 'arrow', and looks different from different directions. It has to go through 360 degrees to look the same.

Spin 2 is like a double 'arrow', and looks the same after a 180 degree turn.

Spin half takes two revolutions to look the same.

In addition to this there is something called 'electron spin', which is not spinning in the normal sense, but jerking up and down.

What this means, is that all these tiny particles are not just static, but are whizzing round at amazing speeds, like mini-gyroscopes. If this is true, it means that everything maintains its stability and balance by behaving like a top. Again, this is nothing new. In Taoist philosophy (Chinese), nothing is static; everything has to keep moving otherwise the world will die.

To make matters even more complicated, each of these tiny particles has, it would seem, an opposite partner. So a quark has an antiquark; an electron has a positron. There are other little factors, such as gluons, and mesons. One wonders how far this can go in delving into the fundamental building blocks of life. It has been likened to the Russian set of nesting dolls; as one pulls out one, there is another smaller one inside, and so on and so on. As one theory seems acceptable, probing into it reveals another theory and so on ad infinitum. Hawking thought we must be near to finding the ultimate building block; but are we?!

There may be some who will regard all this as pure moonshine and imagination. However, even if these quantal entities cannot, as yet, be rationalised, there is good reason to believe that they are real. Perhaps we should give the physicists some credit.

The theological implications of this are various. Firstly, it goes to show that the constitution of Nature is not just some sort of chaotic mess. Every atom, and its constituents, is ordered, balanced and alive with energy. That energy cannot just invent itself; it has to be provided by a superior agency. I would say it comes from the world of the spirit, the very life-force of the Creator.

Secondly, the fact that all these tiny entities have an opposite, or anti-factor, brings us back to the theological factor of theodicy. We live in a world of plus and minus, gain and loss, positive and negative. There is a balance going on between these two opposites. The whole of Nature functions on the juxtaposition of opposites. This is how and why good and evil are a reality which cannot just be ignored.

And thirdly, just as all our attempts at discovering the origins of the Universe, on the mega-macro scale, with the so-called Big Bang, and how everything is believed to have come into existence, the same thing is happening at the sub-atomic end of the scale. The more we delve into it, the more we find, and the more theories have to be devised. When we come to consider the arguments for the existence of God, we shall find that one line of argument, the cosmological one, (7) does exactly the same thing. It goes back further, and further, and deeper and deeper. All our scientific probings and theorisings are nothing new; it is just the same thing using different vocabulary and metaphors.(7)

And fourthly, all this speculation into the very essentials of life, remind me of the way the first century AD Gnostics fantasised about creation, God, and the Logos. Are we sure our scientific phase is not just as fanciful and high-folluting?

One intriguing aspect of modern physics is the urge to find the GUT; this means the Grand (8) Unification Theory (it goes under various names). This

34

is something that Einstein felt he had left undone, and Hawking too, had the same ambition. What it means is that they assumed that there could be a common denominator theory to include all the four natural forces of nature. These forces are, the electromagnetic, the strong nuclear force, the weak nuclear force and gravity. The first three have been analysed and explained. The electromagnetic has a force carrier called the photon, a tiny particle of light; the weak nuclear has a force carrier seen as 3 vector bosons; the strong nuclear is characterised by 8 gluons, which explains the formation of molecules.

But to describe gravity, is altogether a more difficult matter. We all know it exists, but what is it? It is easy to see it as a force which makes things fall down to the ground, in this world. It is as well to remember that on other planets, that force is not the same; on the Moon it is a lot weaker; on Jupiter it is about 11 times stronger. It is all according to the mass of the planet, or star.

There is a sense in which gravity does not exist, according to Michio Kaku.(9) It all depends on what one means by 'exist'. Exist might mean exist in a physical sense. The same can be said of God, according to Paul Tillich, but of course, he did not mean it literally. But gravity has to consist of something. It is easier to say what gravity is not, than what it is; also what it does rather than being seen. In a way, gravity has certain aspects in common with God. Mr. Cox claims that it is gravity that created the Solar system. He declined to ask the question, 'who invented gravity?'

It was Newton that realised that gravity is not just an earthbound factor; it is a universal factor. Anything which has mass has an attraction to something else with mass. The bigger the object, the more the attraction. We can begin by accepting that the moon and the earth are attracted to each other. The connection between the phases of the moon and the tides had been known since prehistoric times. A shallow sea will result in slight tides; a deep sea, such as an ocean will result in a bigger tidal range. When the moon and the sun are lined up, at the equinoxes, it results in spring tides, ie. a much higher tidal range. If one were to think this only works on water, one would be mistaken. The solid crust of the earth also responds to lunar gravity, and can bulge by up to 25 cm. It is thought that earthquakes and tremors are caused by lunar gravity. It is also thought that 'moonquakes' are caused by earthly gravitation. This effect is seen much more dramatically on other moons such as Europa, Io, and Enceladus, where we see bulges, fountains and geysers caused by the major planets such as Jupiter and Saturn.

Looking at the entire Solar System, the fact that the different planets are at differing positions at any one time, their gravitational pull exerts some kind of influence on their orbits. While the moon traces an almost perfectly circular orbit round the earth, other planets do not. The earth's orbit is an ellipse, which is slightly egg-shaped, which helps to explain why the summer solstice is five days longer than the winter solstice. Other planets have slight variations in their orbits, and Mercury, being so close to the Sun has what can be described as a 'rosette' orbit.

It was Einstein who theorised that light is subject to gravity. If it is true that light consists of tiny particles, called photons, that have mass (even if it is very tiny), then it is subject to gravity. To evidence this, in 1919, the experts went off to the Island of Principe (West Africa) to view a total eclipse of the sun. A photograph revealed that the light coming from past the Sun was indeed warped. Gravity has been dubbed as the weakest of the four forces, and yet, it is theorised that a Black Hole would have such intense gravity that even light would be unable to escape from it, let alone anything else.

Gravity is the one force in Nature that has not been properly explained, still less assimilated with the other three forces. No one really knows what it is. It has been suggested that since it is a force carrier, it must have particles, like the other forces. These particles have been dubbed as 'gravitons'. They are completely hypothetical. It is wondered if it has a type 2 spin (as described above), but no one has as yet managed to find such an entity. If one were to isolate such an entity, it might lead on to finding the GUT theory. We recall that every particle has an opposite number, which in this case might be termed an 'antigraviton'. But this is pure conjecture, as yet. Even so, gravity can be calculated mathematically, so much so, that some have dubbed God as a mathematician.

In 1984 a new approach appeared in Physics; the String Theory, and various permutations on it. Can you imagine a one-dimensional piece of string? Not easily! But the pundits have moved away from particle theory in favour of 'strings'. We notice again, the use of macro-world metaphors in an attempt at describing matters purely theoretical. The world-sheet is an open string, but its ends can be joined up. A closed string becomes a loop or a tube. These can be joined up as well, rather like the legs on a pair of trousers. The gravitons are thought to travel down the tubes, say from the Sun to the Earth. After 1984 a revived approach to string theory arose in the form of the 'heterotic string'. Now, it seems, there are four different string theories, with all kinds of interesting metaphors derived from the macro-world. As one theory falls apart, another one is devised. We seem to be no nearer to the GUT theory which is supposed to be waiting to be found. Are we just chasing a mirage?

Hawking boils it down to three possibilities;

1. There is a complete unified theory just waiting to be discovered.
2. There is just an infinite sequence of theories which put together will give an overview of reality.
3. There is no such theory; everything is random and unpredictable.

Number one again raises the issue of free will versus predestination. But all our scientific investigations make the assumption that there are 'laws' to be discovered, and from them, predictions can be made. If we give up on assuming the laws of Nature, we may as well give up on science altogether.

Number one is a tempting proposition, but may in the end be unachievable; it is like the Russian boxes; we go on for ever, delving ever more deeply into these matters and not come to the end of it. Moreover, we would never be quite certain we did have the final answer, from a scientific point of view. From a theological point of view, the answer is that God is the final creative genius behind all of these intricate matters.

Number two is probably more feasible. It could be likened to making a map of the world. It is a globe, so it cannot be represented on a flat piece of paper. There have to be various projections of it, which, if put together, give a fair idea of the geography of the world. So too, various theories, which paradoxically may be contradictory, if considered together, may give us a fair view of the basic building blocks of life.

Theories come and go; interesting metaphors come and go; but the essentials of life are still elusive, and that is especially true for gravity. Every theory that arrives, has some element of truth in it, as well as a few mistakes. What this tells us is that human nature, being inquisitive, is trying to find those laws which are assumed to exist somewhere. Some of them have been found; others remains elusive. Being human, every clever idea has some kind of flaw in it, some kind of rash idea, even wishful thinking. But we all assume that there are laws, and that presupposes someone who frames the laws, a lawgiver.

Looking at the way the Solar System operates, with its delicate balancing act between the Sun and the planets, all based on gravity and the speed of orbiting, I cannot avoid the conclusion that it is a highly intricate system. Going on from that, there are other solar systems, and whole galaxies in outer space, stretching to infinity. Future research may, I expect, discover even more intricate factors, of which we are not yet aware. How can this have just formed itself, all by itself? I say that is impossible. The interplay between those tiny electrical impulses at the atomic level, plus and minus, can hardly have installed themselves. It is one thing to attempt to describe how atoms were formed, in the physical sense, but the overall power, design and intricacy of it demands us to take the creative genius of God seriously.

It is interesting that the most recent ideas, namely the string theories, so-called, look remarkably like a return to 'wave' motion concepts. Even so, they involve the gravitons shooting along tubes between the Sun and the Earth. All very imaginative but completely hypothetical! What strikes me is two things, on reading up information about the Quantum World. Firstly, with all these tiny entities circulating and gyrating like gyroscopes, it gives me the impression that it all contributes to the balancing act of life itself. This is mirrored in the mega world of the Solar System and also of galaxies. It is all a matter of balance. Can such a thing as balance install itself, or just develop by one mistake after another? I do not think that is realistic.

Secondly, on studying these matters, I am struck by the inability of the pundits to dispel one mystery after another. The whole matter of quantum mechanics is clearly functioning on some other system of logic. Attempts at imposing our assumptions of regulation on this world, do not work. Our thought forms, metaphors and vocabulary simply do not fit. One wonders whether there is not some kind of intelligence going on in these tiny entities. What may appear to be randomness, might, for all we know, follow some sort of policy that we do not understand. It amounts to a deep mystery, with so many unanswered questions. But the same is true in theology. Certainly in the faith of Christianity, there are many deep mysteries. Attempts at rationalising them, simply do not work. Holy mysteries are not confined to Christianity; many other religions have such deep questions at their heart. Attempts at sanitising them have been seen not to be particularly successful. The essence of true religion is mystery; it would seem that that would apply to quantum mechanics as well.

One of the dilemmas in this kind of research concerned the issue determinism versus randomness. It was Einstein who believed in determinism, but others, such as Bohr did not. This is where theological considerations enter the picture. The question of predestination as opposed to free will has been a bone of contention for philosophers and theologians since the dawn of civilization. It is politically wrong to agree with predestination in these times of supposed freedom and democracy, but there are still those who believe in predestination. This would be chiefly the Muslims, but not just them. If it is true that there is some kind of inevitability at work in the sub-atomic world, what are the implications for the macro-world? Does it mean that there is some form of determinism functioning in our lives, of which we are not really aware? In the ancient world, it was an important assumption that the behaviour of the stars and constellations had a direct effect on one's life. There are still people who take this matter seriously today. This is where the element of paradox may become helpful. Would it be fair to say that determinism and randomness in the world of quantum mechanics are both true in their own way, just as wave-motion and particle-motion can be seen like this? (10)

What other theological conclusions can be drawn from quantum mechanics? At the very least, we can say that the whole of creation, from the simplest things to the most complicated, are all constructed from the same basic ingredients, namely, the atom, in all its variations. It is not as if some things are made of X basic materials and other things made of another arrangement, call it Y. This must argue for the unity of Creation. It is one plan, one clever arrangement, and one ingenious result. This must indicate that if Creation was caused by some kind of spiritual being, or beings, this must be one God, as opposed of myriads of them. This is in strong support of monotheism. The pagan notion of multi-gods is clearly wrong. Going further, it is claimed, with good reason, that the same quantum mechanical arrangement is at work out there in the rest of the universe, as far as we can reach. This must tell us, that if there is a creator God, he pervades all of the Universe, not just some quiet corners of it.

Another conclusion that one might draw, would be as follows. Clearly there is some kind of energy at work in every single atom. The same energy drives the whole of creation along, but also, we have sensed that some aspects of it (the photon) might display some kind of 'thought' or intelligence. What are the implications in that? Does it mean that the intelligence of the great creator is at work in every single atom? This could be an indication that the Pantheist idea has some validity. The Christians have always maintained that even if God is to be seen in all his Creation, nevertheless, he is totally other than his creation. Here again is an amazing paradox. Can we see that in every atom, there is the energy of the Creator, and yet God is not an atom, nor even billions of them. This reminds me of what Jesus said; "the very hairs on your head are numbered" by which he meant that every tiny detail of creation is known about and energized by God. (11)

I think it is fair to accept, in general terms, the theorizing of the physicists on these matters. That does not have to mean we accept en bloc every claim that they make, and we must remember that they spent a lot of time arguing amongst themselves. It is worth remarking that someone published an article on the subject. It sounded all very clever and high-flown, but in actual fact, it was gibberish! This reminds us of the redoubtable Professor Stanley Unwin, who came out with all kinds of mind-boggling scientific remarks, which were actually complete claptrap! I think it is fair to say, that we should all be wary of taking on trust every word that the scientists serve up. Let us just remember that they are quite adept at changing their minds on matters. Are we waiting for another Einstein to appear, who will throw the whole matter in the air and devise a completely different atomic theory? Let us not allow ourselves to become too dogmatic on these matters.

Another aspect of this is the nature of light. We all know about the electromagnetic spectrum, and types of light that the human eye cannot see. If it is true that the photon (as theorised by Einstein) actually is a particle that has weight, we can understand that these particles are just as much a part of the created universe as everything else. In the first chapter of Genesis, (12) we read that God said, 'let there be light'. This was not the sun or the moon, although they followed on in the next verses. But the whole theory of light as discussed by the quantum mechanics shows us that 'light' is not just a matter of the sun or the moon shining. There are so many different permutations on light, and the one that can see right through us, namely X-rays, reminds us that God knows each and every one of us in tiny detail. This reminds us of the Samaritan woman at the well, talking to Jesus. (13).

Even so, one has to admit that the very building blocks of creation are amazing and beyond our comprehension, at least, for the moment. I cannot imagine these tiny impulses of life just inventing themselves, or gradually taking shape by some kind of evolution; to say that is just pure nonsense. It has to be the work of a superior agency, which is a fancy way of talking about God. In this way, surely quantum mechanics goes a long way to supporting any argument in favour of the existence of God.

**Footnotes**

1. These comments are taken largely from Marcus Chown, The Ascent of Gravity.
2. The experiment is described in detail in Marcus Chown.
3. See chapter 2 for diagrams.
4. See later on in this chapter.
5. More discussion of this comes later in this chapter.
6. Taken from Hawking, A Brief History of Time.
7. See Chapter 12.
8. See Marcus Chown, Time and Gravity.
9. Kaku is an America theoretical physicist who propounded the 'string theory' and also delves into futuristic physics.
10. One of the problems in theoretical physics has been the failure to grapple with the concept of paradox.
11. Matthew 10:30.
12. Genesis 1:3.
13. John 4:19.

# 5

## *Biochemistry and Theology.*

Following on from an assessment of the quantum world it is possible to move on to the way that atoms combine to form the various forms of life that we see on this planet. As to whether the same arrangement applies on other planets, there is much speculation on this matter, but as yet, there is no clear indication of life forms elsewhere. This applies particularly to our Solar System, and may, in time, prove to be true with other planets, now termed 'exo-planets.'

Biochemistry is one area of Science that has made great progress in recent years. It would be very easy to confuse the reader by quoting all kinds of difficult terms and phrases used in biochemical textbooks. My intention is to keep the heavy technical terms to a minimum and where we cannot avoid using them, try to make it possible to elucidate their meaning in simple terms. I have been fascinated by the textbook which Oxford undergraduates are recommended to use, Biochemistry by Hames and Hooper. One wonders if the undergraduates manage to master all those technical phrases?! It will seem, however, that contemporary findings in the area of biochemistry do have some kind of bearing on Theology. I do not claim to be an expert on biochemistry, but I do feel that I can see the main trends and essentials of it and can see its relevance to religious practice and also traditional doctrines, and the assessment of human nature.

Biochemistry is essentially concerned with the chemical basics of living matter, whether it be flora, fauna or the human structure. Before the advent of recently developed powerful microscopes, we had to infer the existence of atoms, by observing the effects that they gave off . One of these effects, is that when heated or burnt, they give off distinctive colours. One example of this would be copper, which gives off an intense bluish-purple colour. When dealing with biochemistry, there is no need to 'see' atoms. The molecules that they form can be seen through very powerful microscopes. There are several such in use now; light microscopy, fluorescence microscopy, electron microscopy with their variants. With these, actual cells and molecules can be identified and analysed. There is no need to go into detail as to how these microscopes work. But I would say that it is fair to say that these methods are giving us a reliable amount of information. In other words, we are not now in the realms of supposition and guesswork.

The main areas of analysis in biochemistry are thus; understanding about cells, the actual building blocks of life; amino acids; proteins; enzymes; DNA, genes and chromosomes; RNA; fatty acids and cholesterol. Each of these will receive closer attention in due course. If the reader wishes to delve more deeply into such matters, I suggest one obtains the textbook cited above. However,(1) my intention is to give a general overview of these matters without confusing the non-specialist with too many abstruse phrases. Also, I will try not to oversimplify these matters, which would have the effect of rendering the matter superficial.

We begin with a few comments on the subject of cells. A quotation from Hames and Hooper, page 1, is interesting;

"Despite the huge variety of living systems, all organisms on Earth are remarkably uniform at the molecular level, indicating that they have evolved from a common ancestor."

This firstly is saying something which can be verified, that all living organisms in this world are basically formed on the same tiny structures which look something like an egg, but which also have one or more tails with which they can move around. This reminds us of the sperm, the male reproductive element, which is needed to fertilise the ovum, or the female egg. What is contained within each cell, in the nucleus, is different, and this is conditioned by the DNA (to be discussed later). But the different types of cells are relevant to the life-forms that they are the basis of. It is also interesting that this comment betrays the notion of 'common ancestor'. This is a notion derived from evolutionary thinking. It was a theory which Darwin offered in his book, The Origin of Species, and it stems from his work on pigeons. Because he worked out that all pigeons are basically derived from the rock pigeon, therefore that was their 'common ancestor', albeit going back millions of years. This is a good example of a scientist arguing from the specific to the general. Just because the pigeons might have a common ancestor, therefore all creatures have a common ancestor. But speculating on what may or may not have happened millions of years ago, must remain in the realms of speculation and guesswork. How can it ever be provable? Nevertheless, it is now assumed that all cells have a common ancestor. I would say that that may be even more difficult to establish beyond doubt.

Cells are of several kinds; firstly, there are the bacteria, such as E.Coli and Bacillus, and also Archaea, which are also harmful. These are termed Prokaryotes, and are assumed to be the original germs. They are thought to have diverged early in the life of the Earth. The other group of cells is the Eukaryotes which are the basis of animals, fungi and plants. They are much larger and more complex on the inside, and are thought to have diverged from the Prokaryotes early in the life of the Earth. What this means is that some cells are harmful and bring disease while others are essential for the structure of any creature. Quite how this comes about must be a puzzle, but it means that at the microscopic level, there is a constant conflict between life and death, or to put it very crudely, an ongoing tussle between the 'goodies' and the 'baddies'. The question must arise; why should the good ones have to be derived from the bad ones? Might it not be the other way round? This is something that is beyond evidence as yet.

This is where Theology enters the picture. We know that the ancient pagan concept of life was based on the assumption of perpetual conflict in the skies, with gods incessantly battling with each other. This is a motif which is still with us, not just in the residual pagan areas of the world, but also in Christianity, Judaism and Islam. They too have an understanding of the conflict between good and evil, except that it is simplified into a tussle between God and Satan. This the age-old question of Theodicy; why is there any evil in the world? This a question that philosophers and theologians have wrestled with since the dawn of civilisation, but have not found a straightforward solution. But we see an ongoing conflict at microscopic level, also at the spiritual level and also at the political level in human world affairs. Even at the level of atomic theory, with the tension between plus and minus, we see the same thing. But atomic theory does offer us an insight into the problem. Each atom is somehow very cleverly balanced within itself, between plus and minus. Is this the answer, that the whole of life at each level, is cleverly balanced so that neither good nor evil gain the ascendency, at least if one of them does, the balance is restored in the long run? This is one example of how biochemistry, and atomic theory, tie in with basic assumptions in Theology.

Another aspect of studying life at the microscopic level is the fact that these tiny impulses of life are so intricately organised. It would be true to say for instance that a bacteria has a different internal structure to a typical plant cell. Even so, the internal plan is the same throughout that particular genus. It is not as if all of life is some sort of amorphous uncoordinated muddle. It might appear so, on a casual glance at how life on earth proceeds. But when we come to analyse in detail how it all works, the impression given is quite different. It is all very orderly, predictable and one ought really be able to admit, planned, or going further, the word might be 'designed'. (2) Once we begin to think like that, it raises the question of how this was designed, or in other words, what about the designer? This inevitably raises the question of a superior intelligence that produced these designs in the first place. It makes no sense to say that all these intricate structures, with their interesting functions, just occurred all by themselves, out of thin air.

The same impression is gained when we look at proteins. All proteins are made up from the same set of 20 standard amino acids. We start with Alanine and finish with Valine (3). It is interesting to see that every variant on amino acids, has a single carbon atom at its centre. Surrounding this carbon atom are all kinds of other atoms, hydrogen, oxygen, nitrogen, mainly, sometimes forming an elaborate 'chain', but still with the carbon atom at its centre. All of these acids have some function to perform. One cannot avoid the conclusion that these patterns, can hardly be some kind of casual agglomeration. It is all very orderly and functions according to what certainly appears to be rules and procedures.

Looking at the human structure, there are two proteins which bind oxygen. These are haemeglobin and myoglobin. Haemeglobin transports oxygen round the body in the red blood copustles and myoglobin stores oxygen in the muscles. The haemeglobin in the foetus is of a different quality from that of the mother, and allows the baby to have a richer oxygen supply before birth. Haemeglobin not only has the ability to transport oxygen to all parts of the body, but also to carry carbon dioxide back to the lungs so that it can be expelled into the atmosphere. Again, we see one central atom, this time, of iron, as the focal point of the haemeglobin, and the iron bonds with four nitrogen atoms at the centre, plus various other atoms. The effect is that carbon monoxide has difficulty in bonding with the structure when breathing normal atmosphere. Again, we see remarkably complex structures, for instance the helical 'chains'. At a glance, the diagrams appear to be haphazard and chaotic, but this is far from being the truth. The long 'wriggling chains' all contain essential atomic ingredients and there is nothing haphazard about it at all. One has to marvel at the intricacy of the whole thing.(4)When comparing this with Biblical thoughts on the subject of blood, we find that blood is a very important factor. In the laws of Moses, in Leviticus, it says that the blood is the life in the (5) animal. This is absolutely true; that the red blood corpustles carry oxygen round the body to feed all parts, and then carry away carbon dioxide which would poison the body. In addition to this, when Jesus said, "this is my blood....." he was offering his disciples his very life and soul to invigorate and inspire them.(6)Another element in blood is the white blood corpustles, the leucocytes, which are not normally visible amongst the red ones. There are no less than five different kinds of leucocytes, each with its own special function. The neutrophils, the lymphocytes, the monocytes, the eosinophils, and the basophils.

The neutrophils, which are the most common in the bloodstream, have the task of responding to any injury or infection, which would allow bacteria to invade the body. If such invaders were not resisted, the body would be overwhelmed and die. The neutrophils rush to the injury and engulf the harmful invaders. When the neutrophils die, they are removed by the monocytes, which are much larger. The lymphocites do a similar task to the neutrophils, but tackle invading viruses, and also have a kind of immunological memory. This means that they have a recollection of various viruses from previous invasions. The eosinophils specialise in fighting parasitic infections, and allergic reactions, an example of which is asthma. The basophils are most active at sites of healing or chronic inflammation. As we can see, the whole thing is most ingenious. It appears that each type of leucocyte seems to know its own function; does that imply that each cell has some kind of intelligence or capability of making a decision? It certainly seemed like that with the photons (chapter 3). It is amazing that since the leucocytes have some kind of memory of previous encounters with harmful intrusions, one gains a kind of immunity to certain diseases. This means, for instance, that once one has had chicken pox, one will not normally have it again. Going further, this factor applies to some kind of inherited immunity. If a forebear has a disease, such as scarlet fever, the immunity is passed on to the offspring, rendering it unlikely that the child we contract the disease. The whole thing is really quite amazing. To reinforce this factor, when the Spaniards invaded the Americas, the Indians died, not so much from warfare, but from infections like influenza and the common cold, because they had no inherited resistance to them. The reverse was true for the Europeans.Again, we see the importance of balance in the composition of the blood, and how the various elements are in the appropriate proportion to each other. If the balance is disturbed in some way, by some kind of harmful intrusion, the body's immune system quickly responds to rectify the balance. A disease may gain some kind of advantage, for a time, but in the long run, the immune system regains the balance.

This goes to show that not just the red but the white blood corpuscles are essential for the life of the creature. The leucocytes are a cleansing agent, relevant to the process of healing. Now we see that St. John's statement,(7) that the blood of Jesus cleanses us from all sin, can be seen in a different light. He may not have realised what he was saying, but now, with twentieth century biological research, we can see a deeper truth in this remark, which can be taken as a prophecy. In this way, the importance of blood, in all its forms, is seen on a theological level and on a biological level. The two levels of truth support and complement each other.

Another kind of protein, a family, is called collagen. They form strong, insoluble fibres in the body. This covers such things as bone, skin, tendons, cartilage, blood vessels and teeth. Thus the extremely hard items like teeth and the elasticated items like skin and muscles are all formed from collagen. Calcium phosphate is the essential material in this kind of protein. Again, there are helical 'chains' formed, often with a thousand elements. Again, the fact that this material is not some kind of chaotic mass, but is organised into recognisable forms, such as helices, is an indication that there must be planning, structure and design in the whole thing. Again, we have to marvel at the intricacy and detail of these structures at the atomic and molecular level. (8)

Just as animals have red blood cells (the haemes), so too do the green plants, except that they are called chlorophylls. They are the equivalent of blood in animals. Just as the human blood is based on one single atom of iron, so the plant 'blood' is based on one atom of magnesium, but with a structure of atoms, nitrogen and others looking very similar. But the effect is the opposite. Just as animals inhale oxygen and exhale carbon dioxide, the green plants take in carbon dioxide, turn it into carbohydrate, but exhale oxygen. The effect is that the oxygen level in the atmosphere remains more or less constant at 21%, which is just right for animals to breathe. This means that the two elements, animals and green plants, are interdependent, and anything that unbalances that arrangement, is most unwise. I would say that this reciprocal arrangement can only be called, most ingenious.

Again, the implications of this in relation to Biblical teaching is worth noting. In Genesis chapter 1, God created not just the human race, but the animals and the plants. In the Laws of Moses, the Sabbath and the Jubilee year are not just for the benefit of the human race, but for all of the natural world. Nature itself has to have a rest, to avoid over-exploitation. (10)

We now turn to the matter of DNA (deoxyribonucleic acid) which has become only recently, an important element in modern life, particularly in the field of forensic science. It also has ramifications for other matters. The double helix, shown below, is now familiar to many people. It goes on for billions of combinations, all of which have some bearing on every physical feature of our bodies. One can go further and say not just physical features but personality, and spirituality.

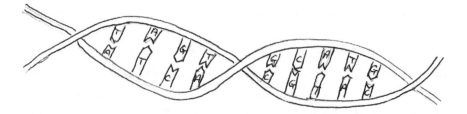

**DNA Structure**

What is less familiar to most people is RNA, which is closely associated with DNA. RNA stands for ribonucleic acid. It is produced from DNA in a process of copying, and acts as a messenger, hence it is abbreviated to mRNA. It has the task of conveying the genetic message to where it is needed and is also a double helix. It has an extra oxygen atom included and of the four bases, thymine (T) is replaced by uracil (U) which pairs with adenine (A). Sometimes it is U/A and at other times it is T/A. It is thought that RNA may be something to do with the origins of life itself; even then, the origins of life are still a mystery. This is a way brings us back to theology and creationism. It is one thing to assemble all the essentials of life at the molecular level, but another thing to make it all come to life. No one has managed to achieve that as yet. Again, we are looking at the creative genius of God. The relevance of RNA to gene editing will be seen later (9) A diagram of RNA is shown below.

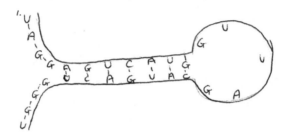

## Single Guide RNA

DNA is basically constructed with four bases; Adenine paired with Thymine; Guanine paired with Cytosine. This time, the structure is predominantly based on Nitrogen atoms with various Hydrogen and Oxygen additions. All four of them have a hexagonal configuration. The partners are held together with a single Hydrogen atom as a bond. The double helix which contains a combination of these partners opposite each other, and the combination of these pairs is different in every creature. Having said that, DNA is an essential element in any living creature, from bacteria up to plants, animals and humans. It is the element that determines heredity, and explains why a child will resemble his parents, and why a strawberry plant will reproduce itself as a strawberry plant, as opposed to a gooseberry bush. Again, we see that there is nothing haphazard or unscheduled in this intricate arrangement. (11)

The importance of this for forensics is as follows; any sample from any living creature, or that has lived, will contain a portion of DNA. That sample is peculiar to that creature. This means, that like fingerprinting and dental impressions, we can identify the person who was in some way involved in whatever deed was committed. We can also determine, or at least, make an assessment, of what relationship there is between one body and another; is this father and son, brother or sister etc? This is now very useful in the field of archaeology. It can be noted that DNA helped to confirm that the remains of a certain person with a crooked back, found in a Leicester car park, was indeed King Richard 3rd.

What are the implications in this for religious faith? Traditionally, several religions have laid great emphasis on the family as a unit of faith. This is particularly so with Judaism and also with Confucianism (and the Chinese mentality in general). It has been inherent in Christianity all along, but now there is the new idea called 'the Family Service' which is an attempt at emphasising the cohesion of not just the physical family but also the family of the Church. Our understanding of DNA underpins this strand of thought in Theology, in religious practice and also in Biblical teaching. It strengthens the instinctive feeling that inheritance and the family name and reputation are very important. This is something we sense all through the Bible. We notice that much stress is laid on those long lists of names (and someone begat someone); (12) it all indicates the continuity of faith over the centuries from the early patriarchs down to New Testament times. Two of our gospels begin with the genealogy of Jesus, showing his regal background (as descended from King David) and also relating him back to Abraham and Adam. This is a roundabout way of saying that he was thoroughly of the Hebrew race and also totally human. This implies that if we had a sample of DNA from King David and from Jesus, we would see some kind of relationship. (13)

Looking at it another way, the metaphor of 'sonship' can be seen as highly appropriate as when applied to Jesus. He called himself 'the Son of Man'. The implication in that is that he had all the inherited traits from his own family, thinking firstly about his mother Mary. Also, as applied to his divinity, he was fully representative of the eternal Father. This is not to say that God has DNA, but as a metaphor, the sonship of Jesus indicates that he has all the attributes of the Father, God. In this way, the modern understanding of DNA ties in with and supports traditional family values, and the doctrine of the Incarnation.

Another aspect of DNA is that even though we all function on the same intricate chemical basis, even so, we are all slightly different. It is the rearrangement of those partners in the double helix which makes the difference. It is claimed that identical twins have the same DNA; even so, there are very slight differences between them, which a parent can tell, but others cannot. The same is true with animals, birds, plants and all living creatures. Every cat is slightly different, even if they are all recognisable as a cat. This goes to show that while there is unity, there is also diversity. This is something we all have to accept as an inescapable fact. Why complain about it? Why can't we rejoice that we are not just clones of each other? The same is true with religious belief; there are no two believers with exactly the same ideas in their heads. Admittedly there are major rafts of opinion, such as Roman Catholic or Islam, but anyone can see that such people are not just clones of each other. They all differ slightly in their thinking. When we come to religious diversity, it becomes even more obvious that there is an entire kaleidoscope of possibilities in religious faith and practice. Can we say that this is a direct result of that DNA which conditions the make-up of each and every one of us?

Now we turn to the issue of cholesterol, a matter which is much in the public eye, not least for its health implications. It is nonsense to say that one should eliminate cholesterol from one's body; we all need it. It is one component of the cell membranes, and that is essential for the texture (and fluidity) of the outer layers of each and every cell in our bodies. Also it is relevant to the production of progesterone, testosterone and cortisol, elements that are related to gender and reproduction. The problem arises when cholesterol begins to accumulate inside the veins and arteries, and if this is not resolved, it can lead to heart problems and strokes. Cholesterol can be regulated medically with the use of statins. The cause of problems is unhealthy eating, and lack of exercise, both of which can be corrected by plenty of physical activity and a balanced diet. Cholesterol problems appear to be a feature of modern living, which involves excessive use of motor cars, sitting in front of computers and generally relying on convenience foods. It is a modern trend which has disturbed the delicate balance of health in the human frame.

How is this related to religious practice? On the face of it, campaigning for a healthier life-style is not confined to those of a religious inclination. It involves anyone with degree of common sense. However, it has to be noted that most, if not all religions, have some kind of dietary restriction. The Hindus will not eat beef; the Jews will not eat pork. This, on the face of it, may seem irrational, but historically, there may have been a perfectly good reason for such rules.An example of this can be drawn from the strictures on imbibing alcohol, which is a feature of many a Protestant group, especially the Salvation Army. This may to some to be unnecessary in today's world, but we have to recall that back in the 19th century, excessive use of low grade alcohol caused all kinds of health and social problems. The teetotallers had good reason to bring in their campaign, and it is worth noting that Alcoholics Anonymous is still kept busy with those who have lost control of themselves in this matter.

In this way, ethics over food and drink are still a matter for religious practice and can also be based on what we know about dietary needs from biochemistry. A responsible religionist will advise a moderate and balanced approach to food and drink, with a view to enhancing the physical wellbeing of the individual.

A final comment on these matters would be, that we can appreciate that the body is a finely balanced mechanism, especially on the subject of cholesterol, but other aspects also. If things go out of balance, we can expect health problems. The same is true for all those other factors concerning blood, collagen, DNA and in fact every other aspect of one's physique. If it gets out of balance because of some deficiency or excess, we can expect trouble. A healthy person is one whose body is well-balanced in every respect. The concept of balance is a ruling factor in every area we have discussed in this book, and also relates to religion.

**Footnotes**

1. Most of this information comes from Hames and Hooper, with a few additions from elsewhere.
2. See chapter on Proofs for the Existence of God, chapter 12.
3. Page 34 in Hames and Hooper.
4. Page 49 in Hames and Hooper.
5. Leviticus 17:11. also Deuteronomy 12:23.
6. Mark 14:24.
7. I John 1:7.
8. Page 58 in Hames and Hooper.
9. See chapter 12 on gene editing.
10. Leviticus 25.
11. Page 173 and 191 in Hames and Hooper.
12. Matthew chapter 1 is a good example.
13. If the body found in the Leicester car park could be connected by DNA to his living descendants, then why not Jesus to King David?
14. Pages 381 to387 in Hames and Hooper.

# 6

## *The Mega World and the Big Bang*

Having reviewed the submicroscopic world, it is now reasonable to assess the big picture, the Universe itself, and its origins. This is where speculation amongst astro-physicists is at its most acute. Does anyone really know how everything came into existence? But there are any amount of ideas based on careful observations of outer space. This has only become possible in recent times because of the telescopic gadgetry that we have developed, plus the observations that can be made from our orbiting satellites which are above the distortions of the Earth's atmosphere. Since it has been noted that the quantum world appears to function according to a different sort of logic to the macro-world, would it be outrageous to say that the mega world out there also operates on a different system of rules and procedures? No one seems to have offered that thought, so far.

Talking of offering a new thought, it was Georges Lemaître, in 1927, who first offered the idea of the Big Bang. At first this idea was ignored, probably as being some sort of cranky idea, but gradually it has become the established doctrine in scientific circles. But what does the Big Bang actually mean? It means that originally, there was a relatively small blob of matter, which decided to explode and scatter material in all directions out into the empty universe. This has been calculated to have happened 13.7 billion (earth) years ago, and that material is still expanding at an accelerating rate. To support this claim, there are various arguments, the chief one of which is the 'red shift' piece of reasoning. (1)

This is how it works. We know that there is the Doppler effect, which means that something making a noise and going away from us, the sound dims down. The opposite effect is heard as something approaches; the sound

53

goes higher. The same effect is claimed with colours of astral bodies. As they recede from us, the red element dims. If they were to approach us, the red element would be brighter; but they are not approaching us. They are flying away at a rapid rate. From this ingenious theory, a whole scale of values relating to astral speeds has been worked out. I would offer the thought that no one seems to consider that this red shift effect might be caused by something else of which we are unaware.

In addition to this, there is a claim made about 'background glow'. It is stated that everything above nought degrees emits radiation, and that indicates its temperature. Everything above 100 degrees, the wavelengths enter the visible range and emits a glow of dull red. Higher temperatures go to orange, then white. From this, we can assess the temperature of planets and other astral bodies. This would seem fair, since contemporary photographs of the night sky do show stars with different colours, which may indicate their temperatures. Going on from this, it is claimed that there is an 'after glow' from the Big Bang. This glow is from 2 to 73 degrees above absolute zero, but to detect this must require highly sensitive equipment.

All this may seem convincing to those who delve into such matters, but one wonders whether they really know what they are talking about. We are talking about vast distances in multi-billions of light years. Some of the light coming from these distant astral bodies will have taken centuries to arrive at our planet. Do we really know what is happening out there at this moment?

It is interesting that the Big Bang is not entirely a new idea. The Chinese (Taoist) creation (2) myth offers us the idea of an original cosmic egg and also a god who banged a drum to initiate the world. The cosmic egg motif is not confined to China. The Greeks had a similar idea. Why they had this idea, would be an interesting question. Is it possible that Lemaître derived his idea from them? If so, this would be a case of mythology influencing scientific speculation! Neither would that be the first time that that had happened!

A slight difficulty with the expanding universe would be; why is it accelerating, as is claimed? One would expect that after the initial force from the explosion, material would continue at a consistent speed and trajectory. In addition to that, we seem to have bits floating in space, going their own way, so to speak. Why is it that we have asteroids and meteorites, and comets, not going in a consistent straight line and sometimes colliding with other planets?

Going on from this, it is thought that the Big Bang emitted vast amounts of hydrogen and helium, and that these clouds of gas formed the first stars. The question must arise, if such an immense amount of gas was pushed out into the universe, how was this material formed in the first place, and from such a relatively small 'egg'? An even greater difficulty arises, when we ask, where did all the ingredients for this material come from? What happened before the alleged Big Bang? No one really has the answer to that, except the religionists, who understand that it was the Creator God who installed the basics of all those billions of atoms.

If it is true that the Big Bang emitted vast amounts of hydrogen and some helium, we may ask where did all the other chemical elements come from? As we see from the Periodic Table, devised by Mendeleev, it goes from hydrogen, the lightest, up to Uranium, and others even heavier.(3) They are thought not to have appeared at the great start of all things. The answer is that the astro-physicists believe that all the other elements came from stars. This is called the Stellar Synthesis Theory. It goes something like this. To make other elements form from hydrogen requires immense heat. We are talking about 50 to 60 million degrees C. The only situation where this heat could be found would be inside a star. The reason for this is that a vast hydrogen cloud such as is needed for a star, shrinks under its own gravity, and thus produces enough heat to ignite the hydrogen. This results in a nuclear bonfire, something which we have managed to fabricate for ourselves since 1945. Initially, the hydrogen is converted into helium, but then, with such immense temperatures, other elements form, such as iron, silica, carbon and others. Experiments done in laboratories have given us the impression that this is feasible. The logic of it is somewhat tortuous, but can be read up in various scientific textbooks. (4)

We then have to ask, how did these heavier elements escape from the stars and form planets? The supposed answer is that as the star reached an explosive situation, such as a super-nova, it spewed out all kinds of materials into space, thus forming the planets. Some of these planets became rocky ones, while others just stayed as gas giants. Our inner planets in our solar system, Mercury, Venus, Earth and Mars, are rocky planets which would allow life to have a firm basis. A gas giant such as Jupiter, might not have a convenient basis for life.

To my mind, there are various questions one ought to ask. It is assumed that the stars are the only possible method by which heavier elements can be formed; how do we know there was not some other process at work, which we do not see today? I would also ask, if it is true that the sun spewed out all these elements, in contradiction to its own gravitational pull, why did these immense amounts of material form into almost perfect spherical shapes, as our planets are? Also, why is the core of our planet active with great heat, while the crust is cold? Also, why is it that various minerals, such as iron, copper, tin, zinc etc. are concentrated in a few selected areas, rather than spread out everywhere? We know that copper is heavily represented in Rhodesia, iron in parts of Canada, tin in Malaysia and so on. Also, why is it that some planets have remained as gas giants and not shrunk down to be rocky planets? It would seem that there are many questions not yet resolved; indeed, can they ever be?

One factor which could be stated with some confidence, is that the vital elements that make up our physical world, appear to be the same, not just in this solar system, but everywhere else. Every time a meteorite lands from outer space, the chemical composition of it does not show anything different from what we already know. It may be a big assumption to say that the whole universe is functioning on one consistent periodic table, but that is the way it seems, so far. It is not as if some parts of outer space function on some other system of reality. If this is true, it is another argument in favour of Monotheism, that there is one Creator God with one method at work, as opposed to different ones with different ideas.

Another factor which appears important in the formation of the various elements, is the factor of balance. As the elements form, each atom feels the need to achieve its own equilibrium. This means that the protons and neutrons in the nucleus need to match the number of electrons in the outer 'shells'. Paradoxically, there are some atoms that do have a degree of instability because they have a slight shortage or superflux of electrons in their outer shell. Sodium and chlorine are such examples. This explains how and why atoms are attracted to each other and form ions or molecules and hence large structures and compounds. Being attracted to each other in some kind of bonding arrangement, gives the atoms a fresh form of equilibrium or balance. We have already seen how balance is an important factor in biochemistry. Can this factor of balance really install itself? It requires a superior agency or planner to devise it in the first place. (5)

It is now the right moment to assess the formation of stars. Our star, the sun, is thought to be a fairly late comer as compared with some of the others. Astronomers believe they can describe the life of stars, as they claim to be able to see new stars in the process of formation and older ones in the process of dying or exploding. The word 'evolution' is freely used in describing this process, but is it really applicable? One wonders.

The 'birth' of a star happens when vast clouds of gas (hydrogen) and dust collapse inwards. As it becomes denser it heats up. Its gravity draws in more material, and as it heats up it begins to glow. Then nuclear fusion reactions begin. The star is now active. Two examples of this would be Orion Nebula M42 and Lagoon Nebula M8. It then moves into its 'adolescence'. It is still surrounded by clouds of dust and gas. Its magnetic field will attract and repel via its poles. The pressure of radiation may blow away lighter elements like hydrogen. It may go through a period of pulsation, known as 'T'-Tauri. It now begins to glow; this is called a Herbig-Haro object. Examples of this are Gamma Cassiopeiae and Trifid Nebula M20.

The main sequence is when the star shines brightly for most of its life. This might be millions of years. Its magnitude depends on its size or mass. Inside it are massive nuclear fires going up to 60 million degrees centigrade. Since no one has ever managed to probe the internal workings of a star, this is pure conjecture. An example is Alpha Centauri, our nearest neighbour.

The star then enters its 'old age', as it runs out of hydrogen and starts to burn helium. It goes brighter but the outer layers cool. It begins to expand into a red giant. Then it shrinks back as long as the helium lasts. Then one of three courses takes place;

1. It becomes a low mass star, collapsing and dwindling down to become a 'black dwarf', after a large red phase.
2. A sun-like star, of solar mass 1, goes into a red giant. The core itself collapses and then it shrinks down to normal until the helium is exhausted. It then becomes a white dwarf. Examples of this are Arcturus, Aldebaran, and Betelgeuse.
3. A high mass star of 8 solar masses. It then turns into a red supergiant (also possibly yellow or blue). It may expand or contract. It may collapse inwards and then explode outwards as a Supernova. When this does happen, it is quite spectacular but also rarely seen. Examples of this are Antares (red), Pollux (yellow), and Eta Carinae (blue). There was a supernova explosion in 1987 in the Tarantula Nebula. After that it turns into either a neutron star (a pulsar). This is a collapsed core, far denser than a white dwarf. They rotate

rapidly, giving off beams of light and radio waves, at the rate of 1000 times a second, blinking like a lighthouse. That is the kind of star that twinkles. Examples of that in the Crab Nebula M1 in Taurus. Otherwise, it turns into a black hole. The star collapses altogether, leaving a gravity which sucks in even light. We notice that this ties in with Einstain's idea that even light is subject to gravity. An example of that is Cygnus X-1.

Single stars like ours are a rarity. Normally stars are in pairs or clusters. Some stay together; others drift apart. Simple binaries are the most common type, but larger groups are widespread. Stars in groups can age at different rates and show different colours. They can go into orbit, if the two are equal in mass. Examples of this are Albireo (Beta Cygni) and Izar (Bootes). They can appear in open clusters, dozens or even hundreds of new stars. They tend to be very hot, blue-white stars, and tend not to last very long (10's of millions of years). Examples of that are Pleiades (Taurus), Jewel box (Crux), and M44 Behive (Cancer).

Also there are globular clusters, of stars that are denser and more structured, thousands or millions of yellow and red stars, orbiting the galaxy. These tend to be older stars, dying and are much further away, such as 20 to 30 light years from us. Examples of this are Omega Centauri (Centaurus), 47 Tucanae (Tucana), and M13 (Hercules).

If it is true that the Big Bang started everything off at the same time, it must raise the question why are all these billions of stars all at different stages of so-called development. Ought they not to be all the same? Why is it that some of them are a lot younger and some a lot older, bearing in mind that this will be a difference of millions of years? We have to realise that some stars are massively bigger than our own sun, and might burn at much higher temperatures. It is predicted that our own sun will eventually run out of hydrogen, turn into a red giant and then engulf all the rocky planets. Then it will shrink down to become a black or a white dwarf. This will indeed be the end of the world, assuming that does actually happen. This is where scientific speculation ties in with the eschatological element in religious belief, namely that the end of the world will arrive, in spectacular fashion. This is another way in which theology and science are in some kind of agreement.

It might be a fair comment to remark that all this prognostication about the stars is just that. Since these alleged 'developments' are claimed to take millions, if not billions of years, how are we ever going to be certain of what is actually happening at this moment? Supposing the stars do not conform to our 'evolutionary' expectations?

This remark can be expanded by an appreciation of what are called 'variable stars.' Not all stars shine at the same brightness; their magnitude can vary by the hour or by the year or can be quite unpredictable. These are described in various ways. There are pulsating variables, going through a period of instability. They can swell up and shrink, which affects their brightness. This is the most common type of variable known. Examples are; R. Cannae, and R Centauri. A Cepheid is a yellow supergiant, three time the size of our sun. They too can expand or contract in a matter of days. Examples of this are; Zeta Geminorum, and Polaris (Ursa Major). Also there are eclipsing variables, when a binary pair pass in front of one another, rather like a solar eclipse. The magnitude rises or falls accordingly. Algol, in Perseus has a ten hour eclipse every 2.9 days. Examples of this are; Delta Librae and Beta Persei. A rotating variable is a star which rotates with some areas brighter or dimmer, like our 'sun spots'. Betelgeuse has a large bright spot caused (it is thought) by hot material welling up from the centre. There are cataclysmic variables, seen in close binary systems, where the gravity of the one pulls material away from the other. A thermonuclear explosion happens, which can increase the magnitude tenfold. This will be termed a 'nova', and this can repeat itself several times. An example of this is Nova Cygni, in Cygnus.

What we are looking at here, is all kinds of strange permutations on what we understand about our sun. There is no doubt that if our sun behaved like these strange entities, life on earth would be very difficult. What it does indicate, is that we are only just scratching the surface of what goes on in deep space. All these prognostications are based on our telescopes, developed within our own lifetimes. Who knows what was happening before that scenario! We have still got a lot to learn about stars and their derivatives. It shows that the field of knowledge is expanding, massively, and that easy dogmatisms on astrophysics are a mistake.

How does the nuclear fireball relate to Theology? For centuries, the pagan world focussed on the sun as one of the chief gods. This was particularly so with Ancient Egypt and the Incas, but there were many other cultures included in this. In a sense, they were right. The sun is the chief source of life for this world; it is the engine that drives just about everything. Even the monotheistic account in Genesis 1:14, shows the importance given to the sun (and the moon). All the other stars, which we have described, were at that time not seen as the same sort of thing as the sun, are also mentioned. For the pagans, all of these lights in the sky were regarded as gods. The Greeks in particular studied the constellations and wove elaborate myths about them. We may think that this was a lot of superstitious nonsense, but the astrologers of the Ancient World went to a lot of trouble in making forecasts about events and people's futures, and still do, to this day. Do we take this matter seriously? Many people do, even in this age of so-called rationality. (6).

At the very least, we have to admit that astral bodies have had an important influence on religious thinking and practice. It is inevitable, that in a world of so many uncertainties, it is only (7) human nature to attempt to find some kind of certainty from what appears to be something fixed in the sky. Now we know that very little of this is 'fixed'; the astral world is anything but fixed.

We now come on to consider that there are billions of stars out there in outer space. They can be seen in whole galaxies. The Milky Way, of which our solar system is a part, is just one of thousands of them. There are several different types of galaxy.

Spiral galaxies, of which the Milky Way is a good example, are flat with extending arms, like a Catherine wheel, and with a bulge in the centre. It slowly rotates. The bulge is mainly old red and yellow stars; the arms contain younger, bluer stars and gas clouds. There are 200 billion 'suns' in our galaxy. It is thought to have a massive black hole in the centre. It is 1500 light years thick and stretches 150,000 light years across. Good examples of this are Andromeda, Triangulum, Whirlpool, NGC 253, M 81, M 64 Black Eye, M 104 Sombrero, NGC 3979, NGC 4414, NGC 1300, Tadpole.

A barred spiral galaxy is when the hub is crossed by a 'bar' of stars from which two spiral arms emerge. The Milky Way might be such, except that the bar is end on to us and we cannot see it. Examples of that are; Large Magallanic Cloud, Stephan's Quintet, NGC 1300, and M 83 (Hydra).

Elliptical Galaxies vary in size from dwarfs to giants. Early galaxies begin as small elliptical and then go through the spiral stage and then back to elliptical. Examples of that are; M87 in Virgo, NGC 5128.

There are irregular galaxies which are just a shapeless collection of stars. They are rich in gas and dust and presumably in the early stages of forming into a regular motion galaxy. Examples of that are the Magallanic

Cloud, LMC Dorado, SMC Tucana, NGC4212, M 82, NGC 604, NGC 1569, Hubble V, and Hubble X.

With this we see that there are galaxies still forming and new stars appearing in them. This means that the process of Creation is ongoing, or at least, that is how it appears. Also, there is that circular motion that we see in our Solar system, the sun itself and of course in the quantum world. It is thought, with good reason, that many stars have their own 'solar system' somewhat like ours. We are now told that there are such things as exo-planets, circulating stars, although no one has actually seen one, as yet. But the evidence for them is quite reasonable. This does not have to mean that every star has such an arrangement, but it is quite possible that the circulating planets have something to do with balancing and stability. Future research will doubtless confirm these matters.

For stars that are not yet formed, or in the process of forming, we note that there is such a thing as a nebula. This is a cloud of gas (hydrogen?) and dust gradually being pulled inwards under gravity, to form some kind of astral body. Nebulae are of various kinds; an emission nebula which glows like a neon sign, usually red. Examples are; M42 in Orion, M8 Lagoon in Sagittarius, NGC 2237, and Rosette in Monoceros.

A reflection nebula is a faint blue colour and difficult to see without a telescope. It is lit by light from other nearby stars. A dark nebula is a cloud of dust and gas with no stars to light it up. Examples are, the Coal Sack, and the Cone in Monoceros. Also there are planetary nebulae, associated with red giants. Examples of this are; M27 Dumbbell, M57 the Ring in Lyra, the Clownface in Gemini, the Helix and the Eskimo.

One might wonder how we come to know all this. It is because in our own times, we have developed very much more powerful telescopes, and can see these things going on. My comment is, that we are only just scratching the surface of what is out there to be discovered and explained.

We now come to consider the formation of planets and their satellites (moons). This is where speculation is rife and there are no definite answers. If we could actually see planets forming round a star, we might gain a clearer idea of how this happens. Let us stick to observable facts (like Heisenberg) and draw a few conclusions from them. All the planets and moons in our solar system, move around in the same direction, and around the ecliptic (which means the sun's equator). It is not random motion, and is consistent with the sun's own spin. The distance between the planets' orbits is consistent and regular, working on a ratio of 1.7. This is called Bode's Law. There are two groups; the inner, small, rocky planets and the large four outer gas giants (or ice giants). The speed (8) at which they orbit is related to gravity and their distance from the sun. This means that they do not swerve into the sun and be consumed by it. All except one (Venus) spin in the same direction. It is interesting that W.Gilbert (1600) thought that magnetism was the factor that held the Solar System together. Somehow, there is a delicate balancing system at work between the Sun's gravity, the distance of the planet from the Sun, and the speed of its orbit. (9) Any 'facts' now adduced may be modified as more research continues with space probes.

Mercury, nearest the sun is 57.9 million Km from it; by day the temperature rises to 437 C and sinks to minus 193 C by night. The atmosphere, which is very thin, is 42% oxygen, 29% sodium, 22% hydrogen, with an array of minority gases. It is about a third of the size of earth. This is hardly a comfortable place for human habitation.

Venus, another rocky planet, almost the same size as Earth, is 108.2 million Km from the sun. The atmosphere is nearly all carbon dioxide (and other gases), and is so dense that the sun is not seen. The heat is trapped in a 'greenhouse' effect, which means the heat is always about 350 C, and then it rains sulphuric acid. Probes to the surface so far have been crushed by the heat and pressure. A human would not last long in this environment. Like Mercury it has volcanoes.

Planet Earth is the largest of the four rocky planets. Distance from the sun is 149.9 million Km, and the atmosphere is 78.1% nitrogen, 20.9% oxygen with other trace gases. This mix of gases is just the right consistency for mammals to breath, and the temperature is just right for habitation. Earth has one moon which is much the same material as the parent planet.

Mars is the last inner rocky planet, and is slightly smaller than Earth. It is 227.9 million Km from the sun. The atmosphere is 95.32% carbon dioxide (with other trace gases) and is a lot thinner than ours. The surface temperature is 25 C by day and minus 125 C by night. Scientists have speculated that Mars could support life, but so far, there has been no irrefutable evidence for this. There have been about 30 probes, to date, some of them landing on the surface, only to find a barren, cold, rocky landscape. It has two moons, which may be asteroids with erratic shapes. Mars' orbit is more eccentric than Earth's which means that the distance from the sun varies enough to alter temperatures. The possibility of sending a human to Mars is now the latest mania. The feasibility of this is questionable; one would have to overcome a whole list of problems. The distance involved would mean a voyage of 6 to 9 months. One would have to stay at least a year in order to return. A rocket ten times bigger than the Apollo would be needed. With no gravity during the flight, the crew would have to do strenuous exercises to avoid muscle and bone collapse. Mars has no magnetosphere (Earth does) which means that radiation from the sun will be lethal. Parachuting down will be hazardous since the atmosphere is a lot thinner. The temperatures are much colder than on Earth. Dust storms rage on Mars. The return trip would need another rocket with enough fuel.

Going on from Mars, we have the asteroid belt, which occurs where one would expect another planet to exist. It is possible that this is a failed planet; just rubble floating round in orbit. Some bits are large enough to be seen as dwarf planets. An example of this is Ceres. Distance from the sun, 414 million Km, and their orbit times are variable. New ones are being discovered all the time.

We now come to Jupiter, a gas giant, 11.2 times the size of Earth. The atmosphere is 89.9% hydrogen and 10.2% helium, surface temperature minus 110 C. It spins so fast that its equator bulges out and its poles are flattened. The gravity is 11 times that of Earth's. Jupiter has four main moons and about 60 smaller, irregular ones, plus a faint ring system, like Saturn. There is also a belt of asteroids leading and following Jupiter, orbiting at the same speed; how they relate to Jupiter is not known. No one has managed to discover what lies beneath the immense gas hurricanes; is there a solid core, or just more gas? Also Jupiter has an immense storm, called its 'eye' for which we have no explanation, as yet.

Saturn is the next largest planet, 764 times the size of the Earth, with a massive gravitational pull. The atmosphere is 97% hydrogen, and the temperature is minus 191C to minus 130C. Saturn is noted for its seven rings; while they are only 10 metres thick, they are 384,000 Km broad. The core of it is rock and ice. It has 62 known moons, but there will be more to follow; each moon is very different from ours, and Titan (the size of Mercury) appears to have what might be termed a 'new chemistry' which shows a different extent of the acid/alkali range. With its fast rotation, it too has flattened poles and a bulging equator.

Uranus, only recently discovered (1781 by Herschel), is another gas giant, mostly hydrogen, and with a massive gravitational pull. It is a featureless blue, with clouds and eleven faint rings, which circulate almost vertically, to match its axial tilt. It has 27 moons and counting, all very different and with irregular shapes.

Another new discovery, Neptune (1846 by Adams and Le Verrier) is also a gas and ice giant, blue, with a storm in the middle. The atmosphere is 80% hydrogen, and there is a faint ring system. There are 13 moons and counting; Triton goes in retrograde motion round Neptune, and its orbit is decaying, which means it will crash into Neptune one day. Other moons are smaller and with irregular shapes.

Beyond Nepture lies the Kuiper Belt or the TNO's (Trans-Neptunian Objects). This includes Pluto but other dwarf rock planets. Pluto was discovered in 1930 by Tombaugh and now we know about Charon, and new ones are being spotted regularly. Pluto has an irregular orbit which crosses that of Neptune and is tilted 17 degrees out of line with the other major planets.

In spite of the probe, New Horizons which went by in 2015, giving us our first glimpse of Pluto and valuable information on the other distant planets, there are still more mysteries than certainties about the Solar System. The worlds we have peered into show that there are all kinds of permutations on our world, and that dogmatisms and certainties about planet formation cannot be sustained, at least not yet, and possibly for a long time to come. We have a lot to learn, as yet. Beyond the Kuiper Belt, is the Oort Cloud, about 1.6 light years away, and about half way to the next star, namely Alpha Centauri. It contains billions of comets, circulating the Solar System, and occasionally one of them darts in towards the sun and back again, or possibly collides with Jupiter. This is enough to show that the whole thing is far more complicated and mysterious than we ever realised before, and will go on amazing us for as long as it takes.

One might think that with all this new information about satellites (moons), we might have some idea of how our own moon was formed. We are still largely in the dark about how this came about. A few general comments about them are interesting but do not really answer the question. The moons we have seen are highly diverse, some being liquid, some solid, some active and others passive. Their orbits are usually elliptical, usually prograde around the equator of the parent planet; others retrograde but at a higher inclination. It is to be expected that there will be collisions. But our moon's orbit is almost a perfect circle, even if it is calculated that it is coming a little closer to the Earth. Even if the moon is thought to be 40 to 100 million years younger than the Earth, it is also thought to have a common parentage to the Earth. (10) There appear to be three main theories about the moon's formation; the capture hypothesis means it was a planet that came near to Earth and became captured into orbit; the fission hypothesis, means that in an early molten phase, the Earth spewed out an immense volume of material which formed the moon; the giant impact hypothesis, which means that a large planet such as Mars collided with the Earth and a chunk flew out and formed the moon. None of these ideas are completely convincing and the moon's formation remains a mystery.

Another important mystery, not often considered nowadays, but was in the Ancient World, is the fact that the Sun and Moon are the same diameter. At least, it appears so, but of course we know that the Sun is much bigger than the Moon, but is also much further away, so they only appear to be the same diameter. But the result of this is that we have solar and lunar eclipses, which of course have much excitement for the astrologers and soothsayers. This is an arrangement not seen on any other planet (as far as we know). There must be some significance in it somewhere. It can hardly have been some kind of coincidence. Coming back to more solid speculation, we know that the moon has a decisive effect on tides on Earth, and that in itself is a healthy aspect of ocean activity.

Looking at the Solar System in general terms, without becoming too enmeshed in speculation and detail which may not be complete, the whole thing gives the appearance of being very carefully constructed, using gravity in relation to orbital speed, and also the spacing of the planets. How is it that the rocky planets are almost perfectly spherical, and behave like giant gyroscopes; why are they not irregular like some of the distant moons? Are we looking at a very carefully balanced arrangement, so that the gravitational pull exerted by each body is just right to keep the whole system from flying apart? We marvel that one planet, Venus, spins in retrograde motion, just like some of the distant moons. Is there a reason for that, relating to the whole balancing of the system? Why is it that all the planets, including the asteroid belt and the Kuiper Belt, circulate in the same way? If they did not, we might expect to see disastrous collisions wrecking the whole arrangement. I cannot avoid the conclusion that the whole system was carefully devised by a superior agency. In addition, the fact that Earth is tilted on its axis at 23.5 degrees is just the right amount to give us the seasons of the year, and that results in different climatic conditions and variations in agricultural products. I cannot escape the conclusion that the whole thing has been careful devised. We add to that the fact that the outer planets all have a massive gravitational pull. The effect of this is that any harmful intrusion from outer space tends to be sucked in and collide with one of those gas giants. This means that only infrequently does a meteorite of any size or threat, manage to invade our atmosphere, and rarely does one actually reach ground level. It is all very providential and wonderful. Why do people doubt that there is a Creator God?

Looking at the theological aspects of this, it is clear that thoughts on Creation and the (11) wonders of the Universe, are all expressed in terms of high emotion and figurative language. The Bible has various passages on the wonders of the Creation, and the metaphors used are some of the highest and greatest examples of literature in the world. But nowadays, we express these matters in another genre of vocabulary, that of scientific analysis, speculation and sometimes plain wishful thinking. Even so, we have to remember that much of this scientific language is just as much metaphor as before. How often do we see earth-bound metaphors applied to astral matters? Is that really appropriate? Just as we have seen that the quantum world appears to function on a logic all of its own, beyond our powers to comprehend, so too does the mega world of stars and galaxies. That too has all the appearance of being beyond us to assimilate in our tiny, earth-bound minds. There is no need for a clash over science and religion here. Those who cling to the mythologies of the past and those who speculate with the scientific mythologies of the future are equally earth-bound. Who knows what is really going on out there? Who knows where it will all end, if ever?

There is one more implication for Theology in all this. We are instructed not to make any idol of God, or gods. Three major religions, Judaism, Islam and Christianity adhere to this, the second of the Ten Commandments. Admittedly, they vary in their interpretation of this command, however, the gist of it, and the relevance of it, is that one must not imagine that God can be reduced to human preconceptions. We regularly do this mentally, but it is a big mistake. God is above and beyond anything that the human mind can concoct; even so he is closer to each and every one of us than we can possibly realise. How is this relevant to scientific investigation? We have seen that the quantum world, and the mega world appear to be functioning on a system of logic that we do not understand. Even so, we regularly assume that our thought-forms, our yardsticks of mental framework can describe what is going on in those different worlds. We only have to look at those strange worlds which are a weird permutation on our ideas of planetry, to realise that we do not know what we are talking about. And yet, we regularly try to describe all these things according to our own narrow preconceptions, based on this planet. This is the modern scientific idolatry, that we seek to make everything conform to our own assumptions. And going on from there, how many of us make the assumption that 'scientists' are the new 'gods' of the modern age? How often have we heard the phrase, 'it is scientifically proved'? Perhaps we should just recall that scientists (even the genuine ones) are only human like the rest of us, and are quite capable of being deluded, misled and plain wrong, sometimes. This is why, in this book, I call for us all to be less inclined to dogmatisms and more inclined to keep an open mind. That way, God can reveal his wonders to us in his own special way.

### Footnote

1. Much of the material in this chapter is derived from Marcus Chown, The Ascent of Gravity. Also, Hawking, A Brief History of Time. Also Astronomy, Ian Ridpath.
2. Details about Chinese creation mythology are found in my book, Myth, Legend and Symbolism, page 183.
3. Uranium is the heaviest natural element, but others heavier have been made artificially, such as Francium and Lawrencium.
4. See Chown.
5. See chapter 12, Proofs for the Existence of God.
6. Constellation Myths, by Eratosthenes and Hyginus. Translated by Robin Hard.
7. A good example is the Magi who calculated the Birth of Jesus Christ.
8. Below is a simplified diagram of the planetary orbits; they are far from pure circles.
9. Hawking in A Brief History of Time, Page 92, tries to explain it in terms of gravitons, and virtual photons. All this does is to underline the intricate balance at work in the solar system.
10. Some think the Moon is coming nearer to the earth; others that it is moving away at the rate of 3.8 cm per annum (Chown).
11. Examples are Psalm 104, Job 38ff.

# 7

## *Life on other planets?*

This is not a new idea, but has become a mania with people in recent times. There is always the feeling that if other forms of life were to be found somewhere else, it would have ramifications for theology. I am not totally convinced that it would; one would have to discover, analyse and give a lot of thought to the matter before deciding that it had anything to do with the reality of God, or not. So far, the idea is only a frantic piece of wishful thinking in the minds of those who think it will overturn all our assumed dogmas.

For a long time, it was imagined that there might be life on our neighbouring planets in the Solar System. The Earth lies within what is termed the 'habitable zone', which means, just the right distance from the sun so that the temperatures are just right for our type of existence. Since Mars and Venus are also in the same range, it has been imagined that there might be life on them too. Since we have sent probes to all our neighbouring planets, there has been much disappointment for the wishful thinkers. Venus is far too hot, the pressure is massive and it rains sulphuric acid. Mars has been a favourite for some kind of life, but so far, nothing has been found. It is somewhat colder than Earth, and the atmosphere is mostly carbon dioxide, and there is no protection from the sun's radiation. Two final candidates could be Europa, one of Jupiter's moons and Enceladus, one of Saturn's. These have been seen as having circumstances favourable for life. However, being so far from the sun means they will be very cold, and as yet we do not know enough about these planets to make any firm conclusions. In total, it looks very much as though us earthlings are on our own in this Solar System.

Part of the problem is that we find it very difficult to understand life as being anything different from what we experience on earth. Many people have assumed that to land on another planet, we shall be shaking hands with cheerful, smartly dressed gentlefolk who are fascinated to meet another version of themselves. This is making far too many assumptions. How do we know that life, if it can be called that, will not appear in a completely different permutation? We might not even recognise it as life. It was interesting to see the assumptions in that film ET. It was assumed that someone from another planet far away, would have a physical form somewhat analogous to our own, albeit with different functionings. It was assumed that ET would be far more intelligent than us; why would that be so? All this is symptomatic of modern day fantasy and (1)wishful thinking. This is where 'science', if it can be called that, is way off the mark and just pure unsupported speculation.

Now let us examine what might be seen as the scientific basis for life elsewhere. We are now becoming increasingly aware of many other solar systems functioning in other parts of our galaxy, the Milky Way. Add to that, there are millions of other galaxies further away. There must be vast numbers of exo-planets out there. What would be needed to form a basis for life, assuming it was a form of life that we would recognise?

Firstly, it would need a rocky planet as opposed to a gas or ice giant. Such a life form, one would assume, has to stand on something firm, as opposed to floating about in clouds of gas such as hydrogen (or so one would think). Secondly, such a planet would need to be in the so-called 'habitable zone', so that temperatures would not be too extreme. Otherwise, the life-form would be either frozen stiff or cooked. So far, we have observed exo-planets that appear to be too close to their suns. Additionally, there seems to be no evidence of planetary spacing according to Bode's Law, like our Solar System. Thirdly, we are not yet at the stage of analysing the atmosphere or water content of any exo-planet. Fourthly, we cannot be certain of anything that could qualify as 'food' for some kind of alleged life. Life, whatever form it takes, has to live off something.

Even so, the Kepler probe, has shown us that in just one sector of space, there are 150,000 stars, and maybe 1000 candidates with planets with possibilities for life. There is a calculation called the 'Drake' equation, which is claimed to indicate the probability for planets sustaining life. All I can say, is that it is so full of unsupported assumptions, that it is meaningless. Until someone comes up with something that can be properly observed and analysed on this subject, it is wise not to go making claims about life in far away places. The question should remain open and not be clouded up with spurious claims. Heisenberg was right in saying, let us confine ourselves to matters that can be observed.

It is difficult enough to cope with the question of how life began on this planet. This is a brief idea of what scientists think happened. Going back 4.55 billion years, to what is termed the Hadean period, it is all guesswork as to what the conditions were. It may have been massive volcanoes and meteorite strikes, but for the Archean period there is slightly more information. It is conjectured that the Earth was lacking in oxygen. The evidence for this is the state of the mineralogy of ancient rocks. The materials that formed the Earth were highly 'reduced'. The Moon still is in this state, having had no life develop on it.

What do we mean by 'reduced'? For those who are not familiar with the workings of chemistry, there is a process called a 'redox' reaction. It is the interplay of 'oxidation' and 'reduction.' A chemical such as iron will attract Oxygen, thus forming rust; this is called oxidation. A chemical that attracts Hydrogen, such as copper oxide when given hydrogen will produce copper (as a metal) and the oxygen and hydrogen will combine to form water. This is putting it very simply; a redox reaction is normally reciprocal; loss of hydrogen; gain of oxygen, or vice versa.

There is something called a 'placer deposit' which is thought to survive from the Archean period, and has been buried so that it did not get influenced by later atmospheres. There is no trace of oxygen in the placer deposits. Life is made up of organic molecules that have 'reduced' forms of carbon. To start life organic molecules must exist stably in their environment. It cannot have oxygen in the atmosphere, which would destroy the first cells. For life to commence, it needs anaerobic conditions, in other words, oxygen-free. That may seem strange, since life nowadays depends on oxygen in the atmosphere.

The development of 'life' is thought to have gone through three energy 'revolutions'. The first one was when autotrophs began to appear. These are the tiny cells which produce their own food by using the sunlight, and from this, plant life can appear. Heterotrophs, however, consume other things as food, such as chemicals, and it is not clear which came first, the autotrophs or the heterotrophs. Also there were chemoautotrophs, which consume material from hydrothermal vents, and are not dependent on sunlight. Also there are photoautotrophs, which harvest the light from the sun.

The second energy revolution, was when the plants began to produce oxygen. This gas begins to build up in the atmosphere, and at first, the oxygen is harmful to the primitive life forms. However, as the oxygen content in the atmosphere builds up, so the reciprocal relationship between plants and animals emerges. Only when the oxygen level builds up to a certain level, can multi-cellular life thrive. This leads into the third energy revolution; plants exude oxygen, animals breath it in; animals breath out carbon dioxide; the plants consume it and produce carbohydrate. We have to realise that the oxygen content in the atmosphere has not always been at about 21%, but is now more or less stable. We notice again, that this is an ingenious example of balancing between one form of life and another. This is why people now are seriously concerned about the pollution of the atmosphere; that it will disturb the balance between oxygen and other gases and turn this planet into some sort of 'greenhouse', rather like Venus. This is a grossly simplified outline of how life is supposed to have arrived on earth, and much of it is guesswork and supposition. If it is true, then that will explain why other planets are not covered with vegetation and animals eating it.

What no one seems willing or able to discuss is this question; given that on this planet, life is based on the subtle interplay between hydrogen, carbon, oxygen, plus an array of other chemicals, how do we know that another ingenious palette of chemicals does not exist somewhere else? For something to be called 'life', as far as we are concerned, it needs to be born and to die, eat something and produce waste, and be capable of autolocation. How do we know that on another planet 'life' is not constructed on another different kind of framework? A different permutation on life, as compared with ours might be possible, indeed, something that we might not regard as 'life'. For this reason, I maintain that to be too dogmatic about these matters is to no purpose.

In general terms, one is inclined to see the whole of the origins of life as something really quite ingenious. I cannot see how all those chemicals can have decided amongst themselves, to initiate life, as we know it. No one as yet has actually managed to make those basic chemicals 'kick start' any life form. That still leaves us with the burning question of how life did actually start, not from the point of view of raw materials, but from the initial burst of energy. Add to that, we still have to ask about the origin of all those chemicals, taking us back to the Big Bang, and the origin of every thing. Inevitably, this brings us back to the question of God the Creator.

It would be interesting, at this point, to compare the scientific view of Creation with the Biblical expression. The scientists relate everything to basic chemical reactions stemming from the alleged Big Bang, to the formation of the sun and then the planets circulating round it. This is fair enough as far as it goes, as long as we remind ourselves, that this is all deduction decorated with much speculation. How we are ever supposed to know for sure what actually did happen billions of years ago, is an interesting question. I think any honest scientist would admit that there are so many aspects of this matter that remain a mystery, that to become over-dogmatic would be foolish.

We can now take another look, from a slightly different viewpoint, at the first few verses in Genesis, in which the Creation is described in theological terms. We can hardly expect a passage like this, which almost certainly was written in the Iron Age, or even in the Bronze Age, to be taken as a scientific analysis. At that time, there was no idea of the quantum world, and the Greek philosophers with their ideas on atoms, were still in the future. The first passage has got to be taken as poetic and non-scientific (Genesis 1:1-2:4). Everybody thought that the Universe was a three-decker structure, heaven, ground level and the underworld. Even so, there are aspects of it which tie in with modern scientific thinking.

1. The earth was without form and void. We now think that since the material to form the earth came from the sun, it must have been a shapeless blob before it settled into an almost perfect sphere.
2. We notice that the waters appear after the earth was formed. That makes sense, since there was no oxygen available to combine with hydrogen to form water, so we are told.
3. The Spirit of God was moving over the face of the waters. We recall that the waters symbolise the powers of evil or death, so this means that the question of Theodicy is already rearing itself, just as the good and the bad bacteria somehow diverge at the start of all things.
4. Then comes the vegetation as the dry land appears. This too is the next step as far as the evolutionists are concerned.
5. Let the waters bring forth swarms of living creatures. Again, it is thought that the first animal life forms emerged from the seas and were dependent on the vegetation.
6. Finally we see the rise of the human race, which although it rules over the rest of creation, is intended to use everything else as food.

In general terms, the scheme in Genesis is roughly the same as that of the Evolutionists, added to which, the awareness of periodic extinctions in the early history of the world, ties in with the way that Genesis has creation come in stages. We have to remember also that every account of Creation has its underlying 'dialectic'. In the case of Genesis, the scheme strongly emphasises the importance of the seven day week, and of Saturday being a day of rest . It is in fact saying that the whole of Creation is framed around the Sabbath. No one in their right mind would try to deny the importance of this; holidays, rest, recuperation, breathing space are all essential. If these are ignored, it is to the detriment of health and the smooth functioning of the natural world too.

If we could just rid ourselves of the idea that Genesis is intended to be a scientific treatise, the matter would be so much simpler. It is a poetic, schematised way of showing that God initially provided a wonderful world, which needed to function on a seven-day framework. Conversely, to take the evolutionist approach and assume it not to be poetic is equally ridiculous. The scientific (or some would say speculatory scientific) approach concerns itself with the raw materials and ingredients of Creation. The theological approach is concerned with the meaning and spiritual framework of life itself. That is a very different matter.

One might fairly ask, what is the agenda behind the evolutionist approach? Let us not pretend there is no such agenda. The agenda for many of them (though not all) is to minimise the theological element, and sideline God, to put it bluntly. This actually is a misuse of Darwin's original intention. He was a firm believer and his theory as expressed in his book, The Origin of Species, does make frequent mention of God as the Creator. There is no need to dispense with the reality of God in these matters. However life on this earth came about, and that is something that in the end we may never know for sure, it still requires that initial energy, spirit, designer, purpose to make it all happen. Unfortunately, for those of an atheistic mentality, the theory of evolution came as a god-given gift to allow themselves to dispense with religious faith.

Another aspect of evolutionism as coupled with a humanistic approach to life, is the question of failure, wickedness and a world not functioning as it should. I would say that no one, not even the humanists, would say that this world is perfectly satisfactory. There are so many things wrong with it. That, of course, is a motive for denying the reality of God. Evolutionism, in its pure form, does not really come to grips with the question of evil, or wrong, or failure, however one phrases it. The religionists do have various explanations, according to whatever mythical framework each religion espouses.

In the Bible, the Garden of Eden concept is of the highest relevance to this question. It is saying, in effect, that there was a time when everything was perfectly satisfactory. It went wrong because of one foolish act on the part of humanity; they ignored just one of God's instructions. From that, flowed all the wrongs, mistakes, evil, crime and failures that dragged humanity down, producing the mess we have on our hands to this day. The Marxists would probably agree with this in substance, that at one time everything was ideal. But then the greedy capitalists came in and began to exploit the working class.

The Taoists would say that it was not the Jade Emperor who made humans out of clay, but a goddess called Nu Wa, the goddess of Creation. But it was the Jade Emperor who left them out in the rain, which meant that they were less than perfect, in other words, a deformity of what they were originally. The Norse mythologists would probably say that with the gods being so violent, bloodthirsty and destructive, it would be a puzzle as to how there would be any good in the world. There is no god who is equivalent to the Devil, but there is one called Loki, who is mischievous and plays pranks on people. The human race plays hardly any part in Norse mythology. The Greeks also had the gods misbehaving themselves in the skies, but the question of evil comes with that story about Pandora's box. Itwas a Golden Age until this lady opened the urn and allowed all the evils of the world to escape. We can see Pandora as the equivalent of Eve; it quietly excuses the rest of the human race from blame. The Gnostics, which were popular in the mid-Roman Empire, had one very good god at the top of heaven, but other gods of lesser quality descending down to a Demi-Urge who was bad. The problem was, how did the good God manage to father other gods who were not quite as good? One answer given was that the good God has forgetful; the word used is 'nescience'. This explains how the world as we know it is a problem world. We notice again that the blame is aimed away from humanity. Later Jewish thought which does not appear in the Bible, (except to say the book of Job), had a fallen angel, called Satan, who precipitated the disaster in the Garden of Eden. We notice again that the blame for evil is diverted from the human race. How convenient!

What has this to do with life on other planets, assuming there is any? If we ever do manage to find such a planet, it will be a matter of importance for theology to see if it a 'fallen' world, or some kind of Golden Age. If there is any kind of life analogous to humanity, will they be totally innocent or will they be encumbered with 'original sin'? If they have no concept of guilt or shame, will they be quite happy to do without any clothing? We notice that on the Sci-fi programmes such as Star Trek and Star Wars, they all seem to wear clothing and accept that aggression and bloodshed is quite the norm, in spite of being highly intelligent! Even if there are no 'humans' on this hypothetical planet, there might be other life forms; will they be 'fallen' or in some kind of golden age of innocence? If they are really nasty creatures, it might be a good idea to leave them alone!

All this is sheer speculation and supposition. It cannot be called genuine science until something genuinely observable is discovered, and so far, that has not happened.

**Footnotes**

1. I agree with Heisenberg, that proper science confines itself to the observable and avoids all kinds of speculation and guesswork until experiments produce facts.
2. Bode's Law shows that the planets are spaced according to a factor of 1:7, in a regular sequence, and that even includes the Kuiper Belt.
3. The Drake Equation. This is an attempt to show by a probability statement that there are 10,000 civilizations out there in deep space.
4. These are described in chapter 5 on Biochemistry.
5. The question of Theodicy, the problem of evil, is discussed in the Theology of Paradox, chapter 2
6. Various myths from round the world are described in Myth, Legend and Symbolism, and each one has its own explanation for the question of Theodicy.
7. Original sin is not described as such in the Bible, but later Christian theologians, for instance Augustine, went into details about it. It is still an important element in Christian theology, in spite of the humanistic climate of today.

# 8

## *Time, Space and History*

We are accustomed to think of TIME as an absolute measurement. Hours, days and years seem somehow immutable. But are they? Our times and calendars are based on the movements of the Sun. Some civilisations have based their calendars on the Moon, but this is nowhere near as (1) convenient. There have been various methods of calendar calculation in the world; the Chinese, the Islamic, the Jewish, the Julian, the Baha'i, and the Gregorian. The Gregorian calendar, so called after Pope Gregory in the 16th century, has now come to dominate the world. This is not to say that it is the absolute truth; it is only so widely accepted because of its ease of calculation and anticipation. The truth is that time and calculation of years is only a human construct. This may seem a damning thing to say, but if one were to go and stand on the International Dateline, one foot could be in today and the other foot in tomorrow, or possibly yesterday!

If we look at the way the Bible treats time, it begins with the start of History and leads through to the end of History. The time span is divided up into eras or epochs, based on the progress or decline of the Israelite people. This approach to history becomes even more emphasised in the apocalyptic material which belongs mainly after the Old Testament was written. The Jews were not the only people to schematise history like this. The Greeks too had their own system, although they did not really consider the end of the world in the way the Jews did. The Christians too continued this line of thought, relating it directly to the coming of the Messiah, not just the first time but also the Second Coming. This is a belief which still dominates Christian thought to this day. It was the Gnostics, a sort of philosophico-theological strain of thought, rampant in the mid-Roman (2) Empire, who took this kind of thinking to extremes. They turned eras, epochs and time-spans into quasi-deities. Gnosticism could be outright paganistic, or influenced by Christianity or full-blown Christian heresy. What we notice is that there is this obsession, on the part of humanity, to calculate times and seasons, and relate them to the divine. It would be fair to say that with Eastern religions, there is less of this obsession, but it was, and still is, not completely absent. There is not the same fixation with the course of history, as in Western religions; even so, calendar calculation is still a factor in the East. (3)

It is Hawking who raises the interesting question; if we can remember the past, why can we not remember the future? (4) For a theologian, or one steeped in the Judaeo-Christian tradition, this is a silly question. Anyone who has studied the Old Testament (not to mention the New Testament), will realise that the factor of prophesy is a very important element in the faith, and also in God's way of dealing with the faithful. The prophets were the people who could see into the future. We think of the Davidic Psalms, the amazing Messianic oracles of Isaiah, Jeremiah and Ezekiel, and above all, the dream-like visions in Daniel. For those who find this material difficult to cope with, I would refer you to the oracles of Nostradamus, who gave detailed forecasts of events leading from the 16th century to the 20th century. (5) Obviously, Nostradamus has his detractors, but these are the people who have not bothered to read the material with a sympathetic eye. I maintain that there is some core of reality in the phenomenon of prophesy; there are a few people, specially gifted, who can see into the future. If this is true, then the logic of it would be that the future is somehow predestined, planned and laid out in advance.

In addition to this, another short comment on the Hebrew language. It has only two tenses; the past and the present/future. The distinction between them is not strong. It is obvious enough in a historical narrative such as the Book of Kings, where the past tense is used freely. But in the prophetic oracles, which are very largely couched in Hebrew poetry, the distinction between the tenses is not at all clear. One example with suffice;

Psalm 79:1: "O God, the heathen have come into thy inheritance; they have defiled thy holy temple; they have laid Jerusalem in ruins."

We notice that this is written in the past tense, and yet it is referring to the future, when Jerusalem was finally ruined by the Babylonians. This must be long after the Psalm was written. We see how the prophetic mode uses tenses in a way that we would not nowadays, with our methods of using verb tenses. It all indicates that there is that feeling of imprecision over time, and that eternity pervades the whole thing.

If this were to seem all very strange, we find that the 20th century has produced a train of thought even stranger! It was Einstein and Rosen in 1935, who devised the theory of relativity, which is all about the warping of time and light. It is Hawking who expands on this in the late 20th century, and if this sounds like a hyped up version of Gnosticism, you will be forgiven for thinking that!

The first assumption, as seen earlier, is that the universe is expanding at an accelerating rate. This is as a result of the Big Bang (allegedly). On that basis, history will go on in a straight line, eternally. However, what if the expanding universe decides to go into reverse and contract in on (6) itself? Does that mean that history will go into reverse? Noticing that everything seems to be going in circles, planets, stars, galaxies and in fact the entire universe is behaving like a gyroscope, what is to stop the universe from doing a loop round and moving in on itself?

The second assumption is that time travel is a possibility. Faced with the difficulty of sending a mission into outer space, we must realise that there are vast distances, measured in light years, and that there is a limit to the speeds that we can achieve at the moment. To reach Alpha Centauri, our nearest star, would entail travelling for four light years. Even if a space craft could achieve the speed of light, it would take four years to make the journey, and another four to make the return journey. A realistic estimate has been that it would require 30 years to reach Alpha Centauri, which is half a lifetime for the man in the capsule. Experiments with accelerating particles show that as it approaches the speed of light, more power is needed, and we can only achieve 99.9% of that (7) velocity. What would happen if we tried to boost an entire space craft, loaded up with fuel, supplies and life support mechanisms, to achieve the speed of light? Star Trek seemed to manage it, but that was pure fiction and wishful thinking.

It was Einstein that had the idea of a 'bridge', or some kind of short cut to achieve such distances. Now, it is called a 'wormhole'. It all hinges on the possibility of warping space time; an idea derived from the theory of general relativity. It would require finding a region of space with negative curvature, as opposed to positive curvature. This would allow a space traveller to arrive at another planet so rapidly, that when he came back, he would land home in the past. Indeed, he might even meet himself coming back!

So this raises the question of time travel and possibility of a time machine. So Dr. Who is not quite such a crazy idea after all, one might think. The implication in this, is that one could go back into history, and possibly rearrange things. Just think, if one could go back to 1800 and shoot Napoleon? How convenient! One of the episodes in Star Trek centred round the preservation of the whales. Jim Kirk managed to borrow a Klingon space ship, scoop up a whale, carry it off into space, and bring it back at a different time in history, and so save the whale! This does raise the question of predestination; whether one could alter the course of history, by going back to previous times with the knowledge of how events were going to turn out. This is all very speculative and fanciful, but even so, there may be some possibilities in it.

What are the implications in this for religious belief?

With regard to the circulatory motion of just about everything, it is worth pointing out that this is by no means a new idea. In Hindu-Buddhist philosophy, everything is circular. This is less emphasised in Hindu thought, but in Buddhist 'mythology', there is the Wheel of Becoming. It is all bound up with Karma, or reincarnation. One circulates from one life to the next, round this Wheel, not unlike the magic roundabout. At the top, one is an angel, or a god, and going down to the right, one deteriorates down to becoming a devil, or something nasty, and then up the other side to the top again. One can continue up and down this Wheel eternally, and one's conduct in life determines where one lands, as something good or bad. Of course, there is an escape available from this inevitable round, provided by the Buddha. Thus one escapes to Nirvana and the whole cycle of life and death is over.

The only difference between this and what Hawking offers is as follows. He proposes that Space is not empty, but filled with particles of different spin, plus and minus. They circulate in pairs (8), in a sort of balancing act, cancelling each other out. We notice again the element of balance between plus and minus, good and bad, and the fact that good has to be balanced by bad. The same motif is seen in the construction of the atom and just about everything else. In a sense the Buddhists are right, except to say that one does not necessarily have to believe in reincarnation. For Hawking, the emphasis is on the physics of electrical impulses; for the Buddhists, the emphasis is on one's personal destiny and worth. Otherwise, it is the same motif but just expressed in different terms.

With regard to time travel, it is interesting that this too is by no means a new idea. The Christians have someone who is the same 'yesterday, today and tomorrow'. That someone is called Jesus, the true Messiah of God. It is Hebrews that describes the Messiah in terms of eternity. (9)

"In the beginning was the Word, and the Word was with God and the Word was God," (10)
And "before Abraham was, I am." (11)

Jesus Christ was quickly seen as spanning the whole of history, and eternity. It was realised that he was pre-existent and post-existent in relation to the Incarnation. The Buddhists, however, devised another permutation on this. They picture the present Buddha, Siddhartha, to be only one of a long line of Bodhisattvas, stretching back into history, and appearing in order to offer salvation to suffering humankind. What this means is that the religionists have understood 'time travel' or coping with eternity, long before Albert Einstein.

The word, WORD, in Greek, is LOGOS, was an important concept in the philosophy of the Roman Empire. Philosophers and scientists at that time threw the word around as if it were the answer to every question. Nowadays, we throw the words 'evolution' and 'quantum' around, without much thought as to the implications involved. The Gnostics pictured the Logos as some kind of spiritual entity, emanating from the eternal God, and that would enter the world, bypassing all the nasty gods, and bring salvation to all who could achieve 'gnosis'. This, in a way, was not dissimilar to the process in Buddhism. One could see a potential equation between the Logos and the Buddha. In fact, one suspects that the new faith of Buddhism had actually influenced thought in the Roman Empire.

However, St. John has here Christianised the word Logos, by claiming that the true Messiah, Jesus, is actually the ultimate instrument of Almighty God, coming into the world to effect salvation. In spiritual terms, he spans the whole of the history of creation, from start to finish. It is no surprise that the Gospels give heavy emphasis to pointing out that Jesus is a prophet. This comes out very strongly in St. Matthew and St. John. This indicates that time, in our parameters, is of no real meaning for God or the Messiah. (12)

The notion that the Creator God had and still does have, an agent in the process of Creation, is strongly emphasised in the Wisdom literature of the Old Testament. So, Proverbs 8:22 claims that the Logos was the first of all God's inventions, long before the physical universe came into being. Job also has the same motif. It answers the question, of how the eternal God, who is spirit, can be involved in the production of the physical world. The answer is that he has a 'right hand man', a (13) 'workman' or an 'agent' who actually brings physical things into being, and is also capable of coming into the world himself, in real terms. In this way, the Christians can see Jesus of Nazareth as fully human, like the rest of humanity, and yet, fully divine, as a complete revelation of the eternal God.

Obviously, there are people who find that impossible to accept. It may seem a crazy idea, but then, how crazy is the notion of time travel, going back into the past, or forward into the future? Dr. Who is great fun as sheer fantasy, but we must remember that that is sheer invention and wishful thinking. Even so, how often have we seen what has appeared to be a crazy idea in times gone by, actually come to pass by the ingenuity of the human race? Personally, I am far more inclined to take Jesus of Nazareth seriously as not just time-bound but eternal and the final spiritual connection between God and humanity. He is the true and ultimate 'time-traveller'.

Who are the people who object to Jesus being the Logos of God? Traditionally, the Jews and the Muslims have not accepted Jesus as the Messiah. Not a few Christians have problems with the Incarnation. We can see from the New Testament why the Jews rejected Jesus, and that remark 'before Abraham was, I am' was probably the basic problem for them; how could a carpenter from a remote Galilean village be the eternal word of God? No wonder they thought he was deranged. It was, however a strange paradox which turned out to be providential. Because he was rejected and crucified, this led on to the resurrection, the greatest triumph of all time. This demonstrated, finally, that in the tussle between good and evil, good will always eventually prevail; life will overcome death; plus will overcome minus.

What this means is, that whatever one believes about the beginning of all things, or indeed the end, essentially does not matter. One may find the Big Bang an attractive doctrine, or unduly frightening. One may be fascinated by the idea of the Sun enlarging into a Red Giant and engulfing us all, or possibly not, according to one's opinion. But above and beyond that, is the promise from the inspirational words of the Bible, that the Eternal God is in control of the matter, and that his Messiah is a spiritual reality guiding the course of history.

## Footnotes

1. A thorough treatment of calendars and time is found in E.G.Richards, Mapping Time.
2. Gnosticism: keeps reappearing in various forms to the present day.
3. The Chinese had a most complicated calendar system but gave it up in favour of our Gregorian system.
4. In A Brief History of Time, Stephen Hawking.
5. A full text of Nostradamus with commentary is found in Erika Cheetham, The Prophecies of Nostradamus.
6. There is a strand of opinion that suggests that.
7. This has been experimented on with the Hadron collider at Cerne in Switzerland.
8. Hawking, A Brief History of Time, page 215.
9. Hebrews 13:8; "Jesus Christ is the same yesterday and today and for ever."
10. John 1:1.
11. John 8:58. The Jews were ready to stone Jesus, on the assumption that this was a claim to being God.
12. Psalm 90:4; "a thousand ages in thy sight are but as yesterday when it is past..." and "from everlasting to everlasting thou art God."
13. Proverbs 8:22 and also Job 28:20ff.

# 9

## *Biology; the animal kingdom*

Certain aspects of this have already been discussed in the chapter on Evolution. There is no need to revisit all the arguments surrounding this issue. What we have to take on board is that just as the human race has a world of logic of its own, as indeed the quantum world, so too does the animal kingdom. One could fairly say that the animal world functions on a system which is basically kill or be killed. From our point of view, this must seem quite brutish and heartless; from their point of view, it must seem like pure common sense. Whether the animals possess any sort of emotion which might equate to sentimentality, is a moot point. We, the humans, constantly attempt to superimpose sentimentality on the policy of the animals; if asked, they might not have any idea of what we are talking about.

It is assumed that animals function on the basis of instinct. This is clearly a fair claim, since we can see that with many species, the minute they are born, they are up and functioning just like an adult. Their behaviour cannot have been learned from the parent; it is innate. An example of that would be the turtles, who never actually see their mother, as they are hatched out, and find their way to the sea and look after themselves. On the other hand, there are many creatures that have to learn skills from their parents. This must raise the question of how much intelligence some creatures have. It is claimed, from testing done by psychologists, that rats are potentially very intelligent. There is no doubt that foxes can be incredibly crafty. We all marvel at the ability of migratory fish, such as the salmon, to find the exact spot in a certain river shallow, to lay their eggs, the same place where they were born, after having been away across the ocean for two years. Must this suggest an amazing degree of intelligence? Can it just be pure instinct?

Even more amazing is the ability of the turtle, who swims thousands of miles across the ocean, to a tiny island in the Pacific, to the very same beach, to lay her eggs in the sand, just above high water mark, and at the right time to coincide with the phases of the moon. No one can seriously explain this, unless we accord them a degree of intelligence, or alternatively, an acuteness of instinct that humans do not possess?

So far, we have touched on what Freud and Jung would call the ID and the EGO, which (1) humans and animals have in common. However, humans have another mental faculty called the SUPER EGO, namely the conscience, or capacity to feel guilt. Do animals possess this element? It can be stated that domestic pets form a strong association with their owners, something that could be termed as 'love' (although they might not see it as such!) A sense of conscience can also be seen, although it would be wrong to generalise and say that all animals are capable of such a factor.

As far as sensory abilities are concerned, the humans are quite accustomed to functioning on the strength of five senses. But for the animals, this functioning is very often on a completely different basis. So for instance, an owl, with its enormous eyes which potentially could read a newspaper at twelve yards and which function perfectly in the dark, his eyesight is far better than any human can manage. So also for certain dogs, whose olfactory skills are outstanding, they can follow a scent, whereas a human cannot. Some animals have whiskers, which enable them to locate prey by the slightest vibration. A shark is thought to have at least two senses that we do not possess, one of which is to sense blood in the water; its eyesight is probably a lot weaker than ours. It is known that for a human to be unsighted, his other senses will become more acute in compensation; hearing, touch and smell. Do we see the same motif in the relation between animals and humans? If they are weak on one element, there is compensation with other elements being stronger. This must raise again the issue of balance.

One fascinating issue concerning animals, is the matter of dominant species as opposed to rare ones. A visit to Madagascar reveals that there are many unusual species, not to be found anywhere else. Three examples of this are; Dumeril's Boa (constrictor), the Leaf Nosed snake, and Jackson's Chameleon. This is often cited in support of Evolution; that because Madagascar is an island, and has presumably been separated from Africa for a long time, the fauna have evolved in different ways as compared with the mainland. This kind of argument ignores the fact that unusual forms of fauna are also found on mainland. A brief look at the fauna of Europe (leaving out the rest of the world), reveals that while there are dominant species which inhabit vast areas of the continent, there are also areas that they do not cover. Ireland is a case in point, which seems to lack all sorts of creatures, not just snakes. In addition to this, there are minority species that are found in specifically small areas. They seem to cling on in spite of being threatened. A few examples will suffice at this point. The dusky shrew, very rare, is only found in Finland, as well as the Flying Squirrel. The Pyrenean Desman in Northern Spain, now very scarce and declining. They are also found in the Steppes of Russia, but may well be a different race of Desmans. The Olm, an eel-like creature, is only found in the Balkans, very secretive, and only discovered in 1875. The Pyrenees seem to favour rare species; a certain frog, the Brook Newt, the Rock Lizard, and the Southern Chamois, although admittedly some Chamois are found in central Italy. Galicia, in north west Spain seems to be a favoured spot for unusual species. It would be tedious to catalogue every rare species tucked away in quiet corners of the world, but the situation in Europe is only 'the tip of the iceberg.' One wonders if rarity of species has anything to do with Evolution. There must be other factors involved. It is obvious that these creatures are at home in the specific habitat that they occupy, and desist from venturing out into other environments. Does this indicate a degree of intelligence in them? I would suggest that each creature has some kind of specific role to play in whatever environment he occupies. The fact that most of them are declining is almost certainly a result of the interference of the human race.

When we come to consider the populations in the oceans, there are even more puzzles nowhere near being solved. The fact is, that while we have maps of the Moon and Mars, we do not have maps of all the ocean sea-beds. We know more about other planets than our own. It is only within the last few decades that oceanographic investigation has really taken off. This is because we now have the gadgets to reach the deepest parts of the oceans, three or four miles down, and discover the world that is going on down there. Again, this is a world that has all the appearance of functioning on a different system of logic, like the micro-world, and the mega-world. The chief ruling factor is that the pressure down there is vastly greater, maybe 100 to 200 times greater. Humans can only view this world in some kind of bathysphere, and the creatures that live down there could never survive at normal atmospheric pressure.

We find that the same picture emerges with regard to commonplace and rare species. There are some aquatic creatures that can be found all over the oceans, whereas there are rare forms only found in specific places. But the important point to emphasise here, is that almost every day, something completely new turns up, especially from the great deeps. Constantly, scientists are amazed at forms quite unlike anything seen before. It is fair to say that those creatures that live so deep that the sunlight never penetrates down there, some of them have their own method of producing light, and others have an ability to produce luminescence in response to the light from another creature. Also, many of them are completely transparent, which means they are very difficult to spot.

One important comment I would like to offer at this point, is that since new forms are being found almost every day, it is no longer possible to make easy generalisations about life in the oceans. Some of the forms found are truly bizarre, and are nothing like anything seen before. The same could be said of land-based fauna, since, again, new creatures keep appearing. A cautionary tale is told about how it was assumed that the coelacanth, a bony fish belonging to the Permian period, an example of it was fished up in 1938 and more have been caught since, and appear to be a different version of the same thing. In other words, let us not make too many dogmatic statements about life in the oceans. We have a long way to go in exploring and mapping all of the oceans.

The sea-beds have all kinds of features one might never guess at. There are trenches going down miles; there are volcanoes; there are mud-geysers, not unlike what we see on Europa; there are mountain ranges; there are methane vents. There is much more waiting to be discovered.

One interesting finding is that each ocean trench has its own distinctive species. There is the snailfish only found in the Kermadec Trench, and another species only found in the Mariana Trench,(2) 8,000 metres down. There are creatures that can do without light and oxygen and live on the edge of a thermal vent, just at the right spot to avoid being over-heated or under-heated. Does this indicate a degree of intelligence in such creatures? It is thought that life on earth began in the oceans, millions of years ago, and these findings may support that claim. It also ties in with what is stated in Genesis, that living creatures emerged from the oceans.

The relationship between land based and aquatic creatures is not as straightforward as might be supposed. One example may illustrate the point.

There is a 'fish' called a leaping blenny, found only in Micronesia (Guam). It spends virtually all its life on a rocky shore, eating algae, mating, guarding his territory and reproducing, just inside the tidal range. But the eggs float out to sea and return as larvae, to feed on the shore. The blenny has gills but no lungs. He needs a splash of water on the shore to keep his lungs wet, but also, he can take in oxygen through his skin, as opposed to having lungs. Though he has no legs, he can leap about to find new food supplies and do mating. Even though this is a unique creature from the point of view of its relationship between land and sea, it is not the only one that can cope with open atmosphere and water. Consider the eel, which can spend months crossing the oceans, but can slither across land to find a pool. Consider the crab, which can spend most of its life on the seabed, and yet can survive for several hours when caught. He has neither gills nor lungs in the normal sense, and scientists are at a loss to know how he ingests oxygen. This all raises the question of how, presumably millions of years ago, aquatic creatures emerged from the water and became land-based.

One important issue is that of food chains, and one example will illustrate the relationship between aquatic and land-based creatures. We start with an aquatic plant, the waterweed. This is eaten by the tadpole; this turns the plant tissue into animal tissue. The dragonfly nymphs eat the tadpoles, thus they are first level carnivores. The dragonfly nymphs are eaten by the perch, a second level carnivore. The fish is eaten by the osprey, which is at the top of the food chain; he has no natural enemies (apart from the human race!). When the osprey dies of old age, his corpse drops down to the ground or in the water, and the tiny creatures, including bacteria, set to work to dismantle his body. Thus, all that flesh starts again at the bottom of the food chain. We see from this, that there is a circular motion involved here. How many other food chains are there? How many of them interrelate? But the disturbing fact is, that if the food chain is disturbed for some reason (usually the interference of mankind) then things go out of balance. So we have a superflux of jellyfish, for instance, or frogs or certain species of fish. Restoring the balance can take a long time. One generalisation that can be made is this; that all creatures of whatever kind, are there for a purpose, in the great workings of things. To persecute one type, just because it is inconvenient or nasty-looking, is to invite a disturbance in the balance of nature, and that can have far-reaching consequences. It is only recently that scientists have begun to realise that the sea is not to be treated as a useful rubbish dump; all the creatures in the oceans, even miles down in the chasms, have a part to play in Nature's plan.

Looking at the oceans with their currents, even though we call them specific names, such as Atlantic or Indian, they are really one great circulatory system. A current familiar to us is the Gulf Stream, which comes up from the West Indies and keeps the sea areas of Western Europe clear of ice during the winter. What is not obvious is that the Arctic Ocean pushes cold water down under the Gulf Stream, as far down as the Antarctic. Thus, there is a circulatory motion going on there, albeit vertical motion. Horizontal circulatory motion also happens in certain places, such as the Antarctic Ocean. It is the interaction of cold and warm water, and this has a distinct bearing on the marine life those areas. This is why the term 'World' or 'Global Ocean' is used. It is one intricate system in which the water manages to circulate all round the globe. As we recall that marine life must be affected by these currents, it is interesting that some creatures manage to stay in one specific location whereas others seem to visit all areas. It would suggest that they know what they are doing; this is further evidence that they have some degree of intelligence. One would hardly doubt that dolphins and porpoises are intelligent, but this might imply that they all have some degree of EGO.

If we look at the world ventilation system, the prevailing winds, a similar pattern seems to emerge. On the Equator, the air is descending, which produces the tropical rainforests. Then the air spreads out, north and south, producing the Trade Winds and the 'roaring forties'. Some of the air ascends, to produce circular motion as it goes back to the tropics. Some of it continues north or south , and encounters cold air descending and spreading out from the Poles. This explains the changeable weather seen in the Oceanic climate (eg. UK). If there were no circular motion, either horizonatal or vertical, and the atmosphere were totally still, there would not be the differing climates seen around the world, neither would there be any rain or snow. The differing climates condition the differing life forms found, not just on land, but in the ocean depths. It is all a matter of movement, and circular at that. We can see that Taoist philosophy also says that for it to be a living world, there has to be movement. Things are never stagnant.

This would be an important truth with regard to the avian population of the world. By the fact that they have wings, they can move around from one area to another, and appear not to be as restricted as various animals and fish are. Having said that, there are many bird species that stay in their normal territories consistently. It is rather like the situation over animals; some common species of animals are found over a wide area while others, minority species, are only found in certain specific places. With the birds, however, we have the element of migration, which is a much more noteworthy aspect of their behaviour.

Seasonal migration of birds is one of the puzzles of the natural world, that is only just beginning to be understood, even if there are still many teasing questions to be answered. Looking at the interchange between Europe and North Africa, we see that a regular pattern is in operation. The Wheatears, Chiffchaffs and Sand Martins come up from North Africa in early March. The Swallows, House Martins, and Willow Warblers come up two or three weeks later. The Swifts, arrive in early May and the Spotted Flycatchers come up in June. Many of them are clever enough to take a route over as much land as possible, in order to avoid too long a journey over the Mediterranean. Even so, some species, such as the Swift, are capable of doing about 500 miles in a day. In May, the Greenland Wheatear comes up from Morocco, via Western Spain, the UK and Iceland but returns in the Autumn direct across the Atlantic. Some species can be seen as arriving on the same actual date each year. There are many other species that perform similar feats of navigation in other parts of the world.

How do they do it?

If it is purely instinctive and nothing more than that, it must mean that they possess some kind of sensory ability that is unknown to humans. Are they sensitive to varying temperatures, prevailing winds, weather of varying kinds? We know that some birds have weaker abilities with some senses, such as smell, hearing, but much more acute abilities with regard to sight and vibration. Some of them appear to have an inbuilt 'clock', which means that they arrive at their normal destination on the same day every year. It may be that many of them possess a sensory ability that is not known to humans. We can consider the skill of the homing pigeon; he can find his way home from wherever he is released; this must mean that he has some kind of inbuilt sense of compass directions, plus the ability to recognise his own pigeon loft when in sight of home. The migratory birds can be seen as two-way homing 'pigeons', but without any interference from humanity.

Instinct may be one thing, but we ought to consider the element of EGO, as opposed to ID. Is it possible that these migratory birds are using something akin to what we would call intelligence? One is struck by the fact that they pass over land masses in order to avoid long sea journeys. Is this an aspect of common sense? Even more intriguing, is how do some species, such as the Brent Goose, the Dunlins and the Bar-tailed Godwits, know how long to delay their journey north, to arrive at just the time the ice is melting in the tundra, in May and June? Is this an example of 'brain-work' and calculation at work? I would suggest that we should not underestimate the abilities of the avian population. They certainly have fine instincts that we do not understand, and almost certainly have anticipatory abilities which we find baffling. It is a world that is kept moving with different species having different mental abilities.

The relationship between the animal kingdom and humanity is a complex one, with differing attitudes shown on both sides. Some animals are terrified by humans; others find us easy to relate to. The same is true the other way round. Fortunately, in recent times, there has been much more awareness on the part of humanity with regard to animal welfare and the importance of not sentencing some species to extinction. It is not just the scientists, but many people, who have at last realised that every animal has some kind of part to play in the general picture and balance of nature.

The theological implications of the relationship between animals and humans is spelt out in the Bible, in Genesis chapter 2. In spite of it showing in chapter 1 that the animals appeared before(3) the human race, it is the other way round in Genesis 2. This is not necessarily meant to be a contradiction, since it may not be intended to be taken literally. After the first rainstorm (Genesis 2:6), God creates a man, and then forms the Garden of Eden with all kinds of trees. The tree of life and also the tree of knowledge of good and evil. Only with verse 15 do we come to the creation of the animals, as company for the man, and when none of these were seen as appropriate to be his helper, we have the creation of a woman. Whether the two trees are intended to be literally two separate plants, is an interesting question; this might be an example of Hebrew parallelism (poetry). However, the main point here is the relationship between animals and the humans. It may not be meant chronologically; the human race is superior and in command of the natural world; that is what it is saying, symbolically. The purpose of the human race is to tend the natural world and be in command of the animals.

Then it all goes wrong, as the serpent tempts the woman and the two of them disobey God. Do we have to take it literally, that the serpent could speak Hebrew and at that stage had legs? The whole thing is figurative, but such a powerful image that this passage has influenced religious thought down through the ages. But we see that the animal kingdom is not exempt from the failures of the human race. The whole of creation is 'fallen', not just the humans. We can see that all through the Bible, the natural world is tied in with God's relationship with humanity. The pattern of salvation clearly includes the animal kingdom, and by implication, the whole of creation.

Now we see the importance of the story of Noah and the Flood. A remnant of humanity was to be saved from destruction; not just humans but representatives of all the animals. If we try to take this story completely literally, it would be quite a problem to take a sample of every animal from all over the world. In any case, the account is not completely unanimous within itself as to what creatures to include. Genesis 6:19 says every living thing, one of each, male and female, and that includes birds and insects. Genesis 7: says seven pairs of clean animals and one pair of unclean animals. Clearly this is not intended to be taken literally; the message of the passage is, that God wishes to preserve a sample of all living things, not just the humans. It is interesting that when we compare this with the claims of the scientists, that there have been various extinctions in remote pre-history, it is clear that the vast majority of life was destroyed, and yet certain species did survive, which meant that creation could actually start again. It also agrees, in general terms, with the Greek philosophical view that there have been various 'ages' of mankind.

It is in the Wisdom literature of the Old Testament, that we see some of the finest poetry in(4) relation to the animal kingdom. The book of Job is an outstanding example, for in many passages, the wonders of nature are extolled. The gist of it is that while the animals appear to behave in such strange ways, we, the humans just do not understand their antics. How true this is still to this day, with all the clever scientific probing into the natural world! The main theme of the book of Job, is the question of theodicy; why does a righteous man have to suffer? And indeed, why is there any suffering at all? It is made plain in the first two chapters of Genesis; it was the human race, in relationship with the animal kingdom, that caused the problem through their disobedience.

We now come to the New Testament, in which another man, who is meant to be the second Adam, overcomes temptation and brings salvation to the whole world. We notice that he is born in a stable, which infers that the farm animals are in attendance. As he goes to Jerusalem, in his last few days, he is riding on a donkey. The implication in this is that representatives of the animal kingdom are clearly involved in the pattern of salvation. It goes even further, when at the crucifixion we have the sky going dark and a great earthquake. Do we have to take this completely literally? Some do. But what is it saying? That the whole of creation is redeemed through the sacrifice of Jesus Christ, not just the religious people, or even the wicked people, but the whole of life, whatever form it takes. Then in Revelation, we have the Messiah coming out of Jerusalem on a white horse, in (5) other words, the reverse take on the Palm Sunday motif. He has triumphed, and a representative of the animal kingdom is included in the procession. The Bible concludes with the image of the tree of life, which links us back to Genesis; that the whole of life and eternity, good and evil, every aspect of reality is now saved and ruled over by that humble Messiah, the Lamb. (6)

If one were to think that this relationship between mankind and the animals is confined to Christianity, one would be mistaken. In that great mythical saga, the Ramayana, as Rama goes to rescue his wife, Sita, the monkeys and the elephants are enlisted to join the army which is needed to defeat evil. Indeed, the trees of the forest are asked to give information as to her whereabouts. In the mythology of Taoism in China, the key figure is the Monkey King. In our culture, the monkey is seen as stupid and a nuisance, but in the East, he is seen as a very loyal creature, clever and very intelligent. But the gist of it is that the animal kingdom is clearly involved in their ideas on salvation.

Just as the Hindus and the Taoists have a special place in their theology for the animals, this is particularly so for the Buddhists. There is not much known in the West, about the Jataka Tales, a corpus of folklorist stories stemming from northern India. They probably predated the coming of the Buddha, but were used by him extensively in his teachings. Their influence has been widespread. In the West, they may have given Aesop some ideas and possibly even Chaucer with his Canterbury Tales. It is even possible that Jesus himself derived a few ideas from them for his parables.

The Jataka Tales centre on animals such as monkeys, quails, swans, parrots, pigs, geese and horses but done in such a way as to personify them, imparting some kind of moral teaching. There are claimed to be about 300 such stories, and they make lovely bedtime reading for children. A couple of examples will suffice.

The Monkey Bridge is about a population of monkeys who were ruled over by a monkey king. The king of Benares realised that there was a wonderful fruit growing in the monkey realm, and decided to commandeer it, and shoot all the monkeys. The monkeys realised what was going to happen, and the king made a bridge over the river so that his people could escape. It entailed he himself being part of the bridge, and it broke his back. When the king of Benares realised the sacrifice that the monkey king had made, he relented, and learned that rulership was about love rather than greed.

The Elephant Girly-face is about an elephant who appeared very kind and innocent, but overheard criminals plotting to commit murder. So the elephant decided to follow their lead, and killed his keepers. Eventually, the king sent in someone who knew Girly-face and realised that he had been influenced by the wrong sort of person. So they brought in two people who talked about being gentle, kind, and not killing people. This again influenced Girly-face, and he decided to be influenced by this good influence.

These examples show that animal stories can be used to emphasise good conduct and sound theological values.

**Footnotes**

1. Freud and psychology will appear in chapter 14.
2. The Kermadec Trench, in the South Pacific near Tonga.
3. Genesis 1:20ff.
4. For instance Job 39ff.
5. Matthew 21:5ff.
6. The Jataka Stories, translated by Felix Adler, Noor Inyat and E.C.Babbit.

# 10

## *The importance of trees*

It is only within our modern times that the importance of trees, for life on this planet, has been realised. We have known for some time that the trees exude oxygen into the atmosphere, during the daytime. During the night they exude carbon dioxide, but this is nowhere on the scale as the daytime production. Trees also take in carbon monoxide which is present in the atmosphere, and is not helpful for the human race. But their importance goes much further than that. They filter pollutants out of the air, as the leaves catch particles of dirt and then, when it rains, the dirt descends to the ground. The roots have the effect of binding the soil so that it is less likely to erode. This means that it is inadvisable to root out all the trees to produce clear, empty fields. This lesson was learned with the Great Dust Bowl in America in the 1930's. Also trees act as windbreaks and noise absorbers.

The internal structure of trees is also amazing. The bark, which is dead cells, acts as temperature control. It splits when the cambium layer beneath expands with growth. Every species of tree has a specific bark pattern, as well as specific design of leaves. The cambium layer is the growth area of the tree. In comprises the phloem and the xylem. The Phloem transports nutrients and energy from the leaves to other areas, including the roots, where starch is stored. The xylem transports water in both directions; from the roots upwards and from the leaves downwards. In this area, the annual growth of the tree takes place and explains the distinct tree rings which indicate the age of the tree. The most interesting tree for this matter is the bristlecone pine in America. These trees can be very ancient, thousands of years, and are now being used as a basis for dating matters in the field of archaeology. (1)

The most important matter for us, with trees is that fact that that green pigment, called chlorophyll, in the leaves, absorbs light energy from the sun. It also takes in carbon dioxide from the atmosphere, combines it with water, and produces glucose and oxygen. This process is essential for those who have lungs and rely on oxygen being at about 21% in the air. There is much concern that with the tropical rainforests being cut down, that this will affect the oxygen content in the atmosphere. It is calculated that the Brazilian rainforest contributes about 20% of the world's oxygen. There are, however, other rainforests in Africa and New Guinea, for instance, plus the fact that there are other starchy plants that work on the same basis as the trees. But the conclusion that we can draw is that trees, mainly, are essential for maintaining the right mix of gases to sustain life for us on this planet.

What has this got to do with religion? The answer is, that it has a lot to do with it. The importance of the tree, in mythological thinking and by association, in theological thinking is profound. We have already seen that the Bible begins and ends with a certain very significant tree. It symbolises life and also knowing the difference between good and evil. Why is that? The image of the World Tree is to be found in so many mythologies, the world over. What is the symbolism in it? The branches reach up to heaven, the bole is visible in this world, and the roots reach down to the underworld. What this means is that the 'tree' is the vital connection between all three worlds. It does not matter which kind of tree forms the image. In ancient Norse tradition, it is yggdrasil, the ash tree. In Germany it is the oak tree. In Druidic tradition it is the holly and also the mistletoe. In the Ramayana, as Rama tries to discover where his wife Sita has been abducted to, he asks the trees in the forest for their opinions. In African lore, there are certain mystical trees which have special spiritual significance, and are loaded with spiritual power. It is interesting that when Siddhartha has his enlightenment, it was under a special tree called the Boddhi tree. We can see the symbolism in that. He came to know about the deep spiritual matters of life and death under the tree of enlightenment; the tree that connects all three zones of the universe.

From this we can see that the terms 'tree of life' and 'tree of knowledge of good and evil' are most appropriate. When we see that a certain very significant tree comes into the Gospel accounts in the New Testament, namely the cross, made of wood, of course, the Messiah is nailed on to it. This symbolises that the connection between heaven, earth and the underworld is a living person and not just a dead piece of wood. This is how Jesus can be seen as the final, ultimate representative of God in this world and below.

Strangely, shrubs and bushes do not seem to assume quite the same significance in theology. It would be fair to say that they too, with their green leaves, contribute much of the oxygen in the atmosphere. The one noteworthy example of a bush being included in the pattern of salvation, is the Burning Bush. (2) The bush is on fire but yet, is not burnt up. God speaks to Moses out of the bush, and commissions him to rescue the Israelites from Egypt. How literally we can take this passage is a matter for discussion, but the symbolism of it is very strong. The tree in this account is an incomplete one, still growing, we assume, which indicates that the connection between heaven and earth is not yet complete. Also, in mythological thought, fire indicates cleansing and purification (as does water), and the fact that the bush is not consumed, is a strong indication that this is symbolic.

It is in the parables of Jesus that shrubs and bushes assume much symbolism. The vine, the fig tree, the mustard tree; all these are symbolic of the people of Israel, and also of the growth of the kingdom of God. In one passage, the fig tree actually withers away, which indicates that the people of the Old Testament are set to fade out. In John chapter 15, we have the powerful image of the vine being pruned by God; 'I am the true vine and my Father is the vinedresser.'

This underlines the importance of pruning bushes and shrubs. Any gardening manual worth having, will go into details about how and when to prune the bush. If this is not done, the bush will become less and less productive, self-defeating, until it is overwhelmed by itself. Pruning has the effect of removing dead shoots, encouraging new life and productivity, and also shaping the bush for the best effect. We can think of the rose bush which has to be pruned carefully by a gardener with experience. If left to its own devices, the bush will just become a tangled mess and suckers will spring out of the ground and stifle the main bush. What this implies is that the intervention of the human race is essential for the health of the natural world. So there is this balance between the energy of the natural world and care with which the gardener controls it to best effect.

If we look at Genesis 2:8, we see that God provided a garden (Eden) and it was Adam's task to tend it. We see here that basically, the task of the human race is to tend the natural world. There is a reciprocal relationship installed here. If the one thing goes out of balance, things go wrong. So if the natural world is allowed to run riot, we lose productivity and weeds take over in a big way. If the human race is allowed to overdo things, over exploit the natural world, we have another set of problems. It was not for nothing that the mega-Sabbath was ordered; every 49 years, the land (3) should have its rest, as well as the human race.

It would be a massive task to discuss all of the varieties of plants in the world, and well beyond the scope of this book. However, there are some very strange and rare species which can be commented on. Just as little fleas have lesser fleas upon their backs to bite them, the same is true for trees; they have parasitic growths that often defy explanation. We all know about the mistletoe which is familiar parasite in this part of the world, but there are many other very weird growths in various corners of the earth, well over 4,000 different species. Because they have attached themselves to something else, such as a tree, they do not use the normal method of using chlorophyll, like normal plants, but suck moisture out of their hosts. Some of them do not even have any roots or green leaves. (4)

A fascinating example is found in Sabah, North Borneo. Rafflesia is the world's largest flower. It starts as a bud looking like a large cabbage but unfolds to about five feet in diameter. It is attached to a tropical vine and produces a nasty smell like rotting flesh, which attracts insects. It is restricted to a small area in a forest in order to prevent it going into extinction. DNA analysis has shown that it is related to the euphorbias, or the spurge. This is a class of plants with about 2040 different variations, some of which are green plants and have tiny flowers. There is also the Rhizanthes which uses the same method to attract flies, except that it produces heat in order to spread the smell it makes. Another one, the Mitrastemon, found in Mexico, grows within the tissues of a certain type of oak, and only emerges when it flowers. It looks quite unlike anything else. But DNA analysis indicates that it is related to the Ericales, which includes heathers, rhododendra and azaleas, an order that includes 11,000 different varieties. One wonders how or why the Mistrastemon is so different from all these others, both in method of living and appearance. Could it be that the factor of DNA is not the only factor determines how plants grow?

What has been dubbed as the world's weirdest flowering plant is the Hydnora Africanus. It lives underground in the semi-deserts of South Africa, and only appears, quite unpredictably, when it decides to bloom. It exudes a smell like faeces to attract pollinating dung beetles. It is distantly related to Dutchman's Pipes. This is a curious species, found on most continents, and dangling from its host tree. Its method of pollination requires insects to be attracted down inside the flower, where they encounter inward pointing spines which will not allow the insect to escape. Later, when the insects are covered in pollen, the spines wither and allow the insect to escape only to find another flower. This way cross pollination is achieved. Dutchman's Pipes appear in all kinds of permutations, some of them totally weird. Perhaps the most ingenious of them would be the Aristolochia Arborea, which lives in the base of its host tree. The blooms very cleverly mimic a certain little purplish-brown toadstool, complete with the correct scent. The fungus gnats are tricked into laying their eggs on the 'toadstools' and in so doing perform pollination. All I can say is that this is highly ingenious, and if evolution is imagined to have made this arrangement, I would be stretched to find an explanation. I have to say that there must be more factors involved then just evolution.

The relationship between plants and insects is not always a negative one; there are various types of 'ant plant' which act as a host to ant colonies, and render mutual support. The Myrmecodia Lamii lives perched on tree branches, found in West Papua. They provide 'domatia' which are a complex labyrinth of hollow cavities with tiny entrance holes. The ants can enter and find smooth-walled chambers, ideal for nesting, and also rough walled chambers used as lavatories. The ant faeces are nutrient-rich which the plant needs. Some plants offer nectar for the ants. Some kinds of ant do some 'gardening' using sap-feeding insects like aphids, which yield honeydew. Also the ants encourage fungal growth inside the domatia, and this is used for their larvae and also transfers nutrients to the plant. This is not the only plant that has a reciprocal relationship with the ants. The Fanged Pitcher plant of Borneo has a close relationship with a specific species of ant. They live in the swollen, hollow tendrils, consuming nectar produced by the plant. In return, the ants attack the weevils that attempt to live off the new shoots of the plant. The ants can dive into the fluid without being poisoned, unlike other insects. The ants remove other insects that have died in the fluid. It is a unique and highly reciprocal relationship, except to say that there are other arrangements that are not quite so ingenious or elaborate.

My comment is, that this is truly amazing, and one wonders how evolution can be the simple answer to it all. We notice also that there is the element of ongoing conflict, seen at so many levels in the natural world.

The relationship between insects and plants can be exemplified by a few words about the Flying Duck Orchid, found only in southern and eastern

Australia. It looks exactly like a duck in flight, and it attracts male sawflies which attempt to mate with it. They land on a hinged lip and try to fly off with what they think is a female, however, the lip swings back and throws the sawfly back into the reproductive parts of the flower. This means that pollen becomes attached to the flies, and eventually, when they do escape, they carry the pollen to another duck flower. Another example is the Bee Orchid, found in the Mediterranean basin. The flowers look just like bees, but also exude a smell just like the female of a particular species of bee. This way the pollen is transferred to the other plants. However, each species of bee orchid targets a specific type of bee, which means that pollen is not wasted with the bees visiting the wrong type of orchid. There are all kinds of strange ways in which pollination is achieved, with a reciprocal relationship between insects and plants.

It does not have to be insects. There is the Bat Pitcher Plant of Borneo, which has an arrangement with the woolly bat. The plant lacks the scents and nectar which would attract insects, but instead, provides a daytime roosting place for the bats. The opening has a quality which reflects the ultrasound calls of the bats, which means they can find the plant amongst dense undergrowth. As the bats roost in the flower for a time, they leave their droppings, which are food for the plant. It is an amazing reciprocal relationship. A similar scheme comes with the King Pitcher Plant of Borneo, except that this time it is tree shrews that are attracted to them. There is a puddle of toxic liquid into which the screws fall and drown. It is even believed that the plant can consume rats. It is now very rare. Low's Pitcher Plant of North Borneo functions in much the same way. Even more bizarre is the arrangement of the New Zealand Flax Plant. This time it is geckos that congregate when the flax plant comes into flower, and using their long tongues, scoop up the nectar inside the petals. The geckos have modified scales on their chins and throats, which become dusted with pollen and so a visit to another flower achieves pollination.

One could describe hundreds of cases like this, with slight variations in pollination, and reciprocal arrangements. What it indicates is that the natural world is a most complicated, ingenious and amazing arrangement. I would find it very strange for anyone to claim that all this just happened by one coincidence after another. Even if it is true that Evolution was the mechanism by which these matters arrived (and that is by no means totally certain), there has to have been some kind of guidance and planning for these arrangements to have arrived. This brings us back to the teleological argument for the existence of God. (5)

This also raises other matters relevant to religion. We see that parasitism is a common factor in the natural world. From the cuckoo to the mistletoe and all other types of parasite, we wonder what is the purpose of it? Does it have any purpose? I suspect, strongly, that all these features of the natural world have some kind of function. It may be that we do not easily see what that function is, but further research from the Botanists may in time clarify matters.

But with religion, in its multiplicity of forms, we may find it strange that the same factor occurs. We have main strand religions, such as Christianity, Islam and Buddhism, but in company with that we have all kinds of splinter groups, schismatic branches, bizarre permutations going on. Some of them seem completely crazy; but then some of these rare parasitic plants do as well. America seems to be the happy hunting ground for strange permutations on religion. I shall not attempt to make a list of them, since they all think they are the real thing and everybody else is wrong. But do they fulfil some kind of purpose in the general picture of faith and belief?

The same picture is seen in politics, where we have main centre parties which tend to behave with some kind of moderation. Also we have extremist parties on both the right and the left. What is the effect of this? It is a reciprocal relationship. The moderate parties have the effect of tamping down extremes, and the extremes have the effect of keeping important issues in mind. The same can be said with religion. There are extremists and moderates. Again, there is a reciprocal balancing situation at work. It is one thing to say that there should be Christian Unity; there are far too many schismatic, splinter groups in existence, just cancelling each other out. But then there is still the major balancing situation between Christians and Muslims, Hindus and Buddhists. This may seem shocking to those who have decided that their particular version of the truth is the truth and everybody else is wrong. However, whatever version of the truth one holds, the opposite version of it, or the criticism of it, is still important. This world, indeed, this entire universe, functions on the tension between plus and minus, good and bad, and the net result is that all things are strangely and wonderfully kept in balance. The balance of Nature is an important factor which no one can deny, and it works in all kinds of strange ways. But the same is true with religion and also politics.

The parasitic growths have their part to play; the strange methods of pollination have their role to fulfil. It might occur to one to see all these different ideas on religion as a method of cross-pollination between various versions of the truth. One simple example would be the way in which the Roman Catholic faith has been influenced by the Protestant ideas, and vice versa, the Protestants have in recent times seen many of the Roman doctrines in a slightly different light. Religions move slightly under pressure from other groups. The Taoists might well say that for a (6) religion to have any life, it must be moving rather than stagnant. This must be particularly true in the modern world, where so many changes have occurred, which do have implications for religious faith. We have only to look at the situation with medical science to realise that hard and fast traditional doctrines must, at the very least, be given fresh consideration and appraisal. Life is moving on all the time, and anyone with a religious impulse, must face up to these new developments. I am not trying to say that we should all be completely carried away by every new discovery made by the scientists, after all, some of their ideas might actually be wrong. But we must be ready to evaluate and come to some kind of conclusion over the expansion of knowledge in our own times.

Another aspect of Botany is the fact that new species are being found all the time. One would have thought that with the botanists combing the world for information, that all species would by now have been identified, but this is far from the truth. At the very least, this must warn us about making easy doctrines out of the botanical knowledge we already have. Just as it is true that the astrophycisists are finding new things in outer space, almost every day, the same is true for the botanists. Why is it that there are dominant species and also minority ones? The same is true with the animals. The same is true with religions. Why is it that some minor religious groups have survived for centuries, against all the odds? Why is it that some theological ideas which were current in the Ancient World have begun to surface again in the modern world? A good example of that would be Gnosticism. It must indicate that all these strange permutations on life, and also on belief have some part to play in the general picture. It suggests that for all things, there is some sort of purpose, some sort of contribution being made to life in general. As the Psalmist says, 'in wisdom hast thou made them all.' Now we can see just how prophetic that verse is in today's world. (7) Without this factor, we would probably find that certain dominant species would monopolise the picture and there would be very little variety. We need to see the proliferation of life in a positive way, and look out for what the strange and rare species actually do contribute.

In addition to this, I cannot rule out the suspicion that like the photons, many, if not all of these plant species have some element of rationality. To put it bluntly, they have some kind of intelligence or decision-making facility. The other side of this is that some species, notably in the insect world, are not quite as intelligent as they ought to be. In other words, they are easily deceived by certain plants, using scent in particular. I think we all know that this world is a world of illusions, mirages and self-delusions. It is not just the insects that are deceived, but the human race also, in so many ways. There are religious groups that deliberately embark on deceiving people and taking advantage of them. Also there are scientists, or pseudo-scientists who set to work to deceive people. In all these matters, where belief, faith, so-called certainty, are involved, we must (8) remember that it is so easy to be deluded by a clever bit of theatrical trick. We ought all to be in search of the truth, but that can be like trying to locate the rainbow's end. This is one of the lessons, relevant to science and religion, that we can learn from the flora of this world.

### Footnotes

1. Bristlecone pine is found in many states in western USA, and is the oldest tree to be found, going back 5000 years
2. Exodus 3:1ff.
3. There is a slight discrepancy in the Laws of Moses in that 50 years is ordered. Leviticus 25:10ff shows that there is some dilemma over whether it is 49 or 50 years.
4. Information for the following plants is taken from Chris Thorogood, Weird Plants.
5. See chapter 12 for Proofs for the Existence of God.
6. Taoist philosophy involves the concept that a world that is not developing is a dead world.
7. See Psalm 104:24.
8. See chapter 19 on the subject of pseudo-science and pseudo-religion.

# 11

## *Medical Science and Religion*

It would be difficult to describe the earliest attempts at medicine as scientific, but the people of the ancient world would probably have thought of it in such terms. We know that a systematic approach to coping with illness and disease can be traced back to Babylon, Egypt, China and India. Their methods were noticeably different from ours today. What has influenced us right through historical times, has been the contribution of the great thinkers of Greece and Rome. We think particularly of Hippocrates (460-361 BC) who placed doctoring on the beginnings of a professional basis. Also of Galen (129-210 AD), whose ideas remained authoritative until quite recent times. It would be unfair to say that all their ideas were wrong; they knew some aspects of medicine which were correct and are still influential nowadays. It was just that they were not right on every matter. (1)

What was the basis of their thinking? An idea stemming from Babylon and Egypt, was that there were three prime constituents of the world; water, air and earth. Fire was added later as a fourth element. The Chinese had five basic elements. In Taoist philosophy there is fire, water, wood, (2) metal and earth. Applying this concept to the human make-up, we were seen as having four 'humours', namely, blood, phlegm, yellow bile and black bile. In more elevated vocabulary, it was Sanguine, Phlegmatic, Choleric, and Melancholic. If these four factors were in balance within the human person, then one's health would be satisfactory; if they were out of balance, then one would be unhealthy in some way. It is worth remarking that the concept of balance has been seen before in the Biochemistry chapter, and will appear again. The answer to the problem lay in three methods; bleeding, purging and some kind of adjustment of diet. We notice that the last one, concerning diet, is still with us, albeit in modified forms. Bleeding persisted until quite recent times and only became discredited in the 19th century. Even so, the idea of applying leeches is even now, beginning to be taken seriously again.

It is worth noting that no one saw any clash between this aspect of science and religious belief. It can be seen in Galen's writings that there is a spiritual element in his analyses. Galen became the authority on medicine right through the Middle Ages until the Renaissance, and even then, his influence continued until relatively recent times. This is a factor in medical thinking, that of authority. A new idea, or a challenge to established thinking, always provokes a negative reaction amongst medical analysts. But then the same is true in other branches of science; they have trouble coping with a challenge to established patterns of thought. The same is also true in religion!

There were three major factors that prevented progress in medical knowledge. Firstly, there was the ban on dissection of the human body. This was in force in the Roman Empire and worked its way into the Christian frame of thought. Up until comparatively recent times it was difficult for scientists to perform any kind of autopsy, and this resulted in 'body-snatching' and other nefarious schemes to obtain information on the internal workings of the body. While it was acceptable to perform dissection of animal corpses, it was thought sacrilegious to interfere with human remains. This difficulty has held up the search for medical knowledge for centuries. Secondly, the other problem has been the age-old superstition that disease is the result of some kind of sin. We see this assumed in that passage in St. John 9:3, where the disciples ask Jesus whose fault it was that the man was born blind. In other words, it might have been the result of some sin, or his parents' sin. To us, this must seem absurd, and yet, there is still this idea current among many people, when they contract an illness, 'what have I done to deserve this?' This is particularly true for anyone contracting cancer. The truth of the matter is that guilt, or fear, or faulty life-style can result in certain conditions. But it is misleading to say that every illness is caused by someone's bad behaviour. Thirdly, another aspect seen in the New Testament, is the idea that an evil spirit has invaded the individual and caused an illness. This was particularly true of mental disorders, and traces of this opinion are still noticed today. In Mark 1:21, someone who is deranged shouts out at Jesus in the synagogue. This is described as one with 'an unclean spirit', and various cases like this are described in the Gospels, especially the Gerasene Demoniac in Mark 5:1-20. I would not like to say that there are no such things as evil spirits, and try to deny that they manage to 'possess' people.

The church has specialist priests who regularly have to cope with this problem; it is called 'liberation' ministry. But to say that everyone who is mentally ill is possessed by an evil spirit is overstating things and most unfair. But the assumption that this is true, has put the brakes on any attempt at finding cures for these conditions. Even now, there is this background fear that anyone with a mental condition is to be shunned, shows that the problem is still there in many people's minds, even if we know, rationally that it is nonsense. The true purpose of those accounts in the ministry of Jesus, was to show that the Messiah had the spiritual power and authority over all things, not just physical but spiritual as well.

When we come to the Renaissance, we see a general questioning of just about everything. This was as a result of Copernicus and Galileo, and the coming of the first telescopes, showing that the traditional dogmas about the earth being the centre of the Universe with everything circulating round it, was wrong. This questioning went further; it now meant that Galen and anything that went before, had to be challenged. This is where Paracelsus (1493-1541 AD) enters the picture. He rejected the four 'humours' and the methods employed to bring about balance. He now said that the body is a chemical system, and that health can be restored by the correct application of some kind of concoction of mineral chemicals. As background to this we must recall that in the Middle Ages, the alchemists were discovering all kinds of interesting concoctions. Again, we can see that there is an element of truth in this, as some conditions can be corrected by the application of some kind of drug or chemical concoction. But to say that this is the total truth is again overstating things.

The same line of thought continues with Descartes (1593-1650 AD), who said that the same mechanical laws rule all things. (How modern does that sound!) The body is a machine. If one is sick, one is like a badly made machine, and vice versa, if one is well, one is like a finely constructed machine. To support this view, it was Harvey (1578-1657 AD) who described the circulation of the blood in the body, and this was objected to by his contemporaries. It was Malphigi (1628-1694 AD) who completed the picture by describing the capillaries that allow the arteries to feed the blood through to the veins. But this presupposes the appearance of the earliest microscopes. This allowed scientists to identify the tiny life forms such as bacteria and cells; not that they realised what these things were at the start, but eventually it led on to an understanding of infection and how to combat it.

We notice that by now there are the beginnings of a chasm between science and religion. It would be a mistake to say that all these medical experimenters were atheists; far from it. But what was happening was that as they explored the workings of the human body and the tiny organisms that could explain our problems, traditional assumptions about disease were now beginning to be challenged. There was no need to lose faith in God over this, but we can see how a traditional, and mistaken dogma about disease being shown to be faulty, can cause failure of faith. As the Age of the Enlightenment (so-called) came in, the challenge to faith increased, not so much over medical matters, but certainly over the issue of political authority. The result was the blood-bath of the French Revolution.

As the nineteenth century progressed, great strides were made in preventive medicine. Vaccination, developed by Jenner and Pasteur, has now managed to control many of the infectious diseases such as smallpox, diphtheria, and scarlet fever. Improved sanitation and health programmes have made such things as cholera and diarrhoea well under control. One might be forgiven for them thinking that all diseases would soon be eliminated. At the same time, there were great strides in pharmacology, and since 1945, the development of antibiotics has given us great hope. The mid- twentieth century saw the rise of biochemistry. This works on the basis of assuming that all living processes are ruled by the laws of chemistry and physics. There is the assumption that molecules are lifeless (!) And now we are at the point where advanced methods of surgery, aided by much more sophisticated anaesthetics, can cope with many more problems in the human frame.

So by now, we ought, in theory, to have eliminated all diseases; is that true? One or two examples will show that this optimism is not quite as valid as one might hope. With the appearance of penicillin in the late 1940's, one would assume that so many unfortunate conditions could be cured. Unfortunately, it is now being realised that the bacteria and viruses are developing an immunity to our antibiotics, which means that the more we use these cures, the less effective they will become. It is a constant tussle between disease and good health.

Another example is worth quoting. Diabetes has been known about since about 400 BC, but it was only in the 1880's that its relationship to sugar was discovered. A 'breakthrough' was found with the isolation of insulin, and that has been a major help, but only to some sufferers. It was then found that some diabetics are non-insulin dependent. It was found that there are different types of diabetes. Diabetes has not been eradicated; it has been brought under control, but is still a reality, and an increasing one at that. It would seem that the more we learn about it, the more complex it becomes. There is the need to find the underlying causes of the various types of diabetes. It reminds us of the Russian dolls; the more we probe into the matter, the more there is to be probed into.

Similarly, the situation over cancer is on the increase. In spite of us knowing that there are various factors which encourage cancer, such as cigarette smoking related to lung cancer, we still do not know for certain the root cause of the problem. All we are doing at the moment, is trying to offset the symptoms and give patients a longer life-span. All the research that goes into cancer has, as yet, not isolated the basic cause, the common denominator, that stimulates all the various types of cancer. We suspect it has something to do with faulty genes, but there other factors involved also.

Another situation is seen with pernicious anaemia. It was realised in the early twentieth century that some kind of deficiency in diet was related to anaemia. In the end, they came to realise that the root cause of it was a deficiency in vitamin B12, and the answer was to eat plenty of beef and liver. Now, it would seem, that a regular injection of vitamin B12 can solve the problem; or can it? We still do not know the finer details of how anaemia occurs and why B12 can appear to cure it. As one problem appears to be solved, we are left with a fine array of questions that are not solved, as yet.

The situation over heart disease and related problems is much the same. Much progress has been made over the 20th century in coping with these problems. Cardio vascular disease accounts for about 40% of deaths in the modern western world. There is an awareness that unhealthy diet, lack of exercise and bad habits such as smoking, are major contributors to these problems. Even so, not everyone who carries on this lifestyle develops heart problems. The narrowing up of the arteries, high blood pressure and the furring up of arteries, which place an extra strain on the heart, are one aspect of the matter, but there is no one simple underlying cause.

We have moved into an era of elaborate gadgetry for coping with heart problems. There is the ECG (electric cardiograph), the CAT (computerised axial tomography) and NMR (nuclear magnetic resonance), all of which sound very clever, but they do not tell us the basic cause of heart disease. Traditionally, Digitalis (the purple foxglove) was known as "good for the dropsy", and indeed it was beneficial if used in the right proportions. But no one knows how or why it works. Nowadays, we have a vast array of drugs developed in laboratories, and many of them are designed to dissolve clotting. Even so, we are still only offsetting the symptoms of the disease, as opposed to finding the root cause.

Along with this, we now have highly developed methods of surgery and invasion for dealing with heart problems. There are heart transplants and the possibility of artificial hearts. There are methods whereby tubes can be inserted to rectify problems without having to perform an operation. All this is most impressive, but we notice that this is only patching up damage or offsetting symptoms, as opposed to finding the root cause of heart problems.

Dealing with a potential heart patient is also not as straightforward as one might suppose. How do we know when someone has had an attack? A pain in the chest may give an indication, but then that pain may have been caused by something else. There might be no pain at all, and yet the patient has still had an attack. The clever gadgetry might show what has happened, but then it might not. There is breathlessness, which might indicate a heart problem, but then that symptom might be caused by something else. To complicate matters, patients respond differently to different drugs. Where one drug might be of major benefit to one patient, the same drug used on someone else might not have any effect. Dealing with heart cases often requires a lot of trial and error, experience, guesswork and a generous application of common sense. It has got to the point where we can control most of the symptoms of most types of heart disease, and make the patient comfortable, and extend life. But that does not mean we have found a basic cause and hence a cure.

The same can be said for many other conditions in other parts of the body. Moreover there are still quite a number of illnesses for which we have no idea of the cause (even less than with heart disease). Asthma, Parkinsons disease, multiple sclerosis, leukemia, are a few examples. It is one thing to give asthma patients a gadget to breath into, which fends off an attack, but that is not a final cure; it is only just coping with symptoms.

How does religion come into all this? All through the centuries of human civilisation, the healing process has been associated with religious belief. One example of that would be the Greek temple dedicated to Asclepius the god of healing, at which many medical processes were performed. We are left in ignorance as to many of their procedures, but they must have been effective, since the Greeks persisted with them for many centuries. In New Testament times, as seen in the Gospels, we are aware of healing processes that were effective, independently of Jesus the great healer. We think of the Pool of Bethesda at which people queued up in the hopes that when the water was disturbed 'by an angel' the first person to dive in would be healed. St. Luke himself is understood to have been a doctor. Then there was Jesus himself, who was noted for being a spiritual healer. He did not claim to be the only one, and indeed, today, there are such healers in action. (3)

The other way that religion impinges on modern medicine is in this respect. Since we have a vast array of gadgetry for prolonging life artificially, this raises the ethical question of how long to persist with this, if the patient is thought to be 'clinically dead'? We are all dominated by that commandment stemming from Moses; "thou shalt not commit murder". This is one of the foundational precepts of any civilised community. But now that we have developed means of prolonging life artificially, or causing it to cease, indirectly, at what point can it be classed as 'murder'? Going further than that, this raises the whole question of euthanasia, in the case of someone who is believed to be beyond hope, or terminally ill. What we do not have, in this country, is a clear guideline from the Government, or the Bible, or indeed God, as to how to cope with this dilemma. What it does show is that the more we delve into the basic processes of life with our clever gadgetry, the more we are taxed with what might appear to be insoluble ethical questions. What we really need is some authoritative voice to give firm guidance on these matters. To put it another way, we need a prophet of God to clarify the ethical uncertainty. At the moment, no such person has appeared.

What is clear, is that the more we delve into these medical matters, the more complicated the analysis becomes. It is like the Russian dolls and the sub-microscopic world. The field of knowledge is not being narrowed at all; it just keeps on expanding as more questions are raised up. In this way, with these ethical conundrums augmenting themselves all the time, we are actually creating a sort of judgment on ourselves, and a disturbed conscience, as a sort of offspin from the Ten Commandments.

To continue the theme, it was in the early 1950's that molecular biology began to develop as a discipline in its own right. This was to some extent stimulated by the atomic explosions in Japan in 1945, from which it was realised that certain conditions must be related to the molecular level. To cut a long story short, it is now being realised that many hereditary diseases are the result of some kind of abnormality in the genes. We now have the possibility of explaining many diseases at the molecular level. It is now getting to the point where we can identify a defective gene which is responsible for some kind of genetic disease. Examples of this would be cystic fibrosis, muscular dystrophy, and Huntington's Chorea; the latter has been pinpointed to chromosome 7 in 1983. This kind of work is not easy, but almost everyday, there is some kind of progress made. One hesitates to call it one breakthrough after another, but the whole field of research is a breakthrough, and opens up the possibility of conquering all kinds of conditions. What we need to remember is that not everyone's DNA is exactly the same structure. For some, an abnormal configuration does not have any implications for ill health; for others, it does. This goes to show that even if we are very close to explaining diseases that used to be a complete mystery, there are many variables that still have to be discovered. Again, it is like the Russian dolls; the more we probe into these things, the more complicated it becomes.

However, the positive side of it is that it may become possible to isolate a 'bad' gene in someone and substitute a 'good' gene instead. The negative side of it is that it is now possible to inform a pregnant mother that her foetus has some kind of defect. This has been particularly true of thalassemia, and the offer of a termination can be made when it is discovered that the foetus has certain abnormalities. I say 'negative', for although this policy has done much to cause a major reduction in thalassemia in Sardinia, Cyprus and Greece, for instance, there is still the ethical question concerning abortion. This is where medical science is potentially in disagreement with many who hold life as sacred and abortion as wrong. Just because it is now common practice in the Western World, does not mean it can be unencumbered by conscience over the seventh commandment. A lot depends on how one defines murder, and to what extent the end can justify the means. My feeling is that the policy of aborting foetuses that are assumed to be defective is a particularly hamfisted and negative way of solving the problem. It is not going to provide a method for correcting the condition. I am sure that no one would object to the substitution of a good gene for a bad one, if this process could be developed and become standard practice. (4)

It can be noted that the explanation for disease has come down from harmful bacteria causing an infection, to the level of micro-biology in which genes or chromosomes and DNA are found to have some kind of defect or abnormality. Does this imply that we need to look closely at the atomic level for the explanation for certain conditions; and then, in the micro-world of quantum physics, could abnormalities at the sub-atomic level help to render explanations? It is just a thought.

Relevant to all this is the situation over Cancer. This has become an increasingly prevalent condition over the last half century, and still we do not know the basic cause. Much progress has been made with treatment, but it must be admitted that this is only controlling symptoms and extending life, as opposed to finding the root cause of it. However, we may be getting much closer to finding the answer; cancer is not such a total mystery as it was a few years ago.

Cancer is not a genetic disease in the normal sense, but it has features in common with genetic diseases, in that the answer lies in the molecular level of analysis. It would seem that some sort of disorder in the cells can be found in all the common cancers. We have to face the reality that there are many different types of cancer, some far more malignant than others; also we have to admit that there may not be one simple cause of the condition; it may require several factors to go wrong to result in a cancer.

It would seem that many tumour viruses carry one or more genes that are capable of producing cancer; these genes are called 'viral oncogenes'. These are termed 'bad genes'. Having such a bad gene does not necessarily result in a cancer. There is also something called an anti-oncogene, which has the effect of keeping the oncogene under control . Here again we see the element of balance, which is so important in all these areas. Also the motif of good versus bad is inherent in this matter; the question of Theodicy. If, for some reason, the Anti-oncogene is not activated, this will allow the oncogene, the bad one, to cause trouble. Another thread is the observation that certain abnormalities in the chromosomes are associated with certain cancers, and this may be related to the oncogenes. We cannot rule out the possibility that these abnormalities are genetic, but normally, we assume they are caused by environmental factors. In other words, the weakness in the genes might be inherited but more likely acquired through faulty lifestyle. The influence of tobacco has already been assessed; also various chemicals and exposure to radiation. These influences can cause some kind of mutation at the molecular level. However, it is simplistic to say, for instance, that smoking causes cancer, in so many words; most cancers need more than one factor to cause a mutation.

These next remarks are purely personal and speculative, but may offer an explanation for the prevalence of cancer in our times. We have just lived through a time when cigarette smoking has been accepted as the social norm, and in fact, actually recommended for its supposed beneficial effects. (!) Now, cigarette manufacturers are going out of business and it is socially unacceptable to smoke. One would expect cancer to be declining, but it is not. Could it be that all that smoking has caused alterations in the genes and chromosomes of our parents and grandparents, and that we are now facing up to that legacy? This does not sound very nice, but then cancer is not very nice, either. This reminds me of that saying of Moses in Deuternomy, that the 'sins of the fathers will be visited on the children to the third and fourth generation.' That too is not very nice, but an inescapable (5) reality. There are so many ways in which the children have to face up to the consequences of their forebears' follies. What it implies is that we, in our times, ought to be very careful about our conduct and lifestyle, bearing in mind that future generations will have to face up to the long term consequences. We think immediately about the use of recreational drugs. This is where ethics (which are derived from religious values) is at its most acute in relation to science.

We may now be very close to finding the basic cause of cancer, but then, there will still be the challenge to find ways of correcting the matter.

Although we are not yet at the stage of finding the basic cause of cancer, we are now a lot nearer to finding it than we were a decade or so ago. It is likely that we shall find that it is not just one single cause, but the coincidence of several unfortunate influences, whether it is bad genes or something stemming from lifestyle or environment. The same may be true for many conditions which are thought to be genetic. It may be possible to identify specific genes or chromosomes that are associated with certain conditions.

Gene therapy, while very much still in its infancy, is beginning to offer hope. There are various avenues of research going on, but there is one which seems to me of particular promise. It has been found that a certain class of white blood cells called TIL cells (tumour-infiltrating lymphocytes), can be extracted from patients, cultured up outside the body, then insert a gene which can kill cancer cells, and then inject it back in. These, it would seem, cause a regression of cancer tumours. What this means is that the treatment is using Nature's own way of tackling malignant factors in the body. That is the purpose of the lymphocytes, the white blood cells, to repel disease and destroy poisons. This is an approach which would avoid using drugs or radiation treatment. All the same, this idea is still in its infancy and has to be proved to work consistently and not cause other problems. Even so, it seems to me to be an approach going in the right way.

How would this relate to ethics, and by implication religious values? There may be some who would raise objections to the whole matter of probing into the very building blocks of life. However, if we are ever to identify the gene or genes that are the basic cause of cancer, I would say that the research into these areas must continue and is well justified. If one of our religious values is concerned with the value and quality of life, then it is inexcusable to cease trying to defeat cancer, and other conditions that are almost certainly related to bad genes. It would be rather like saying, 'we know that smallpox is carried by a germ, but we shudder at the thought of sticking a needle into people with a vaccine'; that is unacceptable.

Here comes another personal thought. The idea of eliminating or removing a bad gene, or some other defective element in the microscopic apparatus of the human body is not just a new idea. We see Jesus, in the Gospels 'casting out' demons, or evil influences, to restore people's health and sanity. Does that approximate to much the same thing? Is the vocabulary just a bit different? Before we reject this idea, it is now being suspected that many mental disorders, including schizophrenia and severe depression are related to genetic factors. That is not to ignore environmental factors, such as severe stress or harsh treatment, which we also know can disturb the mind. The modern phenomenon of 'shell shock' is an acute example of that. As with cancer, and many other conditions which have so far defied analysis, the fundamental answer may lie at the molecular level, and as I suggested before, even deeper down at the atomic level.

Essentially, the seventh commandment, though negative in its tone, is in fact telling us of the sanctity and value of life. This is a precept accepted by virtually every religion and culture in the world. Any responsible process that can enhance the quality of life and bring hope to those involved with a distressing condition, ought to be encouraged and congratulated.

Looking at it another way, the seventh commandment has the effect of placing a limit on what the scientists can do with their experimentation. We have seen the depths of sadism that the Nazi medical experimenters descended to in the Third Reich. There has to be a limit to the experimentation on humans, and some would say on animals, for the sake of basic decency.

One area related to health and religion is that of the aging process. Relatively little is known about this factor, but it would seem that all living organisms have some kind of limit set on their life-span. Aging is not a disease in the same way as heart problems are, but it is thought that it is conditioned by the same genetic mechanisms. It has been determined, by careful analysis, that the human life span is approximately 85 years. So it would seem that centenarians are living on borrowed time.(!)

What has happened in the last century or so, is that many of the diseases and conditions that used to carry people off in mid-life, have been overcome. A whole range of infections are now either eliminated or under control, and mortality in childbirth is now reduced to insignificant numbers, at least in the developed world. This means that people are living longer, well into their 80's and more. This means that they are now more susceptible to other conditions such as heart disease, cancer and dementia. As one gets older, the resistance to disease becomes weaker, for instance a bout of influenza at age twenty is a comparatively trivial matter, but at 75 it can be fatal. It has been worked out that the cells in our bodies seem to know that they must become less productive and the immune system less effective. Also, there is another factor, not normally taken into account by the medical scientists; at a certain age, the will to live is much diminished, at least with some people. Now that we have all kinds of elaborate ways of keeping people alive when in times gone by, they would have died peacefully, it raises the question of life-expectancy and the quality of life. There is no doubt that one's natural faculties, sight, hearing, begin to diminish and more importantly one's sense of balance, which can be the cause of accidents. This is where ethico-religious values should come into the picture.

In Genesis 6:2 it is stated in that mysterious passage about the sons of God marrying the daughters of men, that 'My spirit shall not abide in man for ever, for he is flesh, but his days shall be one hundred and twenty years'. This is in the context of such people as Methusaleh living to colossal ages, such as 969 years. How we take this passage in chapter 5 is debatable. If we take it literally it would mean that Methusaleh lasted the equivalent of living from the Norman Conquest to the (6) present day. But there may be symbolic aspects to this passage, which I have discussed in my book on the subject of Myth, Legend and Symbolism. Those massive ages may be symbolic of something. In fact, the number 120 itself might just be some sort of symbolism. Consider that 12 was the number of the tribes of Israel and 10 was the symbolic number for God, it is telling us that in the wisdom of God and with the framework of the children of Israel, there is a limit on human life expectancy. It is also set against the rapid decline in righteous behaviour, as wickedness permeates human conduct. This is the reason given for the limit on human life.

This can be compared with that remark in Psalm 90:10; 'for the days of our life are three score and ten,' in other words, 70. This is in the context of a song of Moses, and is emphasising the feebleness of the human race as compared with God, who is everlasting. Even if we manage to last up to 80, it is just 'toil and trouble'. This of course, is a much more realistic statement about human life expectancy, and is clearly born of experience in the real world. We cannot rule out the possibility that this number 70 is also in some way symbolic. Threescore and ten in the Old Testament occurs many times and in different contexts. We can see it as 7, being the mythical number for the three levels of the universe and the four corners of the earth. Again, number ten is symbolic of God. So this is saying, symbolically, that as a part of the universe, God has determined your lifespan. We are aware that few people must have survived to the age of 70 in prehistoric times. With battles raging, plagues and famines, hardly anyone would have survived beyond 40 or 50, but a few would have prevailed, and were probably seen as very wise. It is stated in Deuteronomy 34:7 that Moses was 120 when he died. That ties in with Genesis 6:2, but again, it may be partly symbolic. Another situation regarding aging is found in Luke 1:25ff, in which Simeon, a very old man, recognises the importance of Jesus. Also an aged prophetess called Anna, whose age is actually quoted, namely 84, also recognises Jesus. The fact that they were well advanced in years must have inferred that they were very perceptive. We must remember that the use of numbers in the Bible very often cannot be taken totally literally; often they are symbolic. But in this case, 84 might be taken as literally true.

How do these remarks relate to medical science? The fact the scientists have not spent a great deal of effort on researching the aging process, may be an indication that they tacitly accept the inevitability of the aging process. Even if someone did devise a treatment that would extend people's life by a significant amount, would it actually gain anything? The truth is that we all have to die one day, regardless of how fit and careful we are with our health. The challenge to the scientists is to make our departure from this life as comfortable and dignified as possible. With that factor in mind, there is no clash between ethical values and medical care.

It was interesting that David Weatherall, in his book Science and the

Quiet Art, admitted that it is suspected that more sufferers resort to what is called 'alternative' medicine, than what is called (7) 'conventional' medicine. Alternative medicine can take many forms, including acupuncture, herbal remedies, homeopathic preparations, and all kinds of strange procedures. He never seems to make mention of the importance of the soul, or spirit of the patient, even if he does see the importance of treating each patient as an individual rather than some sort of categorised item. There is scant mention of the good old placebo as being quite an effective influence. The importance of this is the element of suggestion. If one believes in one's doctor and believes in the pill he offers, that in itself can be highly effective. If the opposite state of mind prevails, it is no surprise that the patient does not improve.

But it must be commented that with the vast of array of pills and elaborate gadgetry on offer in the Health Service, we are still encumbered with endless health problems, in fact, the complexity of it seems to be increasing rather than diminishing. It is in our own times that the importance of minimising the use of drugs and seeking more natural ways of bringing healing. It is now being realised that gardening or just increased contact with the natural world brings about a healing process. That would be most relevant to those suffering from mental problems, but not entirely. It is now being seen that people with Parkinsons and similar problems can improve or stabilise their condition by engaging with the creative aspect of engaging with the natural world. It may be one thing to find the defective gene that is causing the problem but another matter to reverse the condition, or at least, enable the patient to live with it and think positive about life. It may not necessarily be gardening that has the beneficial effect; there are many other creative ways of expression that can allow the patient to think positive about life.

In a way, this brings us back to the second chapter of Genesis. However literally or not, we take this passage, it is clearly saying that the human race was designed to interact with the natural world, not just the flowers but the animals too. Expulsion from the Garden of Eden meant that they were divorced from their original intention and task. They were cast out and had to work for a living. Everyone knows that idleness has a destructive effect for anyone; we all need to do something constructive, worthwhile and self-rewarding. The problem with modern industrialisation and urbanisation is that people are divorced from the natural world. It increases anxiety, unrest, lack of purpose, and produces stress. Stress may well be the basic problem with health in our modern, high-powered life, never mind the bad genes.

It could be stress that affects the genes to go bad! One wonders what is happening to this generation of school children who are subjected to levels of stress and anxiety, that are unprecedented, in the contemporary educational curriculum.

Returning to the motif of gardens, it is no accident that Jesus used this motif as a background to almost all of his parables. The vineyard, the harvest field, the fig tree, the mustard tree; all of these which relate to the natural world are such a powerful metaphor for the basic truths about God and humanity. To try to forget our natural dependence on the spiritual influence of the natural world is a mistake; it is now being realised and acted upon by many, including doctors. It is interesting that 'Heaven' is pictured as a garden. The healing influence of the garden or indeed the natural world, is now being taken much more seriously. This is true in Revelation, but is heavily emphasised in the Koran. In effect it is saying, 'back to the Garden of Eden'.

One thing never mentioned by David Weatherall, is the matter of spiritual healing. Obviously this is something that does not lend itself to scientific analysis or explanation. It is one thing to talk of 'suggestion', and to be fair, this can be a most helpful factor, as we see with the placebo. But with Jesus of Nazareth, we see someone who had massive spiritual power that could correct all kinds of physical and mental disorders. This, of course, is beyond normal human rationality, but is real enough. In my experience, I have come across various spiritual healers and the patients they have helped. There is no denying that they are gifted with some kind of numinous, spiritual power which can bring healing. It has to be admitted that the healing process is not just purely and simply prescribing drugs, applying fancy machines and carving people up. The spirit, the soul of the patient is just as important as the physical situation. This is where religious faith and medical practice can and do converge and should support each other.

Coming into the most recent developments, within the last ten years, a lot of groundbreaking work has been done in the area of modification of genes. Here I follow the seminal work 'A Crack in Creation' by Jennifer Doudna and Samuel Sternberg. This opens up all manner of possibilities for the eradication of genetic diseases. How this relates to religious faith will be seen later, but for now, a brief and not too complicated account of this research will follow. Anyone wishing to follow in detail this information should obtain Doudna's book. (8)

It would seem that inside the bacterial cell is a thing called CRISPR. This acronym stands for 'clustered regularly interspaced short palindromic repeats'. Inside the bacteria, is a string of squares and diamonds; four squares and five diamonds, as per diagram below. The diamonds are all identical stretches of the same thirty-ish letters of DNA; the squares, numbered one to four, each one constitutes a unique sequence of DNA.

Strangely, the sequences are nearly the same when read in either direction, just like a palindrome. This configuration has been found in many of the cells of the prokaryotes (bacteria and archaea).(9) Clearly this element in the chromosome must be there for a purpose; but what? It has been known that bacteria have natural invasive enemies, called phages. These are a virus that manage to break into the bacteria and using various methods, destroy them, after multiplying many times and then scattering around to attack more bacteria.

Is it any surprise to learn that the bacteria have various defence mechanisms to combat this kind of attack? The question now arose, did CRISPR have anything to do with the bacteria's defence system? By 2007 it was confirmed that CRISPR was indeed a kind of bacterial immune system, although the details of how it worked were still unknown. They found that although the 'diamonds' always stayed the same, the 'squares' varied enormously from one strain to another. This indicated that CRISPR was capable of modifying itself to cope with different kinds of viral invasion. It would seem that CRISPR was able to take snippets of the DNA of the invading virus, and retain them as a kind of 'vaccination' against future invasions. Also this modification would be inherited by future bacteria. Also they found that RNA plays a vital role in this process. The more the research progressed, the more they discovered was the ingenious workings of CRISPR and also in relation to the 'Cas genes' and 'Cas proteins'. Cas9 was found to do the actual cutting of the DNA helix.

In short, it became clear that the DNA double helix, the mechanism that controls our heredity, can be 'cut' in a specific place, or various places, defective genes can be eliminated and something else substituted and the cut ends stuck together again. This can all be done using CRISPR in conjuction with RNA and the Cas genes. In effect, this meant that one could rewrite the code of life, by modifying that DNA double helix.

## DNA Targeting by RNA and CAS 9

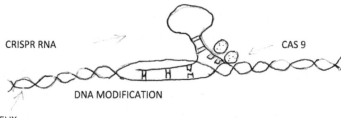

By 2013, at Harvard they had managed to tackle the problem of sickle cell disease. They had managed to cut out the defective gene in the DNA spiral and transplant the correct one in instead. This was using the CRISPR method. They had not got to the stage of trying it out on patients, but the implications in it were vast. It would mean that in theory it would be possible to dispense with genetic diseases altogether, given time and permission from the authorities. It soon became apparent that gene editing could be done on human leukemia cells, human stem cells, mouse neuroblastoma cells, bacterial cells, and one cell embryos from zebrafish. The list is expanding all the time. All it needed was the Cas9 protein, the guide RNA with a twenty-letter code that matched up with the DNA code, and any gene in any cell could be targeted out and edited. This began with modifications to animal life, but of course, plant life was involved as well. The implications in this are fantastic.

A few instances will show its potential. Imagine a cow that has no horns; a pig that never grows to anything larger than a dog. Imagine a human with the powerful eyesight of an owl; or a human with the olfactory ability of a sniffer dog. Imagine reproducing long-lost creatures such as the mammoth or the dodo. Imagine crops that never get blight or mildew. This is all in addition to the human race being rid of cancer and many other diseases that result from mutations in the genes. Clearly there is so much potential for doing good and producing healthy people; however, there is also much scope for the misuse of such a method. What would happen if someone who is evil, unscrupulous, self-serving, should manage to manipulate it. It could cause all kinds of problems.

Jennifer Doudna herself realises this and it is worth quoting her feelings. "First, we had to make the public aware that germline editing was an emerging social issue that should be confronted, studied, discussed, and debated. Second, we had to urge the scientific community ... those who were aggressively pushing it in new directions , to hold off on exploring this one avenue of (11) research....to hit the pause button until the societal, ethical and philosophical implications of germline editing could be discussed...ideally at global level."

The first comment we can make is about 'global level'. It is clear that Jennifer Doudna and her associates are not the only ones involved in this kind of cutting-edge research. There are other variants on gene treatment going on, and it is already an international concern. The stage that Doudna is at is not purely and simply all her own work; she has exchanged ideas with many colleagues in many countries to arrive at this stage.

Secondly, the public at large should be informed of this potentially helpful but also damaging method, and have their say. People of different religions, political stances, moral stances, ought to be able to have some kind of say in this. After all, it could transform life on this planet.

Thirdly, it all reminds me of the old Greek mythical story of Pandora's box. Once you let the 'cat out of the bag' so to speak, or open up the lid on the box of evils, there is no putting them back in. We shall have to live with the consequences for ever. To ask scientists to 'hit the pause button' will be a vain hope, especially if someone who is determined to misuse the method, learns how to work it. One wonders if Doudna could have thought of this potentially perilous situation before it reached this level of success.

It is now time to assess the implications for religious belief in relation to gene editing. Already, the ethical aspects have raised themselves up, and that cannot be unrelated to religion. Is it morally acceptable to interfere with the genes to affect changes in the physical inheritance of anyone, human or animal? I would say that if this method were purely and simply a safe way of eradicating genetic diseases, then it can be ethically justified. Just as we have managed to control so many infectious diseases by vaccination and use of antibiotics, why not carry on the same method with defective genes?

However, there needs to be much caution over how this is done. We have noticed that over-use of antibiotics has had the effect of reducing their effectiveness. To put it bluntly, the bugs are becoming resistant to things like penicillin. How do we know that the genetic apparatus in the cells will not react in some way to as to render gene editing less and less effective? I think the answer is quite simply; try the method carefully and do not overdo it.

But we are confronted with the possibility of the frivolous use of genetic engineering. Why should a cow be engineered to be without any horns? There is the prospect of an animal, say a dog, being provided with a larynx, so that he can speak human language. What would that achieve? We could have 'designer babies' so engineered that they would match the wallpaper or the carpet! Does this sound absurd? The big threat is that a baby's sex could be determined before conception. Think of the ramifications in that! We should be overwhelmed with Chinese and Arab boys and a severe shortage of girls. Also a matter of concern from the political point of view, is that the inequality between the 'first' world and the' third' world could become worse, not better. If the people in the rich countries can afford to have genetic engineering done to their advantage and the poorer countries cannot afford it, it will be like what Jesus said, 'the rich get richer and the poor get poorer.' That was not said as some kind of justification for the chasm between the rich and the poor; it was simply a realistic comment on what really happens in life. (12)

This brings us to the point where what might be called 'creation ethics' must creep in. "In (13)wisdom hast thou made them all" as the Psalmist says. Could we just consider that the way creation came about was not some kind of chaotic mess, one mistake after another, or one coincidence after another? The Bible assures us that it was all carefully crafted, worked out, using wisdom. Nobody really understands why male and female in the human race are roughly equal in numbers. It would be sheer folly to disturb this careful balance. I would conclude that we should have a healthy respect for God's wonderful arrangement of things.

Another aspect in all this, which relates to theology, is the fact that at the genetic level, we see a constant battle going on between the viruses, the bacteria and the cells. It is all about attack and defence. It would seem that the whole of life is a strange balancing act between harmful influences and beneficial influences. The ancient pagan idea of constant conflict in the skies is not so far wrong, except that it goes on at the microscopic level instead. This also goes on at the human level, with the constant tussle in politics between right and left. Also it breaks out into warfare between powerful empires. Conflict seems to be an essential element in life, even if it is an uncomfortable thought. Another way in which these matters relate to Theology, is via the Japanese concept of Kami. In Shinto belief, every physical thing has some kind of spirit inhabiting it. This is not very different from the modern scientific view that all things are comprised of tiny impulses of life, whether it be cells, bacteria, viruses or indeed atoms.

This brings us to the deep philosophical and theological question of Theodicy. Why is there any evil in the world? Why cannot life be all goodness, decency and pleasant? It is the constant juxtaposition of good versus bad, or in spiritual terms, the good angels versus the devils. Why God devised a world like that, is beyond us to explain. But it would seem that the whole of life is somehow dependant on the tension between plus and minus, good and bad, success and failure, however one wishes to describe it. If it is thought that we could eliminate all the bad influences in the world, such as diseases, this must raise the question of whether it is entirely wise to disturb the balance of nature. To put it another way, will Mother Nature allow us to eliminate all those diseases? Will another collection of problems mysteriously appear as a result of engineering genes and chromosomes?

Jennifer Doudna is aware of how much potential for good or bad this latest development in gene editing is. She wants some kind of consensus across the world to place limits on what can or cannot be done with modifying genes, especially the human ones. Already she admits that this is a problem, since governments across the world have differing attitudes on how much restriction to place on the matter, and of course there are differences in values. Some governments have a very tight hold on scientific matters; others are very lax and permissive. It only needs someone in an unregulated country to begin to handle the matter carelessly, and this could spell a lot of trouble. Another quotation from Doudna is appropriate;

"Few technologies are inherently good or bad; what matters is how we use them... when it comes to CRISPR, the possibilities of this new technology – good or bad – are limited only by our imaginations.......deciding on how to use this new technology may be the biggest challenge we have ever faced. I hope.... I believe...that we are up to the task." (14)

I admire her optimism but it has to be said that being realistic about human nature and being aware of a thing called 'original sin', there is almost certainly going to be some unscrupulous person who will exploit the technique for his own selfish ends, and leave everyone else with a collection of problems. My view is that extreme caution should be used when manipulating the very 'building blocks' of life and heredity; the long term consequences may be far worse than just accepting things as they are.

Science and religion have this important factor in common; both of them are only as good or as bad as the humans who employ them. Enormous harm can be caused by careless and selfish implementation of scientific findings; so also can much benefit by be brought about with our new technologies. With religion, of any kind, beliefs, dogmas can cause so much cruelty and give encouragement to violence and destruction; on the other hand, it can bring healing, peace, and cooperation between peoples of goodwill. It is all a matter of the attitude of those who put these things into practice.

### Footnotes

1. Much of my source material for this chapter comes from David Weatherall, *The Quiet Art*. Most of it is slightly out of date.
2. *The Complete Works of Lao Tzu*, by Hua-Ching Ni.
3. Examples are Harry Edwards, Christopher Woodward, and Russell Parker.
4. The issue of gene alteration will be discussed later in this chapter.
5. Deuteronomy 5:9 and other places.
6. The question of those great ages quoted in early Genesis is discussed in my book, *Myth, Legend and Symbolism*.
7. It all depends on what is meant by conventional medicine. Presumably it means treatments which are based on systematic scientific research. Even so, the acupuncturists would make the same claim.
8. Three up-to-date works on this theme are; Douda, *A Crack in Creation; The Gene Machine*, by Venki Ramakrishnan; and *Hacking the Code of Life*, by Nessa Carey.
9. Discussed in Chapter 5 on Biochemistry.
10. This means that bad genes can be removed and good ones put in their place.
11. Doudna, in chapter 8 of *A Crack in Creation*, discusses the ethical, social and political ramifications of CRISPR.
12. Mark 14:7.
13. Psalm 104:24.
14. Doudna's book, page 240.

# 12

## *Proofs for the Existence of God*

So far, each chapter has normally started with some kind of scientific statement which brings in comments from religion or theology. This chapter will tackle the matter the other way round. The theologico-philosophic arguments for the existence of God will come first and receive comment from scientific findings. When talking about 'proof', we normally associate that with (1) mathematical matters, and scientific findings. To talk about proving the existence of God sounds somewhat difficult. If we could see or identify God in some tangible way, proof would hardly be a problem. But we are assured by St. John in chapter one that "no one has ever seen God" (John 1:18). Even so, the Bible records various prophets who claim to have had close encounters with God. Such people are Abraham, Moses, Elijah, Isaiah and Jesus himself. Obviously, for those who do not trust the Biblical accounts, there is the freedom to undervalue or deny such evidence. But one must ask, if we have the evidence, why discount it? Can we not accept that these people were telling the truth?

The nearest the Bible comes to addressing this actual matter, comes in one of the parables of Jesus, where he discusses the contrast between the Dives and Lazarus, the rich man and the poor man. (Luke 16:19-31). The conclusion is that even if someone should rise from the dead, people will still refuse to believe. How true! Human nature is such that if they do not wish to believe something, no evidence will make them change their minds. The opposite is also true, that if they have a fixed idea in their heads, they will refuse to take seriously any evidence to the contrary. When dealing with proofs for the existence of God, we are up against this very mental blockage. If they have decided that they want to be atheists, no argument or evidence will penetrate their defensive system. The word 'proof' is not particularly apt in this context. If these arguments were proof, in the sense of indisputable evidence, there would be no such thing as atheism. Everyone would be forced to admit to the existence of God. It is interesting that the Bible never embarks on such lines of argument. It just assumes that God is a reality and that people know it instinctively.

If one were to assume that proofs for the existence of God were a new idea, one would be mistaken. The first evidence of this approach to theology and philosophy can be traced back to Ancient Egypt and the Greek philosophers. There is a document called the Corpus Hermeticum, a collection of Greek writings stemming from the second century AD, which contains the embryonic basics of this line of argument. But the Corpus is based on much more ancient material stemming (2)from ancient Egypt, and is related to the Egyptian Book of the Dead. Admittedly, the material must have been based on polytheistic assumptions, and indeed, the Corpus itself assumes the Greek god Hermes (hence the term 'hermeticum'). But the document is based on monotheistic assumptions, with various Gnostical additives, something which was probably inescapable in the philosophical climate of the late Roman Empire. The 'proofs' continued through the medieval period with Thomas Aquinas, were taken as read at the Reformation and then were given a fresh impetus (3) with the Age of Enlightenment, with such people as Kant. They are still in use to this day and modern variations on them will be examined. Even if they make no impression on disbelievers, the 'proofs' will not just go away; they keep reappearing in different permutations, very often as some kind of offspin from scientific discoveries.

We begin with the Teleological Argument. This is the argument from Design. It is interesting to see that the Corpus Hermeticum phrases it thus; 'whereby is made this order of the cosmos and the cosmos which we see of order.' It then goes into detail about the intricacy of the workings of the human body, which is an amazing description for what might have been written four or five thousand years ago. The use of the word 'order' is clearly his word for 'design'. This philosopher, whoever he may have been, is capable of seeing regularity, pattern, design, planning, in a world which on the face of it, is chaotic. We know that the Ancient Egyptians were very advanced in their calendar calculations, and this may have induced them to think in terms of regularity with astral bodies. This of course is one inducement to concluding that the universe is not just a chaotic mess, but is designed, and that requires a designer.

Plato certainly thought on these lines, but it was Lucilius Balbus (according to Cicero), who talked of 'the regularity of motion and revolution of the heavens, the distinctness, variety, beauty, and order of the sun, moon, and all the stars, the appearance only of which is sufficient to convince us they are not the effects of chance.' How modern does that sound? So the dilemma over design rather than development by chance was an issue in Ancient Greece, as much as it is today. As stated before, human nature does not change, even if the vocabulary is slightly different.

We then come to Thomas Aquinas with his Five Ways; the teleological argument was the fifth one. To quote him; 'The fulfilment by inanimate or unintelligent objects of an end to which they are evidently designed to work implies a purposive intelligence in their creation and direction.' It is fair to say that Aquinas and other Schoolmen of that period were under the influence of Aristotelian thinking, but even so, the design argument carried conviction in that day and age, and still does for many people now.

The full flowering of the teleological argument came in the so-called Age of Enlightenment, in the 17th and 18th centuries. This was aided by the many scientific discoveries, some of which we have described in other chapters. It was easier to see that so many features of the natural world, in addition to what could be observed in the sky at night, tended to give the impression that the whole of the natural world was the result of amazing design work. The culmination of this can be seen in William Paley's book, Natural Theology, or Evidences of the Existence and Attributes of the Deity, collected from the Appearances of Nature,' which appeared in 1802. The classic analogy used by him was the metaphor of Paley's Watch. Suppose one found a watch lying upon the ground, and was fascinated to see all its intricate workings and one came to realise that its workings were related to the passage of the Sun, it would be idle to say that the watch had just occurred all by itself, or had invented itself. The same would have to be said about the workings of the human body, and also practically all the systems that function in this world. The analogy of the watch has had its detractors, but even so, many people find this argument quite compelling.

In that day and age, there were arguments against it. It was David Hume, (1711-1776) the philosopher, who found problems with it. That does not have to mean that he was an atheist. Hick manages to conflate Hume's objections into five main areas. Personally, I think the basic problem, as with all these arguments for the existence of God, is that they are essentially circular, in other words, begging the question. The human mind has that tendency to see or assume some kind of regularity or order in all things. It is the tendency that stimulates legalism and bureaucracy. If we see everything through 'design-tinted-spectacles', it will be an easy conclusion to arrive at the teleological argument. The same is true for Evolution; if we view everything through 'evolution-tinted-spectacles' the result will be self-convincing, that Evolution is true. It is very difficult to think oneself out of our habits of mind. If it is a case of begging the question, it is no surprise that there is room for the atheist to reject the argument.

With the rise of evolutionary thinking, one might have thought that the teleological argument would have fallen apart. It did not. One might have thought, that with Darwin producing a sort of evolutionary world tree, showing a gradual development from basic forms of life through to more complex ones, that this too might have given support to the teleological argument. After all, a tree, even if it is a diagram, is still a neat piece of design work. But the effect of Darwin's theory was to produce an outburst of atheism and a counter outburst of creationism which reverberates to this day. For many, it epitomises the supposed clash between science and religion. But this is nonsense. However one views the appearance of life on this planet, whether it is creationist or evolutionist, (who knows, anyway), it can still be seen as the intricate design work of God, never mind the methods by which life came about (4)

In recent times, other pundits have supported the teleological argument. F.R.Tennant (1930), A.E.Taylor (1945), Pierre Lecomte du Noüy (1947) and Richard Taylor (1963). There is no need to recount all their arguments, since it is largely a repetition and enlargement on what has been said before. In essence they are saying that the chances of a world (indeed, a universe) like ours just coming along by 'chance', or a series of coincidences, or one accident after another, are practically nil. There has to have been a superior intelligence guiding and planning all things.

Personally, I have to agree with these conclusions, and the more the scientists delve into the intricate workings of the natural world, the more design work we see. To quote just a few examples, we now know a lot more about our solar system, and the intriguing way that everything is balanced with gravity, gyroscopic motion, speed of orbit, distancing from the Sun and many other features, it is surely idle to say that this just occurred all by itself. Looking at biochemistry and the intricate way in which the body works with so many systems interrelating with each other, even if it did 'evolve' somehow, it is a marvellous piece of design work. And just looking at the work done on quantum mechanics, convinces me that right down to the sub-atomic level, it is all very cleverly worked out and not just a chaotic mess. I can understand an atheist saying that as one observes life, there is so much randomness going on. In fact this was one of the bones of contention going on between the great physicists of the 20th century, namely the dilemma between chance and inevitability. This is a question which still goes on, and is related to the theological question of free will and predestination. (5)

I conclude that the teleological argument ought to be receiving much more attention in this day and age. It is a very ancient idea, but is now coming into its own, almost entirely as a result of the scientific enquiries into the full workings of Nature. It could be argued that this theory is essentially emotional, and a circular argument too. That may be so, but then virtually everything in the realms of religion, science and politics is the product of begging the question. Every argument is basically emotional. This is because we are essentially emotional people. It is a trait of human nature that cannot be denied or avoided. One could maintain that God created us as emotional people so that we could see his hand in the whole wonder of Creation. But that again is a circular argument.

The Cosmological Argument concerns the idea of the 'first cause'. This assumes that there must have been a primary spiritual power of some kind that was uncreated but caused creation to begin. In the Corpus Hermeticum this idea is virtually endemic. While God the Father is immobile, everything else is mobile. "For God is not made himself; by thinking-manifest, he thinks all things manifest. Now 'thinking-manifest' deals with all things made alone, for thinking-manifest is nothing else than making." In other words, the Ancient Egyptians could see that God was uncreated, but everything else in the Creation resulted from him. It is interesting that even if polytheism was rife in Egypt, there is some kind of background assumption of monotheism. The same thought can be traced in Plato's ideas.

It was Aquinas who gave much thought to this strand in his 'Five Ways'. No less than three of his ways are related to or derived from the cosmological argument.

1. Motion implies a first mover.
2. A sequence of efficient causes and their effects implies a first cause (uncaused).
3. The existence of things which are not self-explanatory, and therefore might logically not exist, implies some necessary being.

What this means is that we have to accept that everything in the world has to have something making it happen; it cannot just happen all by itself. But going back in time, there must have been a situation where the first things began to happen. They could not have made themselves happen; it required some agent, force, spirit, however you term it, that was uncaused, or eternal. How many people think like that? I would say, many, if not most.

One would have to admit that one religion, namely Buddhism, considers that there never was a beginning, and that everything has been going on eternally and will continue to do so. This is the importance of the Wheel of Becoming, which goes on circulating like a fairground roundabout. The Hindus have similar thoughts on the continuation of life, but they will admit that there had to be a beginning somewhere in the remote past. (6)

However, the influence of Aquinas has been strong down to the present day, not least in the philosophy of the Roman Catholic Church, but others too. It was Leibniz in the Age of Enlightenment, who gave a fresh impetus to the cosmological argument. "For what follows is in some way copied from what precedes... and so, however far you go back to earlier states, you will never find in those states a full reason why there should be any world rather than none, and why it should be such as it is." The way this is phrased may seem a little strange to us now, but what it amounts to is that everything we see has some kind of cause, but we never actually see the ultimate cause.

For many, this line of argument seems highly convincing; for others, it makes no impression. Bertrand Russell was one such atheist who just felt that the universe was 'there' and there was no further comment to be made.

However, in recent times, the doctrine of the Big Bang, which we have already discussed, has become a dominant theme in scientific circles. If one ventures to disbelieve in it, one is regarded as some sort of crank! But what it means, is that the cosmological theory is back on the agenda, and with various bits of evidence to support it. In essence, the Big Bang means that the whole of the (7) universe had to have had a distinct start in life, from a relatively small blob of material, and expanding outwards and at a colossal rate, and still is even now. One wonders why it could not have been God, the eternal spirit who instigated the explosion. No one seems to make an attempt to explaining the origin of the small blob, or indeed, what was happening before the Big Bang, and who or what provided the ingredients for this alleged small blob. But what this indicates is that there is this tendency in the human mind to picture everything as having a beginning somewhere, even if it is a long way back in the past.

The cosmological theory is not dead, by any manner of means. All that is happening is that it is being rephrased and justified on what may be claimed as scientific grounds. For that reason, I would say the cosmological theory ought to be receiving a lot more attention nowadays. No longer does it have to be tied up with elaborate philosophical jargon; it is now being enmeshed in scientific jargon instead.

Looking at it at the other end of the scale, from the aspect of quantum mechanics, we see something that gives further reinforcement to the cosmological theory. Since it is claimed that God created the world out of 'nothing', when we try to peer into the atom, and its constituent parts, what do we find, apart from tiny electrical impulses? Nothing. Inside the atom, are vast areas of nothing, absolutely nothing. This means that out of nothing comes something, and that is highly ingenious. It contradicts Shakespeare who claimed that nothing comes of nothing. If something does come from nothing, we are seeing the Creation not on the astro-physical scale of things, but in the subatomic scale. This is truly marvellous, and anyone who cannot wonder at such things, must be lacking in some kind of mental faculty.

The cosmological theory is a very ancient one, has been restated and revamped over the centuries and is now showing great potential in the modern scientific climate. It ought to be receiving a lot more attention, just as the teleological theory should as well. Is the cosmological argument a circular one, just as the teleological one was? It relies on that basic notion in people's minds, that all things must have a beginning somewhere. It is an instinctive feeling, and is reinforced by the Bible with its essential statement, 'In the Beginning....' which starts things off in Genesis and also St. John's Gospel. One would have to admit that essentially this is a circular argument, but perhaps not quite as much a gratuitous assumption as the other arguments. We are now seeing what might be accepted as 'evidence' to support the cosmological theory. Of course, it depends on what one accepts as evidence, but at the least, one could concede that we are seeing strong indications that the cosmological theory is correct.

The Moral or Aesthetic argument might be taken as two separate theories; however they both work in the same way and there is some suggestion that they amount to the same thing. The idea is that in this world, although we strive for ethical perfection, we never actually achieve it. The same goes for aesthetic perfection; we have an awareness of beauty, largely in artistic work, but never do we completely achieve it. Therefore, perfection should exist somewhere, and that somewhere is in the world of the spirit, namely God himself.

Traces of this assumption can be found in the Corpus Hermeticum, but it is nothing like as heavily emphasised as the other two theories."...the power of our mind's eye to unfold and gaze upon the Beauty of the Good.... Beauty that nothing can e'er corrupt or comprehend..." (page 33)

"...God's essence is the Beautiful; the Beautiful is further also Good. There is no Good that can be got from objects in the world... " (page 24)

We notice here that goodness and beauty are clearly equated, and indeed, there are many nowadays that would make this instinctive assumption. But to assume that there is perfection existing somewhere, out of our reach in this world, is an optimistic idea, but probably also the truth. But to say that no goodness or beauty can be achieved in this world is almost certainly unduly pessimistic. Even so, there are traces of this Moral Argument to be found in the Ancient Greek philosophers.

With regard to Aquinas, this line of thought forms his fourth 'way'. To quote; "The comparisons we make about goodness, truth, beauty, and so on, imply a standard of comparison which is itself perfect." In other words, perfection must exist somewhere, even if we cannot see it in this world.

The full exposition of this theory comes with Kant in the Age of Enlightenment. (1788). We have the same assumption that absolute perfection or beauty exist somewhere. It is an urge in the mind of man to strive for it, and yet we never fully achieve it in this world. The assumption goes further, in that the highest good is not a passive force, but an active one, which apportions happiness in accordance with moral attainment. In this way, happiness coincides with morality, and since we do not always see the reward of virtue in this world, then it will be apportioned in the next world. How many people have this train of thought at the back of their minds? It has become a basic assumption in the liberalistic climate of modern theology.

Modern writers have taken up this theme, for instance Hastings Rashdall. To quote; "A moral idea can exist nowhere and no how but in a mind: an absolute moral idea can exist only in a Mind from which Reality is derived." We see that this goes a little further than Kant. How do we know that a moral idea can only exist in a mind? It might exist in some other form or dimension which is waiting for us to discover, perhaps through scientific enquiry. How do we know there is an absolute moral idea? It would reassure us all, if there were such an entity, but it is still in the realms of emotion and wishful thinking.

In support of this line of thought, it has to be admitted that every culture or civilisation on earth has some kind of moral code or ethical yardstick. Even criminals have their code of conduct! Clearly, these moral codes are not quite the same, but they have a lot in common. What it indicates is that all of humanity has some kind of impression of what a good person ought to be. The same goes for artistic values, even if aesthetic taste varies considerably from one culture to another. Still, there is the urge to seek the good and reject the bad. Defining the good and the bad will vary according to circumstances, but since we now have increasing globalisation which results from colonisation and international exchange of ideas, we are coming much closer to a consensus on what we would all like to have; the same values all over the world. It can be fairly stated that the Ten Commandments have, over the centuries, had a massive influence on global ethical values. How much of our modern international culture has as its foundation such values as 'thou shalt not commit murder' and 'thou shalt not steal' and other precepts. None of these principles would have become axiomatic in life, unless there had been, instinctively, the need to be told about them. It is a short step to realise that God, in creating the human race, has prepared our minds to understand the importance of these values.

One might have assumed that a scientist would have been more likely to have discounted this line of argument than the others. However, what do we find, but a scientist, Francis Collins, who finds this 'proof' carries its own conviction. "Right and wrong as a clue to the meaning of the Universe" is what he refers us to. In other words, this is a moral universe, and that must imply some kind of moral yardstick, or judge, to regulate the whole thing.

He is an evangelical scientist, not a fundamentalist, but a convinced believer. His ideas on creationism and other matters are worth reading up. (7)

How does all this relate to science? Clearly, when we come to consider Psychology and Sociology, and even Anthropology, these matters will become more relevant. However, there are certain aspects of the Moral (Aesthetic) Argument that do connect with the sciences. (8)

Firstly, we consider the importance of 'thou shalt not bear false witness.....'' which is amplified by Jesus in the Sermon on the Mount (Matthew 5: 33-37), which we should take to mean 'just tell the truth and leave out the lies'. How much of scientific investigation relies on experts telling us the truth? We know that it is not unknown for scientists to invent information, refuse to face up to facts as found! All this does is to bring science into disrepute. We need to know that all those amazing findings, whether it be in astro-physics or at the quantum level, are not some kind of fantasy, but based on the truth. This is where religion, based on ethical principles is of the most importance in relation to science.

Secondly, the relationship between the good and the bad, whether it be of conduct or of artistic achievement, is endemic in scientific findings. At all levels, we have the tension between plus and minus, in electrical impulses, the good and the bad, with regard to bacteria and viruses, death and new life in all aspects of the living world. The Moral theory is just so obvious as a ruling factor in all scientific enquiry. The whole of life in the physical world is an ongoing contest between good and bad. This realisation was most notably seen in the religion called Zoroastrianism, which (9) still survives in many eastern countries. But the basic idea of a good god and a bad god has worked its way firstly into Judaism, then Christianity and then Islam. The basic assumption that the whole of life is a balancing act between the forces of good and evil is now a well established strand in theological thinking. Even if modernist Christian thinkers fight shy of talking about Satan, there is still the awareness of something called 'temptation' to do wrong, and avoidance of 'evil'. Always, there is the assumption that in the end, the good will prevail and evil will be defeated.

Thirdly, we have to take into account that instinctive urge in mankind, to enquire, discover and explain. This is the incentive behind all scientific research, and especially with regard to the basic building blocks of life at the molecular level, and further, at the quantum level. It works at the other end of the scale with our probes into outer space in an attempt at finding the answer to so many aspects of life. The excitement over finding life on other planets is clearly fuelled by the urge to find some kind of basis of comparison for the evaluation of life on this planet. In particular, to quote the Psalmist, "what is man that thou art mindful of him... thou hast made him a little lower than the angels...." (Psalm 8:4-5). This speaks of that basic need in the human soul, to evaluate oneself in relation to the world and the rest of the universe. That is a question that any thinking person must ask oneself. What are we here for? How do we relate to the animals? What is the significance of this world as compared with other worlds?

We have to admit that the scientists, as well as the theologians, are doing precisely the same thing. It may be on a different level, and using different vocabulary, but it is still the same basic need in human nature. The theory of Evolution is a good example, since it tries to show how the human race relates to the animal kingdom. All of astro-physics is an attempt at seeing the world in its context, not just with the Solar System, but with the entire expanding universe. The whole of quantum mechanics is about trying to find the basic building blocks of life, which raises the question of whether we can artificially 'invent' life. If it can be achieved, that will inevitably raise the question of how we evaluate life, and how that will affect our relationship to God. It is all about trying to find 'God' on a physical level. One wonders if they ever will! Theology is all about trying to find God above and beyond the physical level; some would say, allowing God to find us. In other words, the other way round.

The Ontological Argument is also a very ancient one, though appearing in various different forms over the centuries. Anselm is the name mostly associated with this idea, but it appears in the Corpus Hermeticum, which might suggest that the Ancient Egyptians had some ideas on this line. The ontological theory appears to be the only one that can be traced in the Bible, though not in heavy philosophical terms, but in real terms of prophetic experience. I refer to that iconic passage in I Kings 19:9-14, in which Elijah has a Theophanous encounter with God in the cave on Mount Horeb. This is typical of Hebrew thought; it has no idea of elaborate philosophical phrasing. It is all very down to earth, but the underlying factors show the first inklings of the ontological theory. Elijah experiences the strong wind, rending the mountains as the Lord passed by, but the Lord was not in the wind. This was followed by an earthquake, but God was not in the earthquake. Then came a fire, but God was not in the fire. We see the cumulative effect, with factors which one would normally associate with the power of God, but paradoxically, God was not actually in any of them. Then came the still small voice, and Elijah knew instinctively that this was really the Lord, a complete contrast to the other experiences. This is telling us two things. Firstly, knowing the reality of God is personal, instinctive and compelling. For those who have had this type of experience, 'proofs', if that what they may be called, are unnecessary. Secondly, it indicates that if you have managed to picture God, you are wrong, because the picture is not actually God; there is something superior that cannot be pictured. With this fine set of paradoxes, we can see that God is evident in so many ways, and yet, he is beyond human evidencing.

How does this relate to the Ontological Theory? Anselm's phrase for it was 'that than which nothing greater can be thought'. This appears in several variants but amounts to the same thing. If you can conceive of God, then that conception is not God, because something greater exists. Even if the Elijah passage cannot be seen as the first stirrings of this idea, it can be traced back to Clement of Alexandria, who talked of 'first principle' or 'primary premise'; if one can prove a 'first principle' it is then no longer a first principle; another principle, superior to it must then be found. (10)

It is no surprise to find that the Corpus Hermeticum has something to offer on these lines. The phrasing is somewhat clumsy and is influenced by the Gnostic mentality. To quote; 'God is first "thinkable" for us, not for himself, for that the thing that is thought does fall beneath the thinker's sense. God then cannot be "thinkable" to himself, in that he is thought of by himself as being nothing else but what he thinks. But he is "something else" for us, and so he is thought of by us.'

Here we see the philosopher groping towards the thought that if one could think of something greater, that greater thing would be God. Another quotation discusses the question 'Why can't God be obvious?' which means observable. This is a perfectly natural question that most of us ask ourselves.

'For all that is made manifest is subject to becoming, for it has been
made manifest. But the Unmanifest is for ever, for it does not desire
to be made manifest. It ever is, and makes manifest all other things.
Being himself unmanifest, as ever being and ever making-manifest,
himself is not made manifest. God is not made himself; by thinking-
manifest, he thinks all things manifest.'

In other words, if God were manifest, or obvious, he would not be God. Whether Anselm knew of this material or not, is an interesting question, but he developed the matter a little further in this way. If God is just a concept in the mind, does he have to exist outside of the mind, in external reality? Up to this point, an atheist or humanist would probably be quite happy to think that God is just a figment of human imagination. But Anselm takes the matter one step further. He says that to exist in reality, as well as in the mind, is greater than to exist only in the mind. If something exists only in the mind, it cannot be that than which no greater can be thought.

Does this sound confusing? There are all sorts of assumptions in this and circular arguments. It gets worse as we progress to Descartes, Kant, and into modern times with people like Norman Malcolm and Charles Hartshorne and James Ross. I do not propose to confuse the reader by attempting to delve into every aspect of their arguments. But this has to be said, that in spite of this theory sounding very strange, it has gathered much more interest in recent times. To put it bluntly, the Ontological Argument, even if it can be argued against, simply will not go away.

The reason for this, I suggest is as follows. There is that innate urge in human nature to investigate, explain and analyse. In our times, this has become increasingly acute as scientific investigation has made more and more discoveries. It works at both ends of the scale. We have probes into outer space, and speculation about the Big Bang, and not satisfied with that, what happened before the Big Bang, and before that and before that. It is simply the Ontological idea in real terms, trying to find the origin of all things. The same is true at the other end of the scale, at quantum level. There is the urge to find the ultimate building blocks of life, even if they are so minute that we do not have the technology to see them. It is all the same urge; the quest to find 'god' at one end of the scale or another. It may be that the scientists will not admit to trying to find God, but that is what it essentially amounts to. In a strange way, it links up with that passage in I Kings, in which Elijah found the essentials of God, and yet, paradoxically, it was deep down in his soul that the ultimate realities of God showed themselves to him.

The Ontological Argument may sound peculiar, clumsy and irrelevant, and a bit of strange Mediaeval chop logic. That is because we find it difficult to express in intelligible terms. But the reality of it is, that this train of thought is more active nowadays than it ever was, albeit in different modes of expression.

A powerful example of this appeared in that iconic Sci-fi series, Star Trek, back in the 1980's. There are various mythological elements in this encounter, in which there is a column of fire and a voice coming out of it. This immediately reminds us of the Burning Bush incident in Exodus 14:19, in which God speaks to Moses out of the fire. Then a massive face appears, with a beard and a stern voice. Dr.McCoy immediately concludes that this is God. How many people picture God in such terms?! But Captain Kirk keeps his head. When the face starts to demand taking over the space ship Enterprise, Kirk has the presence of mind to ask what would God want with a spaceship. McCoy wants to know why this god is angry; this does not fit in with his idea of God. Again, how many people assume that God is angry? McCoy also asks, 'is God really out there?' We can conclude that, as with the ontological theory, if one had managed to picture God, then God is something greater than one's conception. This links in with a strong strand in the Bible, that forbids idolatry. Making, or conceiving of a picture, a statue, a representation of God is wrong, because God is above and beyond human conception. Many people work on the basis of some kind of caricature of God, which eventually goes wrong, because God cannot be conceived by the human mind. The scene ends with Kirk slapping his chest quite contentedly and proclaiming that 'God is in here.' This again is another sort of idolatry of a humanistic kind. Even so, it ties in with the experience of Elijah, in the sense that knowing God is something personal, intuitive, instinctive but inescapable. Proofs and preconceived ideas are superfluous for those who know God in their souls. The scene in Star Trek is interesting in that it illustrates people's assumptions about God and also the validity of the ontological theory.

There is one more approach to proving the existence of God, which will not be found in textbooks on the subject. This is because I have thought this out myself. It has already been alluded to in the chapter on quantum matters, but it relies on quantum theory being the truth. I think we have to give them a generous degree of credit. It would seem that the whole of reality in the physical world depends on the interaction of tiny electrical particles, some plus, some minus and some neutral. All the atoms that are the basic building blocks of life are constructed on this basis, namely the tension between plus and minus. Even if we probe more deeply into the inner workings of the atoms, it makes no difference. The whole of creation relies on the juxtaposition of positive and negative forces. It is not just one atom; it is trillions of them holding the whole world together and indeed everything else in the universe. The question must arise; how does this tension come about? Could this tension install itself? Could a seesaw install itself? Could a piece of elastic produce its own tension? I would say that that is impossible. It would require a superior force, intelligence, designer, however one phrases it, to make it happen, and go on making it happen. Obviously this recalls the teleological theory, but it is not quite the same. The design aspect has to be involved somehow, but it also requires a spiritual force, unseen but real enough anyway to provide the energy, not just in the remote past, but also from day to day. I would say this is the energy of the Creator at work in every detail of the physical world. This conception also recalls the Pantheistic approach, which means that God is actually the created world. This was a theory (11) epitomised by Spinosa. Clearly, there is an element of truth in this concept, as long as one does not allow it to exclude other approaches to the matter. But the importance of this is that modern scientific theory in Physics and Chemistry actually does support the reality of God.

We are now brushing up against an important paradox. The traditional proofs for the existence of God leave us with a god who is distant, mechanical, philosophically correct and remote, even if they are essentially circular arguments. Pantheism renders this concept as somewhat nearer to us, in that God is in and through every created thing. But the Bible shows us a God who is personal, has a distinct personality, relates in a fatherly way to each and every soul from day to day. Abraham, Moses, Elijah all the great prophets of old and chiefly Jesus himself, show how the individual soul can and does know God on a personal level, not just as some kind of machine, but as close as a loving parent. This is the opposite of proving the existence of God by some logico-philosophical reasoning. Both approaches have their own validity in their own way. It is a mistake to say that one is wrong and the other correct. It remains a stunning paradox, that the great Creator of the universe can and does know each and everyone of us inside out.

The word 'exist' itself can confuse the matter. Existence, implies physical existence. If we say that God 'exists' it implies that he literally occupies physical space in the way that every one of us does. I am sure that many people thought like that over the centuries, and now that God cannot be located up in the skies, it has produced a new crop of atheists. Paul Tillich is one theologian who has the courage to say that God does not exist. That does not mean that he is an atheist; far from it. He is the one who has offered us the phrase 'God is the Ground of our Being' and other variants on (12) it. I feel he has derived this concept from Hindu philosophy, but even so, it is a helpful motif. If we compare it with what we know at quantum level, it becomes all the more relevant. We can see it as God being the basic energy, impulse, inspiration that holds the whole of the created world together.

Defining God has always been a problem. In the Bible, there are many names or titles applied to God. Some find them helpful; others find them offputting. Here are a few examples.

'God Most High' (Genesis 14:19)
'The Lord of Hosts is his name.....'' (Isaiah 47:4) and variants.
'The Lord is King.... ' (Psalm 10:16)
'Rise up, O Judge of the earth....'' (Psalm 94:2)
'The Ancient of Days....' (Daniel 7:22)
'God is Love...' (1 John 4:16)

When Moses, at the Burning Bush asks God, 'what is your name?' (Exodus 3:14) the answer is 'I am that I am'. From this we get the name YHWH which is strictly speaking unpronounceable, but is a contraction of the Hebrew of 'I am that I am.' (13) What it is essentially saying, is that God is beyond human description or conception. Even so, we have to use human metaphors to give us some kind of indication of his nature. Even using 'he' and 'his' is only metaphoric. All those titles in the list (and many more could be found) are only metaphors; they cannot be taken literally. But this is where disbelief or failure of faith can arise, if we take all those metaphors far too literally. But then we have no choice but to use human imagery; no human vocabulary can describe the wonder of God. It is so easy to slide into some kind of idolatry over one's perception of God. Idolatry does not have to mean constructing a statue or a picture and worshipping it. Idolatry can be something in the mind, a fixed idea of what one thinks God ought to be.

In a sense, the traditional proofs for the existence of God can also be seen in the same light. The great designer, the ultimate factor that began all of creation, the ultimate criterion of goodness and beauty; all of these require some kind of preconceived idea, and become hardened into some kind of idolatry. The only theory which avoids the risk of idolatry is the ontological theory, which in effect says that if you have conceived of God, then that is not God, because something greater must be sought. We can see it in this light, as a stunning paradox that all of these arguments have their own validity, and yet none of them are totally conclusive. The only thing that is conclusive, is when the human soul becomes fully aware, in real terms, of the reality of God, normally by some kind of Theophanous encounter, something on the same lines that Elijah had.

We are assured that 'God is spirit' (John 4:24)and yet here comes another stunning paradox, in that God appeared at a time and place on this earth as Jesus Christ, the true Messiah. Many would say that would be impossible. Many would accept the reality of God the Creator but would have problems over him coming to earth as a human being. But that is the essential paradox in the Christian faith, that Jesus is actually the final, ultimate and genuine representation of God in this world. In that sense, God does exist, on a physical level, as well as on a spiritual level.

Essentially, the reality of God is not provable, in the sense of some kind of logical process. It only becomes provable when it encounters a mind that is predisposed to accept it in the first place. But for those who have some kind of understanding of love, or beauty, or truth, or justice, or wonder, or hope, or of caring, then, I would say you are half-way to believing. To go the whole way to faith, requires that input of inspiration given by God, and the simplest way to do it is by focussing on the true Messiah. Faith is not something that one can invent for oneself, any more than a atom can invent its own protons and electrons. Any true believer will understand that faith is a gift from God, but it also requires a mind that is ready to receive it. This is above and beyond anything that science can provide for us.

**Footnotes**

1. Much the material in this chapter is derived from John Hick, *Proofs for the Existence of God*.
2. Corpus Hermeticum, OMTO publication, originally translated by G.R.S.Mead.
3. Aquinas is famous for his 'Five Ways', as proofs for God's existence.
4. Francis Collins, and evangelical scientist discusses these matters in his book, *The Language of God*.
5. Einstein thought in terms of predestination; other pundits disagreed.
6. In the Rig Veda, Agni, the fire god is seen as being the Creator.
7. The Big Bang is discussed in chapter 6.
8. Francis Collins in his book *The Language of God*, finds the Moral Argument compelling.
9. Zoroastrianism was the ruling religion of Ancient Persia, but still survives in the East.
10. A Christian philosopher of the second century AD in the Roman Empire.
11. Spinosa, a 17th century Dutch philosopher who advocated Pantheism.
12. See Paul Tillich, *Shaking the Foundations*.
13. YHWH, which has been rendered as 'Jehovah'. This is a hybrid word, based on vowel applications to the tetragrammaton, YHWH.

# 13

## *Various levels of Truth*

I feel that one of the problems that hover in people's minds, is the fact that Science and Religion are talking on two different levels of truth. It is very easy to confuse scientific realities with theological realities. The problem over Genesis chapters one and two is the best known, but there are others. There are some that take Genesis as an historical, scientific textbook, and because it makes no mention of dinosaurs, it must then be mistaken. The question over Adam and Eve is also central to this dilemma. In terms of cold logic, there should be the first man and the first woman, but looking at the earliest fossils that are relevant to the appearance of the human race, must indicate that humanoids, or hominids, as they are termed, seem to have appeared in widely separated parts of the world, and not just the central rift valley in Africa.

To take early Genesis as a biological textbook is a big mistake. It may be taken to some extent as having a geographical background, but that is not the main intention of the author(s). The main intention with the seven days of Creation, is to emphasise the wonder of it all, its perfection, orderliness and how it is all the amazing product of one God, as opposed to myriads of them. The processes by which he achieved this are not the central point. Whether it was by evolution or by some other process that we do not as yet understand, is beside the point. The work is a theological scheme, with strong implications for the hebdomadal scheme, and also with various mythological ingredients worked in. (1)

The mythological element is found to be much stronger as we read about the Garden of Eden. Again, this is not a biological textbook, even if we are reminded of that awkward question of why a man has one fewer ribs than a woman! The main thrust of the account is to emphasise the supremacy of mankind in relation to the animals, and that no animal is a suitable partner for a man. This is the importance of the human race appearing first, followed by the animals. It is not meant to be a time scheme or even less, an evolutionary scheme. An indication that this account should not be taken literally comes when the serpent speaks in human language, assumedly Hebrew, and does not have to slither about on his stomach, at this stage. The account does have important sociological and psychological implications, some of which one would find a matter of contention for nowadays. But we must recall that this account must have been written in the Iron Age, or possibly even in the Bronze Age, and as such, is an amazing understanding of human nature. From my knowledge of ancient texts of roughly the same era, there is nothing to compare with it. The only material that comes near to it is derived from the great Greek philosophers and writers such as Homer, but that kind of thing must have come a lot later than whoever it was who wrote Genesis. Whoever wrote it, must have been a theological genius, when we consider how this passage has had such a massive influence on people's religious thinking right through history to the present day. In addition, his use of mythological imagery is also stunning and appeals to the deepest instincts in human nature. I cannot think who else could have written it, apart from Moses, but then we are talking about two writers as opposed to one. (2)

But the main thrust of the Garden of Eden account is to show what went wrong with this world. No one, apart from the most self-deluded optimist, could claim that this world is perfectly satisfactory, then and now. The reason given, is that it was the human race that were incapable of following one simple instruction. They ignored God's strong advice. How true this is of human nature! Does it really need any proof? From that one act of disobedience, all the other problems in life began to emerge. It is no mistake that the first murder comes straight after this account. As Genesis unfolds, we are told about how all of humanity descended into corruption. The exception to this was the line of Patriarchs going down to Abraham, who were faithful to God. This too is a strong Biblical theme, that even if everything goes wrong, there is always something or someone, the faithful remnant that prevails and in the end re-establishes the truth.

Other accounts can briefly be alluded to. There is Psalm 104. There is no way that this can be taken as a biological, systematic account of Creation.

What it is emphasising in the strongest poetic terms, is the wonder and majesty of God. It uses the most powerful metaphors, many of which are derived from mythological thinking. As anyone can admit, poetry cannot be taken just at face value, literally. It is a powerful expression of emotion, and indeed the Psalm ends with a burst of praise coming from the believer. I cannot see how anyone can avoid one's soul being caught up with the emotion of this marvellous piece of hymnody. It underlines the fact that knowing God is at its root, a matter of emotion, rather than a matter of logical deduction.

Another creation account comes in 2 Esdras 6:38ff, found in the Apocrypha. This account follows the pattern in Genesis 1, but the main thrust this time is not so much about how things went wrong; it raises the question of why the Jews, who are understood to be God's chosen people, are being lorded over by the Gentiles. So, the Creation account is now applied to a real historical situation in which the Jews were being persecuted, and that would assumedly be during the Seleucid or the Roman period. (3)

The only passage in the New Testament that can be seen as a Creation account, comes in the first chapter of St. John. This deliberately begins with the phrase 'in the beginning...' which clearly recalls the first verse of Genesis. But St. John does not attempt anything that could be called biological, or historical, or indeed anything to do with Science. His purpose is to show that Jesus Christ was a spiritual reality with God right from the start of Creation. And just as God said 'let there be light', so St. John stresses that Jesus is the true light that enlightens everyone. This may be an indication that Genesis was not taken totally literally even in those days. It is saying that the Light of God, which is not the sun or the moon, is Jesus himself. He is not talking literally now; 'light' is a metaphor for inspiration, truth, deeper understanding, and most poignantly, the contradiction or reversal of evil. The implication of that is, though not spelt out directly here, is that the Garden of Eden situation is now reversed. St. Matthew and St. Luke do, however, go into details about how the temptation was resisted. This passage is talking almost completely on a theologico-philosophical level and has no implications for Science at all. (4)

It is now appropriate to examine different levels of truth or reality, and see how they relate to each other. It may go some way to reducing the confusion in many people's minds, which concerns what appears to be a contradiction between religion and science.

143

## Mathematical truth

This is the easiest one to cope with, at least at the elementary level. When two plus two result in four, there is little doubt about the truth of that. So many aspects of modern (and ancient) life are underpinned by mathematics. This has been going on from ancient times, with people like Euclid and Pythagoras, but even before that, in ancient Babylon, there were the first stirrings of mathematics. Why is it there are 360 degrees in a circle? It is because the Babylonians decided that the year was 360 days (the extra five were just an inconvenient irrelevance!), therefore the circle was to be divided into 360 parts. The Egyptians had roughly the same idea. Whoever it was that devised the pyramids must have been a mathematic and civil engineering genius, but it shows that going back to the Bronze Age, mathematics was an important issue. (5)

One might be forgiven for assuming that maths has no relevance to religious faith. Wrong! Numbers of all kinds are found quoted in many places in the Bible. Admittedly, some of them are intended to be taken figuratively or symbolically. But on reading the book of Kings (and the Chronicles), one is struck by the systematic attempt to date all the regnal years of the kings of Israel and Judah. From this scheme, which incidentally does not quite work out, we have a fair dating scheme going back to the second millennium BC. This has worked out well with the findings of archaeology. But why is this important for faith? It has to be understand that Judaism (followed by Christianity) is an historical faith, based on real persons and events. It is not some kind of vague, introspective, subjective, internal system of thought. That sort of thing is found in the Eastern religions. Judaism is based on the active intervention of a living God in human history. This means that timings and dates are of acute importance for the life of faith. This comes out even more strongly in the Gospels, particularly St. Luke. He is at pains to show that Jesus clearly fitted in with the political situation under the Herodian Kings and the Roman Caesars. Jesus was not, therefore, some kind of airy-fairy vague notion that gradually gathered momentum during the mid-Roman Empire. Christianity is at root, based on real times and places and real people of the day.

Mathematics is still of vital importance today, as it underpins all three of the major sciences. As we have seen with the great physicists of the twentieth century, a lot of their work involved high-flown maths. Of course, maths can become a less than precise discipline. We only have to think of the process known as 'probability' to see that it can become pure guesswork. The discipline known as statistics can be, and has been, highly misleading. There are lies, damned lies, and statistics, to quote a famous adage! But statistics can be manipulated to support anyone's favoured policy, given a clever enough pundit. I would say the most absurd use of maths is the so-called Drake equation, which is supposed to convince us that there must be ten thousand other civilisations out there in the depths of space.

But the most acute relevance of maths nowadays is on the issue of distances in outer space. We are now aware of billions of light years stretching out to somewhere or possibly nowhere. These are mathematical figures that are mind-boggling; the human mind cannot really assimilate such quantities. How does this relate to religious belief? If it is true that there is such a thing as 'eternity', in other words, some kind of reality that goes on for ever, then we are now seeing eternity in real terms of mathematical distances, as opposed to some kind of vague, imaginary thing which has been applied to God. It is still fair enough to talk of God as being eternal, but used like that it means that he was a reality before anything occurred, even the alleged Big Bang, and will continue as a reality for ever into the future. That is not quite the same thing as distances in space, but not completely different either.

The importance of mathematics cannot be denied. As a discipline, it infiltrates just about every other level of truth or reality which will be seen forthwith. If God is basic to all things, and maths also is basic to all things, it is tempting to say that God is a mathematician. That idea has been tried! Better to say that it was God who invented mathematics.

## Scientific truth

This is one area in which people assume there are unassailable facts; this of course is a fallacy. The three main areas of Science, Physics, Chemistry and Biology are closely interlinked and dependent on each other. The common factor underpinning them all, is the experimentation with some aspect of the physical world, with a view to determining some kind of 'Law'. Many of these laws have already been found, but it would be fair to say that there are many more yet to be discovered.

The experiment which is designed to find an explanation for some feature of the natural world, may render some kind of interesting result. That result can be meaningless unless a 'control experiment' is carried out for purposes of contrast. A simple example would be thus; suppose a collection of mice had a certain condition and the scientist wanted to try out a preparation which he expected would correct the problem. He ought really to have two groups of mice, both with the same condition, apply the preparation to one group but not the other, and wait for the outcome. If one group made a full recovery and not the other, then it would be fair to say that the preparation worked. If, however, both groups made a recovery, including the one not given the preparation, then the effectiveness of the preparation could be doubted. Many experiments have been, or should be, carried out with a control group, otherwise the results can be meaningless. Also, the experiment has to be repeatable, which means that if another experimenter tries the same procedure, he should obtain the same result. All this means a lot of painstaking hard work, but there is an awareness that some experimenters have made short cuts and deceived themselves as well as the public.

The other problem with scientific research is that scientists regularly argue from the specific to the general. The correct way round is to argue from the general to the specific. A simple example of this would be; we can see that Tiddles, the cat, has got whiskers. That is a fair observation. Now comes the gratuitous assumption, that because Tiddles has whiskers, therefore all cats have whiskers. That may be the truth, but not necessarily. There may be some cats that do not have whiskers, unless of course, one has managed to observe all cats in the world.

An important example of this occurs in Darwin's Origin of Species. He did experiments with pigeons, and determined that all types of pigeon are descended from the rock pigeon. That may be a fair deduction. But here comes the argument from the specific to the general. Darwin then concludes that just because pigeons (one species) are so related, having a common ancestor, the same will apply to all creatures, including humans. Can you see the logical flaw in that? But scientists regularly make this kind of gratuitous assumption. In addition to this, he did not explain how, or why, the pigeons could have decided on a policy which would lead to them having various different versions of themselves! Perhaps they were far more intelligent in antediluvian times!

The public may not be aware that arguments rage amongst so-called 'experts'. This is usually about trivial matters, but not always. We only have to recall how the 20th century physicist pundits argued with each other, and at first regarded Einstein as a quack! Regularly we have bold statements in the press about some amazing new discovery or procedure, couched in dogmatic tones, which is supposed to impress us all. Can we just remember that in the late 19th century there was a scientist who managed to prove conclusively that heavier than air flight was impossible! Now we have all kinds of vehicles sailing through the skies; jet planes, helicopters, gliders and space rockets. Let us just not get carried away by the latest scientific doctrine; let us be free to question and express doubt.

Going further than that, extra caution ought to be applied if a new procedure is claimed to solve such and such a problem. A good example of this comes from the late 19th century doctrine concerning Eugenics. It involved measuring the distance between the patient's eyes and other absurd criteria. Those who were deemed unfit to breed were segregated from society and confined to special institutions. Massive cruelties were inflicted on the basis of this flimsy theorisation. Added to that, the Nazis took the matter to extremes in the Third Reich. A policy of deliberate murder was justified in aid of freeing the German 'race' of undesirable influences. We now know that Eugenics is complete claptrap, but at one time, it was the prevailing scientific doctrine, and no one seriously challenged it.

If one were to think that late 20th century science was free of this kind of problem; think again. It was common practice in mental hospitals to subject patients to electric shock treatment. This may have been helpful to some patients, but the mistake was to assume that it would have the same effect on all of them. Now, it seems, this treatment is out of favour (thank God!). Are we free of this kind of mistake today? We should be looking carefully at the treatments in use now and ask ourselves whether it is unnecessarily cruel in relation to the expected results.

What are the prevailing scientific doctrines circulating today? How about Evolution? How about exo-planets that are expected to have some sort of 'life' on them, just waiting to make contact with us? The Big Bang is another doctrine that no one really dares to argue against. This is where science goes beyond its remit. Speculation, guesswork and wishful thinking are not truly scientific, and yet many people just assume that because an 'expert' has dogmatised about it, therefore it has to be the truth.

I am not trying to say that all science is untrue. That is going to the other extreme. What I am saying is that we should not be carried away by the latest clever idea. Let us apply common sense, caution, rejection of cruelty and willingness to discuss in a calm frame of mind. It is so easy to be deceived by someone who has a political, social or religious agenda, and has managed to manipulate some kind of alleged scientific 'fact' to support such a doctrine. The Nazis were brilliant at that sort of thing; so too were the Communists. (6)

To be fair to science, we now have so many technological advances in the modern world, all of which are the result of experimentation. It is a testimony to the inquisitive nature of mankind and also his inventiveness. All this is a spin-off from mankind being created in the image of God, who is the ultimate and final creator. For us, however, there need to be boundaries surrounding our experimentation. Ethics (which we discuss later) must have an important say in limiting our experimentation. This is something that the Nazi doctors, such as Mengele, ignored. The lesson from that is that science can so easily be perverted into something monstrously cruel.


## Historical truth

If anyone would doubt the importance of studying history, I would say he was seriously mistaken. It is not possible to understand our present circumstances in the world, without an understanding of history. As each successive development in world affairs unfolds, we can see that it is a result, directly or indirectly, of events that preceded it. This is not just factors that are occurring in our own times, but we have to take into account matters that arose in the Ancient World. We are still under the influence of Greece and Rome and before that, Mesopotamia and Egypt. This concerns very largely mythological matters (which will be discussed later), and theological criteria, but also economics, tactics in warfare, social mores and many other factors in the modern world. One important example of this would be the Gregorian calendar that is now dominant throughout the world. This goes back to Julius and Augustus Caesar, and it was not just their own clever idea; they recruited the priests of Egypt to lend their expertise in tidying up the calendar. Admittedly, the calendar has had to receive various adjustments over the centuries, but the basic framework of it comes from ancient Egypt, and that includes leap year. (7)

As we all know, the problem with historical truth is that history is almost always written by the winners. If it were to be written by the losers, it would almost certainly sound completely different. A modern example of this would be how to understand World War 1. We all know that the assassination of the Austrian Archduke was the trigger for this conflict. But one isolated assassination does not necessarily have to stimulate a disaster such as a world war. The truth is that over the previous decades there had been a shift in the balance of power in Europe, and also an arms race, as tensions became more acute. From the Allies' point of view, they saw Germany, and the attitude of the Kaiser, as a major danger. This was probably a fair assessment, since he is reported to have refused to entertain peace initiatives on offer. From the German point of view, there was the feeling that they were hemmed in by hostile powers, plus the fact that they felt they had a claim on parts of France. There was the feeling that there could be a return to the wonderful days of the Holy Roman Empire. As the outcome came, the Allies could reassure themselves that in winning, the right result had been achieved, since neutral Belgium had been invaded. From the German point of view, it was the wrong result because, they felt, they had had the best army, with a just cause, but they had been stabbed in the back by undesirable elements at home. It is all a matter of how we see it. History is always seen by someone with a certain colouration in their spectacles.

A good example of this is seen when we compare the two books of the Maccabees in the Apocrypha. The Jews regarded themselves as having 'won' in the conflict with the Seleucid kings, but the two books display a slightly different attitude towards the Greek kings and Greek culture. The same is also true of the difference between the book of Kings and of the Chronicles in the Old Testament. Clearly the Chronicles was written by a priest, who hardly made mention of the prophets; Elijah and Elisha are hardly included. It all depends on who you are and what is your bias.

A classic example of history being manipulated for political ends centres on the Arthurian traditions in Britain and indeed Western Europe. It is reasonable to assume that there was an important military leader operating in south Wales and Cornwall as the Roman Empire faded away. But by the time we arrive at the Norman kings, whose claim on the English throne was somewhat shaky, there was the need to relate oneself to King Arthur. Thus he was decorated with all kinds of wonderful traits, so that the Norman kings could be justified as they claimed to have been (8) descended from Arthur. The same happened when Henry 7th managed to capture the throne in 1486. A most ingenious family tree was devised, showing how the Tudors were descended from King Arthur! This was comprehensively supported by Edmund Spenser who managed to relate the Tudors right back, through Arthur, to the original kings of Celtic Britain. This was especially useful for Elizabeth 1st, whose claim on the throne was not only rather shaky but had the problem of her being female, and, in the opinion of some people of a certain religious stance, illegitimate. All (9) through this process, Arthur was endued with all manner of magical, mythical attributes. By the time we arrive at the 20th century, Arthur is now decorated with all kinds of imaginative traditions, all of which serve to reassure the British people that they have such wonderful historical traditions underpinning their distinctive way of life. This is a good example of how a faint legend can be augmented into an entire political doctrine and a cultural reassurance for a people who have a high opinion of themselves (namely 'us').

What I am saying is that when dealing with history, it is very difficult to disentangle fact, from interpretation of fact, distortion from warping of memory, and political agenda. Added to that, there is always the tendency to romanticise the past. The phrase 'the good old days' sounds attractive, but is it just another illusion or self-deception? Romantic ideas about the past have very often been used to justify all kinds of policies, not least, the rise of one Empire after another. Mussolini with his fanciful ideas about reviving the Roman Empire is a prime example of this. Was it really such a wonderful epoch in human history? The same goes for Hitler's Nazism. That was imbued with all kinds of mythological fanciful ideas, supported by what was seen at the time as pure scientific common sense!

It is an interesting relationship between mythology and historical account. The same goes for theological assumptions; they too are often inextricable from mythology, as we see in early Genesis. We shall see that so many of these areas of truth are interrelated and inseparable. Certainly with the Judao-Christian tradition, history cannot be avoided. It is a major factor in the theology and religious practice of the two. On the other hand, the opposite is almost true in the Hindu-Buddhist tradition. I would not like to say that history is an element totally lacking in this area, since there are references to real historical situations. However, both these religions can, and do function regardless of historical realities. It is a different situation with Sino-Japanese thinking. With regard to Shintoism, particularly 'State Shintoism', the importance of the Japanese Emperor is clearly linked to historical matters, even if mythology does lend an important element to it. With regard to Confucianism and Taoism, the status of the two founding sages is axiomatic to these two traditions, but after that, their religious practice can continue without serious historical backing. The slight exception to this would be that of the status of the Chinese Emperor, which has been an important element in Taoist mythology, but since the Emperor is no longer a factor, that is irrelevant to Taoism.

If one were to think that the truth about history can never be totally clarified, this would be unnecessarily critical. We have another discipline, a scientific one, called archaeology, which can very often provide us with indications as to the truth. This is particularly true for the historical material in the Bible, but it does not stop there. All kinds of claims about historical events and personalities, from other eras and parts of the world, can be seen in a constructive light by the findings of the archaeologists. (11)

**Geographical truth**

Essentially, Geography is concerned with coming to terms with the physical features of the earth, and depicting them on maps. One might assume that this is straightforward enough, and that the land can be mapped with theodelites and other surveying equipment. This works reasonably well for a small area, but when coping with the entire world, we are up against an impossible task. The world is a sphere, and so it cannot be depicted accurately on a flat piece of paper. There are various ways round this problem, the best known of which is the Mercator projection. The problem is that it turns the world into a flat entity, which has the effect of exaggerating the size of areas near to the Poles, such as Russia and Greenland. The advantage of it is that all the compass directions are reliable, but distances and areas are distorted. This goes to show that something which can be seen as scientifico-literal, can also become misleading in certain respects. How much of science could have that said of it?

The exciting challenge in our own times is that as we manage to send probes to other planets our skills in map-making are even more needed. We now have accurate maps of other planets, such as the Moon and Mars, except that since they too are spherical, the same problems emerge. Also, since there are no artificial features, such as roads, cities or frontiers, it is more difficult to include features that are meaningful. Even so, that task of mapping has to be done, so that manned landings (if they are possible) will be able to determine the best places to land.

Another important aspect of Geography is the description and explanation of physical features. Hills, valleys, rivers for instance are there waiting for us to render an explanation in terms of physical forces as opposed to theologico-mythological ideas on the subject. So when Psalm 104 says, 'the mountains rose, the valleys sank down to the place which thou didst appoint for them,' this is talking on a theological level as opposed to a geographical level. The geographer will tell us that mountains and valleys are formed by 'folding' and 'rifting', which is fair enough on that level of truth. But the whole process can be understood as God's careful planning, never mind the methods by which it came about.

One aspect of geography, namely geology, does have acute relevance to religious belief. The geologist will tell us that, taking into account the different types of rock, these can only be (12) understood in terms of massive ages of the earth, going back to Cambrian times and earlier. On the face of it, a literal acceptance of Genesis chapter one contradicts such an analysis. But as we have already discussed, that chapter does not have to be taken as a literal, geological account. I am quite happy to take the findings of the geologists as realistic, in that the age of the earth must be seen in terms of millions of years and quite distinct epochs. But a theological understanding of the world does not have to be tied to literal time schemes. As Psalm 90:4 puts it, 'for a thousand years in thy sight are but as yesterday when it is past, or as a watch in the night.' Or to put it another way, time schemes in the human orbit are as nothing compared with the eternity of God.

However, we may see this as paradoxical, that geography, like history, is an important element in the Bible. The faith of Israel, and by implication of the Christians, is closely related to geographical matters. We are told about real places in Egypt, Palestine, and later on Asia Minor, Greece and Rome. The maturation of faith is not some kind of imaginary matter that never comes down to earth. It is closely based on real places, and brings religious belief down to basic realities concerning the world. Mountains, rivers, valleys and many other features have a strong influence on faith. Many geographical features are used as imagery in prophetic utterances. A good example of that would be Isaiah 40:3ff, 'In the wilderness prepare the way of the Lord, make straight in the desert a highway for our God. Every valley shall be lifted up and every mountain and hill shall be made low.' It is a mistake to take this literally; it is talking about the rectification of all that is wrong in this world. Geographical truth ties in with the imagery of theological truth.

We have only to think of the importance of Mount Zion in prophetic thought. This is where God is assumed to reside, in his Temple. Hills or mountains have an important influence in theology, since, in a sense, they reach up to Heaven. Many would claim that climbing a mountain is a spiritual experience, in that it lifts one above the banality of ground level. It is no surprise that Jesus delivered the Sermon on the Mount from a mountain; it reminds us of Mount Sinai and the first lawgiving by Moses, and augments the authority of the precepts delivered. This is not confined to Biblical thinking. The Hindus have various mountains such as Mount Meru believed to be sacred, as well as certain rivers. In this way, geographical features have a strong influence on the life of faith. For many, life is seen as a pilgrimage, a progression along a road, to reach a destination that is significant for belief. Jerusalem is for many such a destination. For the Moslems, Mecca is of such importance. For the Buddhists, Benares is such. For the Chinese, Tiananmen Square and the regal palace, which is an exact copy of the heavenly one, is significant. All of this shows how geography underpins many aspects of theology.

## Linguistic truth

All humans have some sort of language, and there must be thousands of different tongues in use all over the world, not including dialects. One could claim that English is the lingua franca of the modern world, but that of course, is an accident of history. If King Harold had not defeated Harold Hardrada at Stamford bridge, the whole world might now be speaking Danish (or something similar)! The problem with language is that it is always some kind of approximation to the truth. It takes a conscious effort of the mind to express any fact in terms that are free of distortion, emotion and prejudice. Our language (and I assume all the others) is riddled with worn out metaphors and (13) inappropriate metaphors and acute metaphors. "The house was dilapidated" is in common parlance even if the house is built of wood, or straw or anything else apart from stone. This is a worn out metaphor. "The ship ploughed through the sea" is an inappropriate metaphor even if it is in common use. Ploughs only work on land, not in water! An acute metaphor could be "the crowd was fired up with excitement". One might be surprised at how much of our normal language was originally some form of figurative expression, as opposed to precise language. This matter is very true with regard to language used in worship and in rendering the Bible. Is Science free from this problem? Certainly not! We have seen in the quantum physics chapter that they had the same problem. Maybe it is inescapable, to avoid the use of imagery in normal expression. (14)

The matter becomes more acute when translating the Bible from the Hebrew and the Greek. In the history of the church, the Bible was translated into Latin and then eventually into vernacular languages such as English and German. It is difficult enough to translate from one language to another, but even worse moving on into a third language. The original flavour is so easily lost, and the presuppositions of the translator so easily become worked into the result, especially when it is a paraphrase. At the Reformation, it was decided that a direct translation from the original languages into whatever vernacular was needed, in order to achieve a more accurate rendering. Even so, this is not easy. A good example of this would be, when rendering a phrase such as 'your sins will be as white as snow', what would this mean to someone in a country where snow was never experienced? The answer has been to render it 'your sins will be as white as the insides of a coconut'.

Even two languages which are very close in vocabulary and ethnic background can present problems in translation. English and French are often seen as an easy option for children in school. But we have to remember that both countries have a very different cultural background, not just in religion but in social mores. An example of this would be that 'monsieur' in French is used on every male, and it means or is equivalent to 'Mr.' in English. But if you use the word 'mister' in English, it carries a different connotation, and on its own, it is slightly disrespectful. For an American, it is even more disrespectful. Why is that? In France, they had a bloodthirsty revolution on the premise that equality should be enforced, so everyone was to be termed 'Monsieur' or 'Madame', regardless of wealth or influence. But Britain never had such a revolution, so calling someone 'Mr' does not carry this connotation. The same goes for 'Madame'. A strict translation into English, gives us Madam, but that has very different connotations as compared with the French. To call a girl 'a proper little Madam', means the girl is a bossy little spoilt brat, and to call a woman a Madam, is suggestive of something really quite nasty. These two examples go to show that translating from one language to another is not as straightforward as one might like to think.

The matter is more difficult when attempting to render a language which is completely different from a European language. Here are two examples from the Sanskrit of the Bhagavad Gita, chapter 3 verse 1:

"O Krishna, you have said that knowledge is greater than action; why then do you ask me to wage this terrible war? Your advice seems inconsistent. Give me one path to follow to the supreme good." (15)

"If thy thought is that vision is greater than action, why dost thou enjoin upon me the terrible action of war? My mind is in confusion because in thy words I find contradictions. Tell me the truth therefore by what path may I attain the Supreme."

One might be forgiven for failing to see that both of these quotations are a translation from the same Sanskrit original. The first one is more of a paraphrase, using vocabulary derived from modern religio-philosophical terminology. The second one is more old-fashioned in tone, and may be closer to the literal rendering of the text. What this shows is that the assumptions and the skill of the translator will always condition the result. Most successful translations are a subtle balance between the literal rendering of the text and a certain degree of paraphrasing. This was very true with the Bible, and still is, with modern paraphrasing such as the New English Bible and the Jerusalem Bible.

We have to admit that just as mathematics is fundamental to all the sciences, human language is basic to all forms of expression. Some languages lend themselves to support scientific matters; others less so. The same is true for religious belief. We only have to compare the Hebrew of the Old Testament with the Greek of the great philosophers, to realise that here were two very different mentalities at work. That is not to say there was nothing in common, for there were a few basic assumptions shared between the two cultures. But with the Old Testament, we see a culture which is very down-to-earth with hardly anything of what we would call philosophy. A prime example of this would be the encounters that Moses and Elijah had with God. This is reflected in the language itself, for it has hardly any abstract nouns, and only two verb tenses. The Greeks however had a whole array of verb tenses and permutations on them, plus abstract nouns with use of adjectives, which indicated much more of philosophical thought as applied to religious belief. One of the interesting features of the New Testament, especially St. Luke, is that he tries, quite successfully, to continue the frame of thought seen in the Old Testament, and particularly the way in which the Septuagint rendered the Hebrew. St. Luke must have been a Greek, and also a very clever linguist. (16)

If one were to claim that the truth is not to be found in human language, this might be a fair assertion. However, we have to use language of some kind, whether basic or elaborate. It may be unnecessarily cynical to say that language is only ever an approximation to the truth. What we have to observe is that careless use of language, loaded up with emotionalisms and pejorative words, can so easily obscure the truth. Precision and a proper use of terms is always to be sought, both in scientific dialogue and theological discussion.

The whole matter of interpretation is not confined to the translation of languages. Seeing the significance of things is fundamental to every area of truth. This is very true in the field of archaeology. There are many artefacts coming to light, which defy explanation. We have no idea what they were used for. All too often, we try to interpret these matters through the eyes of 20th century humanism. All too often we forget that in the ancient world, religion, belief, superstition and rudimentary philosophy were the ruling factors in people's minds, in contrast to today's (17) assumptions. An interesting example comes from the archaeology of Palestine. A set of bronze pots and shovels were found. There is no indication of a date for them; they might have been Israelite, or Canaanite or even from somewhere else. It is tempting to label them as artefacts from the Temple, or a temple. But the truth is, they could have been used for all kinds of things. There are all kinds of things that happened in the Ancient World that we do not know about. This applies to the Roman period as much as any other. New discoveries from Pompeii simply underline the fact that there is still so much to be learned and interpreted from that era.

## Artistic truth

This is probably the area that is most underpinned by interpretation. Every picture, piece of music, dance routine, sculpture, stage drama has to receive some kind of appreciation in order to discover its deeper meaning. What the original composer intended is one thing, but a gifted performer can place his own interpretation on the artwork. We all know the difference between a 'note-producer' and a gifted musician; it is a matter of what the performer can give to the music regardless of what the composer had in mind.

This is where truth can be at its most acute, for artworks of all kinds can convey so much to the human soul, about the realities of life, the human condition, the meaning of life, truths about God (or gods). Emotions about this kind of thing can be expressed in artworks of one kind or another, regardless of language. It is seeking the truth, but on a different level.

If one were to think that artistic truth has nothing to do with these other areas, one would be wrong. One instance is that music is heavily reliant on mathematics, not just for the calculation of rhythm but also for the recognition of different kinds of vibration which make the rich variety of sounds. A gifted musician will instinctively know how to harness these factors to produce a result which appeals to the human soul. Another instance is the chemistry of the composition of paint and stained glass, and stone and metal used in sculpture.

Every religion or secular faith has its own collection of artworks to express its deepest feelings. We only have to think of the Psalms to realise that this is Hebrew poetry at some of its best, and recall that all this was set to music at one time, and still is, in the traditions of Christianity. If we look at the Guru Granth Sahib (Sikhism) we see a faith entirely based on their own collection of sung poetry. The Muslims, with their extreme ban on idolatry, have developed some amazing colour patterns in tiles and stained glass. At the Renaissance, a whole tradition of pictorial art emerged, particularly in the Netherlands, as underpinning Biblical scenes and themes. As we move into the modern world, artworks of a different mentality have appeared. We only have to think of Jesus Christ Superstar, and Joseph and his Technicolour Dreamcoat, for instance, to see that every generation has to express its deepest beliefs in some form of artwork. The value of the new Coventry Cathedral cannot be underestimated. Here is an artistic gem which epitomises the mentality of the late 1950's. It has so many original ideas which offer new insights into the Christian faith, in contrast with the traditional medieaval or Renaissance church buildings. This is a good example of how architecture, combined with artworks, can be a powerful expression of religious belief.

## Literary truth

This area is not much different from artistic truth. There are three main areas involved here; poetry, drama and literature. All three of these can be a powerful conveyer of the basic impulses in human nature. We have already seen that poetry is an important form of artwork. Much of the Bible is expressed in poetry, and not just the Psalms. Anyone who tries to take poetry purely at face value, literally, is missing the point. Poetry, especially if it is set to music, heightens the emotion and connects with the human soul more deeply than other vehicles. To take a powerful example from Isaiah 40:9; "Get you up to a high mountain, O Zion, herald of good tidings... O Jerusalem, herald of good tidings..... say to the cities of Judah, 'Behold, your God'." Anyone who takes this in a purely literal sense has got it wrong. Zion is not a high mountain like Everest, but just consider the emotion and excitement in this passage. Isaiah is completely carried away by the realisation that the Messiah is coming, and that the message of hope is fantastic. It is no surprise that this passage became one of the most well known of the arias in Handel's Messiah.

Something similar happens with the novel. We are accustomed to thinking that the novel is a relatively modern development, but is it? Essentially, it is an invented story but with some kind of agenda or analysis of human nature. Just because it is an invention does not mean that it is nonsense. We only have to think of the parables of Jesus, to know that an invented story, albeit rather brief, can appeal to the deepest impulses in our souls. A good example of a modern novel with a powerful message would be Animal Farm and also Nineteen Eighty Four. The latter is particularly interesting since it involves all kinds of scientific, biological aspects, with babies being born in jam jars. Whether or not this would be feasible is beside the point. The writer is trying to show how ghastly it would be if we were all turned out to be 'tailor made' and exactly the same.

The drama too is important as exploring the deepest impulses in human emotion. The plays of William Shakespeare are still popular and regarded as iconic. His understanding of human nature is second to none. In each of his tragedies, he has a hero who has some kind of shortcoming. So with Hamlet, it is indecision; with MacBeth it is overriding ambition; with King Lear, it is stupidity. A modern drama which is also iconic, is An Inspector Calls. Here we see a family that has done well in life, very pleased with themselves and with little concern about anyone who has fallen by the wayside. Inspector Goole comes in and manages to shake their complacency with a shuddering guilt about how they treated 'Daisy Renton'. The play ends with a classic climax and anticlimax, for just as the family think they have excused themselves from guilt, the telephone rings and the poor soul has committed suicide after all. It is a powerful political statement about the stand-off between the rich and the poor, and has the effect of jerking everyone's conscience. In this way, a stage play can be a most powerful political tool.

In general terms, literary productions can be a powerful conveyer of ideas, whether it be political, religious or social. By heightening the emotion, a literary production can make more impression on people than a plain factual statement. It can also lead people astray by some kind of distortion or false idea.

## Philosophical truth

We are all philosophers in a way, in fact if there is anyone who is not, he is not really thinking about life and the meaning of existence. It is difficult to separate philosophy from theology and ethics, but philosophy pure and simple (if there is such a thing) can be seen as a secularised version of theology. Modern philosophy tries to leave God out of the picture, but this does not really seem to work.

Philosophy goes back as far as recorded material can be traced, and probably before that. It may be that Chinese Taoist philosophy is the oldest known material. This was heavily tied up with (18) their version of physics and also medical practice. If we look at the ancient Mesopotamian myths we see philosophical impulses worked into such material as the Myth of Gilgamesh. The myth of Innana is a good example of how they understood the meaning of life and death.

The Hebrew scriptures are noted for not having much in the way of abstract philosophical thought. Their whole mindset was dominated by an awareness of God's imminence. The nearest we come to philosophy is in the Wisdom literature of the Old Testament and the Apocrypha. In this, Wisdom is personified as a woman who was with the Creator at the beginning of time. This of course, has to be taken as figurative; if we take it literally, it would mean that God had a partner in the skies, which be an infringement of Monotheism. When the Messiah, Jesus of Nazareth appeared, he became equated with Holy Wisdom, and was seen as a fulfilment of everything that the wisdom writers offered.

The full flowering of philosophy in the ancient world came with the great Greek thinkers, such as Plato, Aristotle, and Epicurus and many more. It may be that their heyday appeared after the Wisdom tradition of the Old Testament had begun, since it was Solomon who stimulated their tradition. It is quite likely that the concept of 'logos' (the word) worked its way into Greek thinking from the poetic, and prophetic idea of Wisdom in the Old Testament. At any rate, the two traditions continued side by side into the Roman era and the birth of Christianity.

The early church, in its attempts at coming to terms with the unprecedented phenomenon of Jesus Christ, resorted to Platonic imagery to reach an explanation. Traces of platonic phrasing are found in the Nicene Creed, in which it is emphasised that Jesus was really human and yet divine, and also monotheism is stressed along with the Trinitarian configuration. By the time the schoolmen of the Middle Ages began to examine theology, there was a shift over to Aristotelian thinking. Thomas Aquinas and others offered much profound philosophical material, especially when assessing the nature of the elements in the Mass. Thomist thinking still pervades the Roman Church to this day.

As we come to the Renaissance and the Age of Enlightenment (so-called), we see a separation between philosophy and theology. People like Descartes and Rousseau were concerned mostly with equality and freedom. This, of course, was basic to the American Constitution and the French Revolution, and reverberated through into the 19th and 20th century. But this is where atheism begins to make a stronger appearance. There had been atheists in the ancient world, for instance, Socrates, but the main outburst of it came when it was seen that the Pope had insisted on the world being flat and central to the Universe. If he could be wrong on one matter, how about all the other dogmas? Strangely the American Declaration of Independence attached itself to God; the French Revolution attached itself to atheism.

In today's world, we have philosophers of all different types and shades of opinion. It could fairly be said the Bertrand Russell has been one of the most influential in our times. He was an atheist, or so he thought! There was Teilhard de Chardin, a Roman Catholic evolutionist who was highly influential in the late 20th century, but is now largely forgotten.

The difficulty is that modern philosophers tend to invent new words and phrases, which are not readily understood by others. There is the tendency to produce material that is so obscure that one is left totally confused. But what is in common between them? What are they aiming for? It must be fair to say that they are attempting to find the TRUTH, about life, death, reality, existence, all these matters. That is not really much different from what the theologians are aiming at. The special, secularised vocabulary, the trains of logic and the attempt to leave God out of the picture are what distinguish it from theology. I would say that anyone who is genuinely attempting to find the truth about life, cannot avoid considering the reality of the divine, which means, in effect, trying to find God.

## Ethical truth

Just as we are all amateur philosophers, so too are we all moralists. In fact, it is often difficult to distinguish ethics from philosophy. Western religion has always been tied up with morality; this less so with eastern religions, but is nevertheless a factor. We all have a code of conduct to adhere to, no matter what culture we are born into. It is obvious that virtually all the artistic and literary material we produce contains ethical assumptions of one kind or another.

What are the essentials of ethics? In the Old Testament, ethics are largely assumed until we arrive at the Ten Commandments in Exodus 20:1ff. People have commented on the 'Sacrifice of Isaac' as being cruel, immoral and illogical. By our standards, it would be. But we have to remember that in the Bronze Age, in that part of the world, it was perfectly normal to sacrifice one's firstborn son, and in fact, if one did not, one could expect to receive no more sons. Abraham was only following the normal mores of his time. But God intervened and showed him that child sacrifice was wrong, in fact human sacrifice altogether.

If one were to think that the Covenant of Sinai was the first instance of a lawcode being enforced by a god, one would be wrong. We only have to think of the Code of Hammurabi, which was given by Shamash the sun god, to realise that enforcement of morals had to have divine (19) sanction. It was not enough for a moralist or even a king just to invent a law code and persuade everyone to observe it. This feeling is still there in people's minds today, with the thought that if we commit a crime, we are answerable not just to the Police but to eternal justice, namely God.

161

Ethics develop, and progress, just like science and mathematics. As we come to the Sermon on the Mount, by Jesus, we see that 'thou shalt not commit murder' is intensified to 'every one who is angry with his brother.... and insults his brother....' (Matthew 5:21ff). In our own times, the concept of warfare has undergone a sea-change. It was thought to be magnificent, and courageous to prosecute a war, but now, with the experience of World War 2, it is politically wrong to glory in violence. As science and medical advances have progressed, we are left with various moral dilemmas over such things as abortion and euthanasia. The ethical questions intensify and become more guilt-producing, the more we probe into things.

Freud would tell us that in our instincts there is violence and self-gratification. I would claim that instinctively we have a sense of fairness, of balance and justice, which interplays with the other urges. If we see something that is out of balance, there is the urge to restore the balance. If someone is treated unfairly, there is the impulse to compensate him somehow. This is the foundation of ethics, and is an instinct implanted by the eternal judge himself. Even Hitler, the archetypal warmonger, found it necessary to arrange things so that it would appear that Poland had attacked Germany in September 1939!

The main difficulty now is that with the impression of God very much weakened in people's minds, there is no ultimate authority to enforce morality. The Police are known to be capable of corruption; the courts are quite capable of reaching a wrong verdict, which means the criminals manage to escape justice; it is now quite possible to get away with all kinds of malfeasances and convince oneself that there is no penalty to face. Hell, as a penalty for behaving badly, is no longer taken seriously. Until we discover or come to admit that there is an ultimate criterion of ethics, we shall not have a convincing method of moral enforcement. This is, of course, a secularised way of talking about God. Ethics used to be bound up with religious belief, but the humanists have managed to separate the two issues, and that is not very wise (as far as I am concerned).

## Mythological truth

Virtually every religion or secular faith has as its basis some kind of mythology. But what is mythology? It is speculation about the origins of life, the beginnings of the world, the three tier system of the world, heaven, hell, different grades of people, such as giants and pixies. And since this concerns the beginning of all things, by extension, it concerns the end of all things, in other words, eschatology.

How is this different from theology and philosophy? Mythology employs a number of images that can be recognised in just about every system of thought. There is the snake which is symbolic of life and also death. There is the tree, which symbolically connects the underworld with ground level and heaven. Gold, silver, jewels, crystal, mirrors, translucent stones symbolise royalty and eternity. The sword, the spear or an arrow indicate eternal justice and truth. Water and fire are agents of cleansing, and sometimes blood. These are just a few of the symbolisms that mythology employs. It is easy to say that 'myth' is a lie or a misapprehension, but that is a misunderstanding of the word. Myth, in its proper sense, is an expression of our deepest needs, fears, speculations and aspirations, but in rich imagery as opposed to elevated abstract vocabulary. This kind of expression is found worked into the theology of almost every sacred literature in the world, but also in non-religious material. We only have to think of the traditions surrounding King Arthur to realise that this is a secular, political statement, which is underpinned by rich mythological features.

In the Bible, we start with Genesis chapters one to eleven. These early statements about human origins are heavily intertwined with mythological images. The same is true even more with the finale of the Bible, Revelation, in which just about every aspect of mythology is worked in. People have tried to take Revelation on a literal level, but this is to miss the true significance of the book. It is all about the final defeat of evil, the cleansing of the world and the acceptance of humanity into the presence of God. If we were to think that mythology is absent from the rest of the Bible, that too would be a mistake. It is in many places heavily worked in with other types of literature, not least some of the historical accounts. A good example of this comes in the account of Elijah being taken up into heaven in a fiery chariot, 2 Kings 2:11ff: '.... a chariot of fire and horses of fire separated the two of them. And Elijah went up by a whirlwind into heaven...." We can see the mythological elements in this; the fire indicates cleansing, and the whirlwind, which came at Elijah's encounter with God, is symbolic of God's intervention. It takes a certain degree of skill to discern what is factual account and what is mythological symbolism in the Bible.

The best known mythological system is the Greek one which can be read up in the great Greek poets, Homer and Hesiod. Much of Greek mythology is still influential on us to this day. Other mythologies from around the world are fascinating to study. The Chinese and Japanese ones, being isolated from Europe, have had very little influence on us, but nevertheless have many aspects of symbolism in common. They are fascinating to study.(20)

Just to mention one sacred text from Hinduism, the Ramayana, we see that it is almost all couched in mythological imagery. It is a fantastic story of how Rama's wife, Sita, is abducted by Ravana, and the ensuing battle to retrieve her. It is all about the stand-off between good and evil, and includes many images of death and resurrection, which is a fundamental theme in virtually every mythology, the world over.

Mythology is important. Not only is it closely intertwined with theology and religious practice, but also employs factors from most of our other areas of truth. Mythology appeals to the deepest instincts in our make-up, and talks about the ultimate aspects of life and death, evil and goodness, and hate and love. However, it is not necessarily tied up with religion; it can be the basis of any system of thought, sacred or profane. If one were to think that mythology is a thing of the past, think again; what about Star Trek, Star Wars, the Water Babies, Dracula, Frankenstein and most notable of all in our own times, Harry Potter! Mythology does not die out; it simply moves into a different mode using all the traditional symbolisms and imagery.

## Theological truth

Theology is the element that underpins all the religions and secular faiths in the world. One's theology may be monotheistic, or henotheistic, or polytheistic, or agnostic or atheistic. This line of truth is concerned with the reality of the divine (or non-reality as the case may be). It is talking on a completely different level to mathematics and the sciences. The problem is that people tend to confuse the two, by assuming that a theological statement is some kind of physical, literal, factual claim. An example of this can be found in Revelation 5:10; '.... around the throne and the living creatures and the elders, the voice of many angels, numbering myriads and myriads and thousands and thousands....' This is not some kind of mathematical statement. It is a good example of exaggeration which is often seen in the Bible and other sacred literature. We must recall that number symbolism is a common feature in the Bible. As for angels, that is not a matter for scientific analysis. That is a theological statement which involves an understanding of the world of the spirit. Even the philosophers fight shy of talking about angels and devils. But the truth is that every culture on earth has had some kind of awareness of the world of the spirit. This is particularly true in what might be termed 'primitive' societies that rely on shamanism for their religious beliefs. But it is still true in so-called 'advanced' societies; there is the need for or awareness of some kind of understanding of the divine. Attempts at removing or just avoiding spiritual needs in people have been seen not to work. Prime examples of this can be seen in ex-Communist Russia and the new capitalist China. A theological understanding of life may be out of favour in modern western life, but it will just not go away.

Obviously, theology is closely intertwined with mythology and philosophy, and just about every other expression of truth. If one were to think that science has nothing to do with it at all, one ought to think again. There is the Society for Psychical Research, which attempts to investigate in a systematic, scientific way, the world of the spirit. One obvious approach is the phenomenon known as the 'out of the body experience', which may not be taken seriously by some people, but is taken seriously by those who have had this kind of experience. Obviously this area of research is in its infancy, but may hold promise of interesting results in due course.

Christian Theology has been dominated by many important theorists. Irenaeus, Origen, Anthanasius, Augustine, Thomas Aquinas, Duns Scotus, Luther, Calvin, and coming into the modern world, Karl Barth, Paul Tillich and Hastings Rashdall, to name but a few. The main areas of discussion are the attempts at analysing the Incarnation, the Trinity and the Atonement. In spite of the Council of Chalcedon laying down the doctrines for the Trinity and the Incarnation, all these matters are up for re-examination and differences of opinion in today's world. There was a time when people were branded as heretics, but that kind of intolerance is now history. What they failed to realise and still do fail to do, is to realise that they are attempting to analyse three profound paradoxes at the heart of God's intervention in human affairs. I would say that the future for theology ought to be about coping with these paradoxes and discussing the ramifications of them. There is no point in (21) becoming over-dogmatic about matters which are beyond human comprehension in the first place.

## In Conclusion

We have taken a brief look at eleven main areas of truth or reality. Some are more distinct than others, but it is clear that they are all interrelated in some way, some more than others. It is to no purpose to say that one is correct and the others are wrong. They all have their own validity in their own way. A person with a balanced view of life will be able to see which type of truth is involved on experiencing any given thing. It would be true to say that some people have given one or two areas of truth an excess of emphasis to the loss of others. Each level of truth appeals to human nature in its own way; it is our instincts which produce these areas of truth, which means that they all, in their own way, appeal to us in some way or other.

So when we hear people saying that the Bible contradicts Science or science contradicts the Bible, what we are hearing is a failure to understand that both areas of knowledge are working on different levels of reality. Science is largely but not entirely concerned with the physical, practical, experimental side of life, while Theology is talking about the world of the spirit in relation to this world. It is a mistake to confuse the two, even if at times they become intertwined.

The way that these eleven areas have been presented is not in any order of importance. I have started with Mathematics simply because it is probably the easiest matter to grasp, and Science next because they are all heavily dependent on Maths. I have kept the ones that are most relevant to Religion to the end. Philosophy, ethics and theology are heavily interrelated, and traditionally, theology has been dubbed 'the queen of sciences'. It could be maintained that all of these areas are fundamental to each other in various ways. At the very least, it is to no purpose to undervalue any of them on the assumption that some have more validity. What this means is that a scientist can be a religionist; an artist can be a scientist; a philosopher can indulge in mythology; a historian can be any of these things. Any of these can indulge in any religion of their choice, but I would venture to say that the Christian religion, in all its permutations, is the one that lends itself best to coping with all areas of truth in a fair balancing situation.

### Footnotes

1. Hebdomadal; the pattern of seven days in the week, which now dominates the world.
2. It is commonly supposed that chapters one and two were written by two different writers because of the difference in literary style.

3.  The Jews were persecuted by Antiochus 4th Epiphanes, a Greek king based in Antioch, circa 167 BC. Also the Romans made life difficult for the Jews, cg. Caligula.
4.  St. Matthew chapter 4 and St. Luke chapter 4.
5.  A. Thom has demonstrated the reality of the 'megalithic yard', which would indicate that the ancient celts had mathematical inclinations when devising their stone circles.
6.  The Nazi's managed to convince themselves that their racial theory could be proved scientifically.
7.  See *Mapping Time*, by E.G.Richards, page 150ff.
8.  See my book, *Myth, Legend and Symbolism* on the subject of King Arthur.
9.  Edmund Spenser, the Fairie Queen, gave the Tudor monarchs all kinds of supernatural attributes, but not, however, Mary 1st.
10. See my book on *Myth, Legend and Symbolism*, chapter 7.
11. See chapter 16 on the subject of Archaeology.
12. Cambrian times, when it is thought that life began to appear on this planet, is reckoned to be about 500 million years ago or more.
13. 'Delapidated' literally means 'all the stones are falling out'. Lapis means a stone in Latin.
14. See the chapter on the Quantum World, chapter 4.
15. *Bhagavad Gita*, translated by Eknath Easwaran.
16. The Septuagint is the Greek translation of the Old Testament. It is so called because it is claimed that it took a team of translators seventy days to complete the task.
17. A puzzle. Bronze artefacts found in a cave in Judea, have all the appearance of being sacrificial implements for use in a temple. They appear to have started life as Greek, but with the faces of the gods filed off, that means the Jews had stolen them and defaced them. Quite what their significance is, is a matter for debate; interpretation is an interesting matter. Page 109 in Yigael Yadin, *Bar Kokhba*.
18. The myths of ancient Mesopotamia are quoted in M. Coogan, *Ancient Near Eastern Texts*.
19. The Code of Hammurabi, a Mesopotamian King about 1750 BC is depicted on a stele, receiving a law code from Shamash the Sun god. See Winton Thomas, *Documents from Old Testament Times*, page 38.
20. For Chinese mythology; *Understand Chinese Mythology,* by Teresa Moorey, and *Japenese mythology; The Holy Kojiki* by Cosimo Classics.
21. See my book on *The Theology of Paradox*, for an extensive treatment of paradox in relation to Theology.

# 14

## *Psychology and Religion*

This is the right moment to investigate the social sciences, so-called. Some would take them seriously as scientific; others would not, or at least question their validity as sciences. Either way, the relevance of them to religious faith is very interesting . In many ways, modern psychology lends support to faith and theology. The same is true the other way round. It is well known that many practising psychiatrists are also believers. Some of them are ordained ministers of churches. It would be burdensome to investigate every aspect of modern psychology. It will be instructive to comment on those aspects that have most relevance to religion.

The 'science' of probing into the workings of the mind goes back to the 19th century. That means that this field of knowledge is still comparatively new. A paradigm of how to describe psychology was given to me by a psychology lecturer in 1967, and it went like this;

"There was a drunkard hanging around a lamppost in a street. He was clearly looking for something. Someone asked him what he was seeking. His reply was most interesting, 'I've lost my watch somewhere, and I can't find it.' The helpful question came, 'Do you know where you dropped it?' The drunkard replied, 'Yes, I know roughly where I dropped it.' 'So why can't you find it?' 'Because I dropped it in the next street." The helpful person offered, 'Why don't we go into the next street and see if it's there?' 'No, no," reasoned the drunkard, 'that won't be any good'. 'Why not?' 'Because there isn't a light on in the next street; at least there's a light on here.' Everyone laughs at that story, but there is so much truth in it. With Psychology, we are dealing with matters that are so difficult to quantify and generalise about, that rather a lot of it is guesswork, speculation and wishful thinking. All these aspects of it are not really supposed to be involved in the true sciences. But what I have noticed, with experience, is that psychological 'experts' can be just as hard and fast in their thinking as any other kind of scientist and also certain types of religionist.

As with the philosophers, the psychologists love to coin new words or phrases to which they attach subtle meanings, but which can easily be misunderstood by the general public. Such words as 'complex', 'fixation', 'sublimation', 'libido' and 'ego', have worked their way into the language but are not always used in quite the way that the early psychologists intended them to be meant. I shall attempt to avoid some of the specialised vocabulary of psychology and use words that are commonly understood by normal people. Mind you, it depends on what one means by 'normal'.

The first major figure in psychology is Sigmund Freud, and even if his speculations are largely outdated now, they still do have a major influence on psychiatric practice. His major contribution (1) was to point out the existence of the unconscious mind, a matter which in itself is improvable, and yet it is also an inescapable factor. His theory of the mind, or of personality went something like this. There are three main levels of consciousness; the id, the ego and the superego. Id is what we are born with, our basic instincts, which reside in the unconscious level. The essentials of the id are pleasure seeking and impulsive, consisting of the sex drive and the aggressive and destructive urge. The ego, which is mostly at the conscious level, is concerned with rationality. The use of common sense means that the urges coming from the id must be kept under control. It becomes clear that one gets what one wants more effectively by using rationality as opposed to violent outbursts. The superego is concerned with the intake of moral values, and can be termed 'conscience'. A sense of right and wrong develops, justice and fair play. This exerts an influence on the other two. It can be seen that if these three elements are in balance with each other, then we have a well-balanced person. If one of these elements is to some extent overriding the other two, we then have someone who is maladjusted. We notice immediately that the factor of balance has crept in, an aspect which is so important in many other spheres of life, not least the physical sciences.

To give a few examples, someone who is given to violent, irrational outbursts, has clearly not managed to develop the ego or the super ego sufficiently to control these outbursts. Someone who sees everything as totally logical, never loses his temper but does not see how something rational can cause upset to someone else, has too much ego in relation to everything else. Someone who is obsessive about rules and regulations, and is overburdened by conscience to the extent that they become neurotic; such a person has too much super ego and forces the other two elements down to a minimum. Such people can be termed maladjusted and may need help to see things in a more balanced fashion. The task of the psychiatrist is very often to free the mind from this imbalance and also to help one comes to terms with a bad conscience and cancel out excessive guilt.

How does this relate to religious faith? An important element in many religious faiths is the factor of conscience, which is the internalised law code given by one's God. The Ten Commandments is a prime example of the factor of ethics, flowing from one's awareness of God's expectations for us. But there are other law codes, some of which are derived from the Ten (2) Commandments (eg. The Buddhist one) and others appear not to be. Nevertheless, the factor of conscience in relation to the expectations of the divine, whether it be moral or ritual, is an important aspect of religious faith.

Another way in which Freud's analysis is relevant to religious belief, especially biblical, is that his scheme of id, ego and super ego is simply an internalised version of the three tier universe. Below, we have the underworld where the devils live, ie. irrational, destructive and selfish urges. At ground level we have the normal rational world of ordinary human relationships. Above (in heaven) we have a god who supplies us with a conscience. One wonders if Freud ever thought of it this way? One might say that the three tier universe is now discredited, but even so, that is how people's minds still work; God above and Satan below! This is regardless of the geography of space travel. Another way to see it is to turn the whole thing upside down (something that modern man has managed to do in so many ways!). The rational element can stay as ground level, the ego. The skies contain all kinds of violence and sexual urges, as in many world mythologies, especially the Greek one. The underworld, equating to the super ego, is the hell we subject ourselves to with regard to bad conduct and outrageous behaviour, which results in an over-burdened conscience.

Another aspect of this is how Freudian analysis supports the traditional Christian doctrine about original sin. It was Augustine who expounded this dogma and it has been an ongoing (3) assumption in Christian teaching ever since. It means that tendency in people to go wrong, and it stems from the calamity in the Garden of Eden. One does not have to be a Genesis

170

fundamentalist to accept the idea of original sin. I think we all know that there is that tendency in human nature to destroy something that is good and play up awkward with people just for the sake of it. Also, ask any newspaper editor and he will tell you that trying to sell a newspaper with positive, wholesome material in it is a loser, but selling a newspaper with something disgusting, horrific and degrading is much more successful. It is all evidence of original sin. As such, it ties in with Freud's concept of the id as something destructive, selfish and degenerate.

Personally, I would disagree with Freud about the nature of the id (assuming it does exist). I do not accept that it is all negative, violent, destructive and selfish. There are other instinctive impulses in human instinct. What about a sense of balance and fairness? What about an awareness of deity or of the world of the spirit? What about love for one's mother or possibly a substitute for one's mother? What about the need to be loved and valued? I suggest that that was one of the major failings in Freud, that he did not take into account the spiritual element in human nature. In addition to that, we have seen, in the case of certain animals, that instinct is not all aggressive and sexual. Much of it is positive, such as the homing or migratory instinct, which must, in my opinion, rely on some kind of rationality that humans do not possess. This would mean that the id does have elements of the ego worked into it.

It would be fair to say that the long term benefit of the Freudian approach has been the method known as counselling which involves talking through people's mental problems. The patient lies on a couch and the psychiatrist delves into one's past as a child and tries to unravel one's hang-ups. Very often, the patient is found to be weighed down with guilt, over some past misdemeanour, or imagined misdemeanour. I think we all know that excessive guilt which is not assuaged, can ruin one's life and be the cause of various illnesses. In this way, the mission of Jesus Christ was much the same, in that he came to lift the burden of guilt from such persons. "Your sins are forgiven" is a (4) reassuring comment often given to sufferers. This means that the psychiatrist is attempting to do the same as Jesus, only using secular terms rather than spiritual ones. One wonders which method would be more effective. A religionist would be expected to say that a Christian minister, in the tradition of Jesus, is empowered to give absolution. A secularist, humanist person might find that unacceptable and prefer to be reassured by a psychiatrist. Which ever way one sees it, the task is the same, but the method is somewhat different.

Modern psychiatric methods, which can be traced back to Freud, are mainly concerned with mental illnesses of various kinds. A very common condition in the modern world is depression, which can be very severe. Also there is schizophrenia, which means, literally, 'two minds'. All kinds of strange methods have been attempted, with mixed success. It might seem that the causes are linked to abnormalities in the genes or chromosomes, and there is some evidence that these conditions may be inherited, or at least potentially inherited. Even so, there is the environmental aspect of it, in that one can be induced to descend into a mental condition by one's situation at home or work. To put it very crudely, one can be 'driven mad.' One positive way of dealing with this is to remove the cause of one becoming deranged, before it is too late. To take an instance, if at home there is someone deliberately engendering guilt or trying to destroy one's self-esteem, the answer is to remove the problem. This could involve leaving home in favour of a different atmosphere.

In general terms, even if Freud's influence is still very much with us, his theory of human personality remains improvable and for some mildly unconvincing. The difficulty here, was that like many 'scientific' theories, it was a case of arguing from the specific to the general. He based his ideas on neurotic patients that he treated in Vienna. With Roman Catholicism being a ruling factor and the effect on people's approach to sexuality that went with it, it was easy to arrive at the system that he did. But does everyone, right across the world, have an inbuilt system like that? There are many Protestants, and indeed, many religionists of vastly different kinds, whose minds work in a very different way. Many people, regardless of religious background (or none) see sexuality in a very different light, and it is possible that a different theory of personality might be sought, something that fits more closely to their basic assumptions about life.

As the 20th century advanced, other initiatives in psychology appeared. Rorschach (5) developed the so-called Rorschach ink test. It consisted of cards with different (random) displays of dots or designs, to which the psychiatric patient was asked to say what he 'saw' in the picture. It was intended for the diagnosis of schizophrenia in the early days (1921) but this kind of testing is still in use now as a method of analysing the personality. Not that everyone would agree that it is completely reliable, but it may, in some cases, offer some leads for psychoanalysis.

The use of ambiguous pictures raises the whole question of perception.

How we perceive things has a very important bearing on our approach to life and our conduct. If one is seen to be behaving erratically or irrationally, it may be because one is seeing things in a distorted or confused manner. How one sees things has a very important bearing on religious faith, or no faith, as the case may be. If one makes the assumption that the whole of life is the product of God, the Creator, then one will treat everyone and everything with a degree of respect and admiration. If on the other hand, one discounts the reality of God and regards the whole of life as just an array of facts (or less than facts), then a certain degree of disinterest is very likely to permeate one's pattern of life.

We can take a few examples. There is a drawing called 'the Necker cube'. There are two (6) ways of seeing this; firstly (A) with the square ABCD as the front face; secondly (B) with the square EFGH as the front face. Either way is a valid perception unless someone puts dotted lines to show which lines are out of sight.(C) Then the ambiguity ceases. What does this indicate? Does it mean that the first one shows a forward-looking person, but downward-looking, ie, pessimistic, or looking downwards? Does the second one indicate a forward –looking person, but optimistic, or looking upwards?

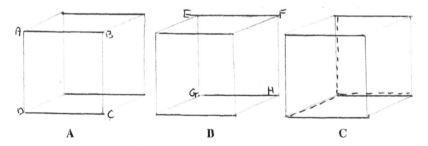

|       A       |       B       |       C       |

Another well-known test is the Rubin's Vase, which might be two equal faces. The question will be, which do you see first, the vase or the two faces? Is this supposed to indicate whether you are a person with dark thoughts or light thoughts? From the point of view of theology, we see here the contrast between light and darkness, good and evil. One wonders if the psychiatrists see it in the same light?

Another interesting test, devised by Bayes, concerns the shading pattern on two identical pictures. The two ellipses with a feature on the top are identical as drawn, but the way they are shaded gives a very different impression. I have rendered a simplified version of this, but a full rendering of it can be seen Brian in Rogers' book, Perception. What is actually the difference? (7)

 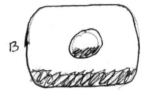

Figure A looks like a crater with a hole in the middle. Figure B looks like a mound with a 'tor' on the top. Why is this? The basic assumption here is that the light source is coming from above. This is a fair assumption, since in our experience, light always does come from above, whether it be the sun, the moon, or an electric bulb. If, however, the light source were to come from below, the reverse effect would be seen, but then we seldom experience light from coming down below.

This factor is interesting from the theological point of view. There is this basic assumption in the human mind, that light comes from above. Light is equated with goodness and with God. Dark is equated with evil, the underworld and Satan. This figure of the crater versus the mound gives us an indication that the human mind is essentially optimistic, is inclined to see things in terms of goodness as opposed to evil. In this way, this finding is a counterblast to the pessimism of original sin and Freud's concept of the id. If it is true that our basic instinct is to look up rather than down, that suggests that we are all searching for God in some way, even if we are degraded by original sin.

At the moment, there are three main theories of perception; the direct theory, the indirect theory and the computational theory. It is interesting to see how the pundits' ideas on these matters change with further research and speculation. But the basic truth remains, that how we see things makes all the difference to our patterns of life. If, like the Hindu philosophy, one sees life as purely an illusion, and that the real world is the next one, and that one's lot in this world is a direct result of one's conduct in a previous life, then there is no incentive to help the poor, since they have deserved what they are now having to cope with, and this life essentially does not matter, since it is purely an illusion. If however, one sees life as a time of preparation and testing for what is to come in the next world, then one is motivated to make the best of this life. One will assume that both worlds are real, and that one's conduct now will have a distinct bearing on one's lot in the next world. It is very largely a matter of how we see things; our basic assumptions shape our patterns of life. If, like some people, there is the assumption that there is no world of the spirit waiting for us at the end of this world, why make any attempt at good conduct now? Why not just do as one pleases? Why not indulge in deliberate cruelty just for the sake of it, as has been seen with certain persons of an extreme ideology in recent times? 'You cannot make omelettes without breaking eggs'. (8)

This is where religious faith and the element of perception as investigated in psychology relate most closely. Unfortunately, in the main, psychology has not really come to grips with the life of the spirit. This is a major element in human nature which cannot be ignored and must have an important bearing on psychological research.

Another interesting feature of work on perception is seen in the following two drawings. The question is, is the central line shorter in figure B or longer? If we take a ruler, it emerges that the central line is exactly the same in length, but the fleches on the ends, pointing in different directions, give the impression that A is longer and B is shorter. (9)

This is an interesting mirage or illusion. It raises the question of how many features of life are some kind of illusion or even self delusion. How many political theories could be labelled thus?! We have already discussed the ancient view of the universe as three tiered and flat; another illusion. If we look out into space, how many illusions are there, never mind the Hubble telescope? The latest possibility is the recently discovered collision between NGC7714 and NGC7715, 100 million light years from Earth. So it appears that the blue spiral galaxy is being torn apart by an orange galaxy, having drifted too close. There seem to be explosions of stars. Or so it appears to be. At such a distance, how can we be sure of what we are really seeing? Is this another mirage? If it is true that 'facts' about our Solar System are constantly being corrected and modified, how much less can we be dogmatic about what appears to be happening so far away? The point is that we tend to see things in terms of our own limited experience. I would raise the question, if it is true that the universe is expanding, how is it that two galaxies can collide with each other? It raises the question of how we interpret such a sight; does it have any implications for religious faith?

Another conundrum for perception is taken from the world of archaeology. Quite often excavations produce some kind of artefact which is a complete mystery. It may be a one-off and may have no obvious purpose or meaning. Often, the context in which it is found might give a clue as to its purpose, but not always. Is it a grave-good, or in a shrine, or a household knick-knack, or just found with no context at all, like the Saxon hoard found in Staffordshire. The precise significance of an artefact is always an interesting question; how seriously do we take it and what are its implications for us in the modern world, if any? Below is a drawing of a curious object found in the Hittite capital, dating from the second millennium BC. It is quite unlike anything seen before anywhere else. (10)

The temptation is to explain it in terms of 21st century assumptions. We think of ducks as comical and tasty for eating. Did they think of it like that? Did it have some kind of ritual purpose? Or was it just a knick-knack made for fun in someone's home? My guess is that it represents some kind of mythical creature which holds some kind of symbolic importance, but that is because I have a wide knowledge of mythology from round the world. Others may see it differently.

How does this relate to religion and psychology? Seeing something which is completely outside one's experience can have a two-sided effect. The first one is to fail to come to terms with it and refuse to admit that it is genuine at all, simply because one has never seen such a thing before. That applies to the miraculous claims, such as healing miracles seen in the Bible. There is the tendency to try to explain it away in terms of one's own experience. When it is pointed out that such healing miracles have been experienced in recent times, this causes confusion and denial. But of course, for those who have had such an experience, the healing miracles of Jesus, and others, make perfect sense. The second response is to force some kind of explanation on to the artefact and take it far too seriously. Thus, one might claim that this was a Hittite god and was the centre of their rituals, and the fact that the duck has two heads, might indicate that the god was schizophrenic! And so, with the material in the Bible, one can take the whole thing completely at face value. So for instance, the Jehovah's Witnesses will refuse a blood transfusion on the grounds that Moses forbade us to eat meat with blood in it. This is a case of literalism gone mad! But this goes to show how people's perceptions of things from the ancient world, and indeed the modern world, can go completely out of realism and proportion.

Perception is a very important factor in human life, and a certain degree of patience, common sense, and application of experience are all needed to prevent us being carried away by any new experience.

An important issue in the field of psychiatry are the attempts to cope with mental illnesses. There are many kinds of mental illnesses, but the one that is of most relevance to religion is the condition known as schizophrenia. The term itself was coined by Bleuler in 1910, a Swiss (11) psychiatrist, and literally it means 'split mind', but he intended it to mean and 'loosening' of the mind. In the public mind, the fictional novel Dr. Jekyll and Mr. Hyde seems to typify this condition, but a multiple personality disorder like that is very rare, and is not actually schizophrenia. There are many misconceptions and superstitions about this condition, and people will go to great lengths to avoid admitting to having it. It is, however, quite common but still not really understood by experts as well as the public. In ancient times, it was believed to be some kind of divine punishment or possession by demons. There were a few people in the ancient world who rejected this hypothesis, but the common assumption was that this condition was related to the world of the spirit. But then, most illnesses were seen in much the same light in those days.

We now know, or rather suspect, that there is a genetic basis for schizophrenia, and that is indicated by the fact that if one has a history of family members suffering from it, then one is much more likely to go the same way. However, just having defective genes does not necessarily result in schizophrenia. There are also environmental factors which trigger the condition. Such factors can be undue stress, upset, severe disappointment, shock, and misuse of drugs such as cannabis, but undue stress is by far the most common contributory factor. All kinds of methods for dealing with the matter have been tried, but now we have antipsychotic medicines and methods of counselling which are far more effective in restoring people to normality.

Schizophrenia seldom occurs overnight, like some conditions, but as we can see, it follows the same pattern as many of the as-yet unsolved problems in medical science. (12) It may take several weeks, months, even years to develop. This is called the 'predromal' phase, and if it is realised what is happening, there is a very good chance of halting the problem and avoiding full-blown schizophrenia. This is where family, friends and medics ought to be vigilant and take action before it progresses too far. The symptoms may be quite slight to begin with, and can be mistaken for other problems.

The main symptoms of schizophrenia are as follows; hallucinations (auditory or visual), delusions, lack of attention, concentration and memory, restricted thought or speech, inappropriate emotions, loss of drive or motivation, social withdrawal. A patient may not display all of these symptoms, and the process of diagnosis may take some time and care by a trained psychiatrist. Just because one has memory lapses, does not have to mean that one is going schizophrenic, for example. Where this becomes relevant to religion is as follows; one may have delusions of grandeur, such as believing one is the Messiah or some great religious leader. One might have delusions of guilt, of having done something really dreadful and being in line for horrendous punishment. One might hear voices or see apparitions and conclude that this is angels or devils attacking one. It is now easy to see how in the New Testament, it is assumed that someone who is deranged is under the influence of evil spirits, and that the solution is to have someone drive out the demons. However we see this, whether as spiritual or as some kind of brain abnormality, the fact is that there are and always have been, certain people who have the gift of exorcism. This is not to undervalue the healing miracles of Jesus in relation to those who were mentally ill. We have to see that in the Gospels, it is described in the terms used in those days. We have to remember that it was a world peopled with angels and devils; this is a sensitivity which is very largely lost in modern western industrialised society, but is still seen in many other parts of the world. Incidentally, it is noted that schizophrenia is more commonly encountered in industrial cities.

That having been said, we can see that the work of the psychiatrist and the work of the exorcist are essentially the same. The difference lies in the methods employed. Counselling and a bottle of medicine can be effective, but essentially the root cause needs to be found. That can, or should, mean, removing the stress or guilt that triggered the condition in the first place. For someone who cannot believe that he is forgiven, that might mean a continuing problem throughout life, unless he comes to believe that Jesus is the ultimate source of forgiveness. This is a roundabout way of saying that schizophrenia may have a physical and environmental starting point, but the spiritual side of it should not be neglected. This is where religious faith and psychiatry should go hand in hand, and very often do, to good effect.

It is useful to remember that many sufferers, if handled with care and understanding, can make a full recovery and resume a productive and fulfilling life. Some of them go into 'remission' which means they could relapse if they failed to maintain their medication or began to misuse drugs again. The old idea of locking them up in an institution for life has almost completely gone. The only exception would be for those very few that are violent and resistant to treatment, and pose a threat to themselves and the community. But the vast majority of schizophrenics benefit from being out in the community, making secure friendships, relating well to family and carers. That is the positive way forward which offers a long-term cure.

One aspect of Psychology which has touched almost everybody in the modern world, is the matter of intelligence testing. It has been and still is a most controversial matter. In spite of the gradual refinement of this method of finding a person's IQ, the whole matter is still a matter debate and with some people, rejection. It began back in the 1920's, with an attempt at deciding which children ought to be defined as incapable of a normal education. The word 'imbecile' was used, but is probably now politically incorrect! Gradually, this type of testing spread to all children in an attempt to place them in an appropriate school which would best match their interests and abilities. The problem was, and still is, that any test of this type has some kind of cultural bias. Even today, with all kinds of refinements, IQ tests tend to favour upper middle class white people. Others from lower classes and the third world can find this type of testing not to their advantage. In the early 1950's and 60's, the Eleven Plus became the deciding factor in placing children in Grammar Schools or something else less exalted, and that produced massive controversies. It soon became apparent that some who had failed this examination, eventually went on to do A levels, University and even higher. Clearly there was something wrong with this kind of testing.

One of the basic assumptions behind IQ testing, is the idea that one's intelligence is conditioned by one's innate ability, in other words, one's genes, and that means whatever one inherits from one's parents. In this we see that IQ testing has something in common with mental illnesses, genetic illnesses and cancers. Environmental factors were considered, but that was a matter of debate. Taking a test that was purely a puzzle using symbols was supposed to reveal one's innate ability. Personally, I find that very strange; someone who has never seen a test like that, might be forgiven for assuming it was just a lot of nonsense, and would not take it seriously. It is certainly true that if one is able to rehearse such tests, one's score can go up quite dramatically!

The basic framework of the IQ test is the following pattern. A score of 100 is supposed to be the average for the population. Should one score 150 or more, one is assumed to be very intelligent. A score of 50 or less would indicate someone who is mentally incapable.

By the mid 1960's the Eleven Plus was seen to be unreliable, and placing far too much pressure of children of that age. The push to move from a tripartite system to the comprehensive system swept it aside, for the most part. It was soon realised, however, that with no intelligence testing at all, teachers and employers had no real idea of young people's IQ. This has resulted in a plethora of testing in schools, Cap tests and Sats, now taken every year with the intention of spotting able children and allegedly helping weak ones.

It would be fair to say that a child's intelligence does bear some relationship to the intelligence of his parents. There is a genetic factor involved. However, we all know that two extremely intelligent parents can produce someone who is educationally subnormal, and vice versa, two parents scoring low on the tests can produce someone who is very bright.

This must mean that while genetics do have something to do with it, there must be other factors in the background, apart from environment. The advent of Gene-editing, which is now becoming a reality, might eventually give us a way forward to enhancing the intelligence of those with a low score, but this is by no means an easy matter. Just as it now appears that we can edit out bad genes that produce cancer and other genetically based conditions, it might be possible to edit out genes that produce low IQ, or edit in the ones that produce high IQ. (13)

One of the problems with the Eleven Plus was that even if it did delineate children who were bright, it did not tell us other essential factors in the human personality. I am aware that contemporary testing now tries to assess on a much more complete basis, but this is a highly specialised area, and not the run-of-the-mill IQ test. Have you ever been given a test that assesses ambition, or business acumen, or laziness, or spiritual awareness, or hate? IQ alone is not enough to determine whether a child is suited to preferential treatment in school. To take an example, I know of a child that passed his Eleven Plus (which must have indicated that he was very bright), but when he arrived at Grammar School, he was far too lazy and idiotic to make any positive use of it. I know of someone whose business acumen is very acute, but his IQ is conspicuously low. I know this is arguing from the particular to the general, which is a faulty procedure, but how often has one encountered this sort of thing? One could take the case of Adolf Hitler, who was advised to leave school at 14 because of his poor academic record, and yet he went on to rule all of Germany and nearly win the Second World War. His abilities lay somewhere else, in the realms of the demonic! The problem with IQ testing is that it only tests one dimension of human personality. We are all endowed with a number of dimensions, with varying strengths and weaknesses.

How does this relate to religion? There are people who assume that having a religious faith is an indication of stupidity. That is a very strange assumption. I can point out that believers are to be found at all levels of intelligence. Doubtless the bright ones see things in a different light compared with the not-so bright. But their faith is real enough. We know that there are religious frauds, and that must take a certain degree of intelligence combined with unscrupulousness. We think of Joseph Smith who managed to produce the Book of Mormon; he was either very clever (if the book is genuine), or a complete deceiver (that's my opinion!). We think of Ron Hubbard whose religion, Scientology, is so clever that non-members are not allowed to learn its secrets; or is it so clever?! (14)

I am glad to say that no one persuaded Jesus Christ to take an IQ test! Even so, the Romans regarded him as being particularly stupid, for having allowed himself to be crucified. But that was the wisdom (or folly!) of this world. It was through the death and Resurrection of Jesus that everlasting mercy and forgiveness were given to the whole of humanity, and that was a wisdom on a far greater level than anything that this world can conceive. St. Paul phrased it as being 'fools for Christ's sake'. This showed that the early Christians knew their faith went against all the normal worldly canons of common sense. The Christian faith still does, for those who take it seriously. What I am saying is that IQ may tell us something about a person's mental ability, but it does not tell us everything about them. It certainly does not get to grips with people's spiritual qualities, strengths and weaknesses.

This just goes to show that something that superficially might be a very clever idea, might in the long run turn out to be a serious blunder. This is a dictum that all scientists could take to heart, especially the ones who are eagerly exploiting genetic editing. Vice versa, what might sound like a foolish idea, might eventually turn out to be correct. Just think of the scientific doctrines nowadays that rule everyone's thought patterns; Evolution being one of them. Anyone who questions Evolution is regarded as cranky, stupid and just plain awkward; what happens one day when Evolution is found to be 90% wrong?! Intelligence is not everything; stupidity has its place in the great workings of things.

One important aspect of Psychology is assessment and explanation of memory in relation to forgetting. Much experimentation has been done in this area, from the 1920's onwards to the present day. I have not found any attempt at correlating the factor of 'good memory' with intelligence level. I would maintain that memory is a different facility in the brain and is not reliant on IQ. It may be that those who have a high IQ tend to avoid forgetting things, but there are many of a lower IQ who still have a good memory. I am aware that many people claim, in their old age, to remember very clearly things from their childhood, but the middle years seem to be a blank. This may tie in with what I am now going to say in relation to religious belief.

Many religions are strongly grounded on their 'founder members'. So for instance, Confucianism is based on the sayings of Confucius, which are recorded in the Analects. The same goes for Taoism with its reliance on Lao

Tzu and the Tao Teh Jing. We must remember Guru Nanak and the Guru Granth Sahib. It is clear that recollections of these people are enshrined in some form of 'scripture' which goes a long way to ensuring that their memory is not warped or faded in some way. Of course, the classic case of remembering is with the Jewish faith, which is heavily dependent on the Exodus event and the way it is recorded in the Pentateuch. The book of Deuteronomy at 6:20 heavily underlines the importance of the memory of the Exodus event.

"When your son asks you in times to come, 'what is the meaning of (all the laws)' you shall say to him,' We were Pharaoh's slaves in Egypt, and the Lord brought us out of Egypt with a mighty hand....'"

This, of course, forms the core of the Passover celebration every year, as a little boy stands up at the party and asks this very question. The memory of this crucial event underpins virtually everything in the Jewish faith. The account of the opening of the Red Sea is recorded in detail in Exodus 14 to 15, and decorated with a lengthy song of triumph. I would say that the passing centuries have not distorted or diminished this account, in the way that memories are apt to do.

With regard to the Christian faith, this too is heavily dependent on memory work. A lot depends on accepting the witness of the four gospel writers. It would seem that in the early years after the Resurrection, it became clear that eye witnesses were being martyred and that written records were urgently needed. It is to the credit of the early Church, that they allowed four different versions of the ministry of Jesus to be in circulation, each with its own bias and interpretation. Three of them were broadly in agreement, barring a few minor details, and St.John presents Jesus in a rather different way. But it does not contradict anything essential about the other three. These four different versions give us a fair indication about how people's memories and interests vary, especially after a lapse of time. One observation I would make is that the four accounts of the Resurrection are all to some extent different. This can be explained by the factor of stress. The psychologists have demonstrated that with people under stress, panic or fear, we see various distortions of their memories. Reading the accounts, one is struck by how the disciples were terrified, confused, absolutely stunned by the events (which is only natural). This easily explains why the Resurrection accounts differ, but even so, there are many aspects of them that are in agreement.

To focus on one event recorded in the Gospels, The Miraculous Feeding.

This is the only miracle that appears in all four Gospels, and actually there are five accounts of such an event. (15) St.Mark has two such accounts. Why is this? It must be that they saw this occasion as particularly significant and wished to give it much emphasis. It may be that St. Matthew and St.Luke copied from St. Mark, but that is beside the point. They all saw that event as a crucial element in the ministry of the Messiah; it indicated that the Messiah is the essential spiritual element that sustains the entire world.

I once did an experiment with a class of teenagers, asking them to decide which account of the Feeding of the Five Thousand was the closest to the real event. I gave them a printed sheet with no indication of who wrote which one. They all concluded that St.John's version was the closest, possibly eye-witness account. That was my attempt at a psychological test, and I think it worked.

When we compare the canonical Gospels with later material, the so-called apocryphal gospels, we can see the difference. The early Church did not allow this material to become canonical, and we can see why. There is so much exaggeration, fantasy and unreliable recollection in them, that sometimes it becomes laughable. But this just goes to show how claimed recollections of events at a later date, can become so distorted and influenced by some kind of spiritual agenda. The main problem was that the Gnostics, with their elaborate speculations about the world of the spirit, were interpreting the plain gospel material with all kinds of speculative terms and claims. But there were others too.

For the Christian faith, the written recollections of the ministry of Jesus of Nazareth are of the highest importance. Many people's spiritual life is heavily dependent on the testimony of the first disciples. But the findings of the psychologists, with their work on memory and forgetting can be a considerable help in seeing things in proportion when assessing the Gospels. It is no surprise that St.John states twice at the end of his Gospel, the importance of taking his words seriously;

"This is the disciple who is bearing witness to these things; and has written these things and we know that his testimony is true." (John 21:24).

The problem of remembering and forgetting is not a modern problem; it is of much importance when dealing with outstanding events. We, in our times, have methods of recording events which were not available in New Testament times. For instance, the 9/11 event in New York is plain for all to see and there were hundreds of witnesses to it. But in the ancient world, they were much more reliant on eye-witness material, and that explains why St. Paul stresses that the risen Christ was seen by no less than 500 on one occasion. (I Corinthians 15:6) The importance of this is that many people were denying the Resurrection and attempting to smother the witness of the first disciples.

There are many other aspects of Psychology that could be mentioned, but the most significant development in recent times is the factor known as 'Positive Psychology'. The book to read on this aspect of the subject is Positive Psychology, a Critical Introduction by G.B.Moneta, which goes into detail about it. It is a new and in my opinion, a much healthier approach to the whole matter.

It seems to revolve around what is called 'The Big Five'. It is all about assessing traits in people's personality. The five are; extraversion, neuroticism, openness to experience, conscientiousness and agreeableness.

To expand on these, firstly, extraversion means engaging with people, plenty of energy and friendliness. Secondly, neuroticism means anxiety, moodiness, depression self-consciousness and vulnerability and a general feeling of worthlessness. Thirdly, openness means being unconventional, showing curiosity, imagination and aesthetic sensitivity. Fourthly, conscientiousness is about being self-disciplined, hardworking, and down to earth. Fifthly, being agreeable is about being altruistic, empathetic, accommodating and helpful, and that would be a kind and forgiving person. Much work has been done in assessing how much of this is hereditable as opposed to being the result of one's environment. The result has been, in general terms, that it is 40% the result of our genes, 40% due to our environment and 20% due to other factors that are not known. One could add a comment here; what about religious faith (or lack of it) as occupying that 20%? Admittedly that might be a component of one's environment, but not necessarily.

Talking of five major traits of personality immediately reminds me of the ancient tradition of the four humours that have dominated Western civilisation for so many centuries. But Positive Psychology has five! This immediately reminds me of the Taoist doctrine of the Five Great Performers! This is a physico-theological system of thought stemming from Lao Tzu, the founder of Taoism, and it is set out in his scriptures, the Tao Teh Ching and the Hua Hu Ching. This system of thought has five basic elements; fire, water, wood, metal and earth. This is one more than the Western philosophers had. One wonders if modern Psychology has gleaned something from ancient Chinese philosophy, namely the T'ai Chi system.

Here is a tentative scheme, to relate the Big Five to the Five Great Performers. Extraversion could be wood; metal could be neurotic, heavy-going and generally depressed; water could be openness, showing curiosity; conscientiousness, being hardworking and down to earth, like earth; agreeableness could be fire, with a warm attitude to everyone. Of course, the Taoist philosophers go on to give all kinds of ingenious permutations on this. Also it goes on to relate how one moves on to the realms of eternity and perfect peace in the presence of the Jade Emperor. This is something that modern Psychology, of whatever permutation, fails to address, namely the spirituality of mankind and the reality of the divine.

However, to be fair, Positive Psychology does take into account much of the thoughts of Confucius, and Aristotle, even if it does not engage with Taoism. This new approach can be commended for its positive look at such matters as hope, love (in its various permutations), happiness, mindfulness, emotions and much more. It can be seen that the basic elements of Christianity have now begun to be taken seriously, and this a healthy sign. The only thing still missing is any attempt at assessing or coping with the spiritual side of human nature. The nearest that Psychology ever did come to becoming involved with such matters was when Jung included Alchemy in his assessments. Coming back to Confucianism, one of their important themes with regard to social and personal harmony is the concept of inner balance and the avoidance of extremes, or the state of Equilibrium. This, it would seem, is a factor that is being taken seriously by this new development in Psychology.

How interesting that religious doctrines and philosophies should now be influencing a discipline which has been characterised (in general terms) by atheism.

**Footnotes**

1. The founder of psychiatric counselling; still has a strong influence on psychiatry to this day. Born 1859; died 1939.
2. The Buddhist Noble Eightfold Path has much in common with the Ten Commandments.
3. Augustine of Hippo, has had an enormous influence on Christian theology down to the present day. See Documents of the Christian Church, Bettenson, pages 83ff.
4. Mark 2:5 for example, and other places.
5. Rorschach; a Swiss psychoanalyst (1884-1922). He devised a method using inkblots to analyse peoples' personality. This method is still used by some, but largely discredited.

6.  Louis Albert Necker, born 1822, a Swiss psychoanalyst. Devised the Necker cube, an important optical illusion which is supposed to indicate aspects of personality.
7.  The full test is a lot more complicated than this but this is enough to show the point. It all depends on where one assumes the light source is coming from.
8.  The famous remark that the Communists used to justify all manner of cruelties.
9.  Franz Karl Muller-Lyer, a German sociologist in 1889 devised this test. There are several variants on it, and it can show how the eye can be deceived with a simple illusion.
10. A duck with two heads from Boghazkoy the Hittite capital. The main empire was about 1380 BC.
11. Eugen Bleuler is noted for his pioneering work on schizophrenia.
12. See chapter 11 on Medical Science.
13. Gene editing is discussed in Chapter 11 on Medical Science.
14. We should be suspicious of any religious group that is closed and not prepared to explain its policy to the public.
15. Mark 6:35ff, Mark 8 1ff, Matthew 16:32ff, Luke 9:10ff, John 6:5ff.

# 15

## *Anthropology and Religion*

In common with Psychology and Sociology, Anthropology is a relatively new discipline. It can be called a 'social science' in the same way as Psychology, but then there would be those who would wish to deny that. The formal discipline itself begins in 1748 with the book Spirit of the Laws by Charles Montesquieu, who is regarded as the 'father' of Anthropology. He was a philosopher of the Enlightenment.

Thoughts on the subject of Anthropology must have arisen on the discovery of new territories away from Europe. The great explorers found peoples with very different traditions, lifestyles and religions. Anthropology became initially at least, as the study of these peoples who had not been influenced by what might be called 'civilization'. Examples of these would be the Maoris of New Zealand, the Aborigines of Australia, and various races and tribes found in the Amazonian jungle and New Guinea. It is interesting to note that still to this day, despite the spread of modern civilization, there are remote tribes that are only just being contacted by the outside world. Some of them are quite resistant to being assimilated into 20th century modes of living. Who can blame them?

All through the age of imperialism, explorers and empire-builders set to work to 'civilise' what they called 'barbarians' or 'savages', usually introducing them to laws, customs and religious ideas which they must have found very strange. Describing the lifestyle of a people only just contacted is frought with the problem of seeing things through the eyes of one's own culture. It is easy to criticise a people for being 'barbaric'; difficult to see the matter objectively. One might almost say it is impossible. One wonders how these indigenous peoples would have evaluated us if they had had the opportunity to invade our territories!

Naturally the colonists assumed that their culture and religion were the correct things and that the indigenous peoples must therefore have to learn from them. This was rather strange, since every colonial European power had its own set of values and differing religious ideas. The natives could be forgiven for being confused. This is certainly what happened in India, where the Hindus stated plainly that they could not see why Christianity had to be about a dozen competing versions of itself. This, in time, led to the formation of the Church of South India, and the North later. It may have occurred to a few of the colonists that what they found might have been something worthwhile, and this helps to explain why modified versions of indigenous religions have worked their way into modern British society.

It would be fair to say, that of all the sciences, Anthropology is the closest to religious belief and practice. To put it another way, if one cannot understand religion, how will one understand the beliefs and practices of these indigenous peoples? We all know that religion is no longer central to life in modern western culture; but the opposite is true with these indigenous peoples. Religion is endemic in their culture and to attempt to divorce it from other aspects of their culture is to fail to appreciate what is going on.

What sort of religion do they adhere to? The answer is almost always, some form of Shamanism. In a tribal, rural, pre-industrial, pre-urban setting, it is easy to understand that the people rely on Shamanism for their theological horizons. What is a Shaman? A Shaman is someone who has spiritual capabilities that most people do not have. These abilities might involve being psychic, having healing powers, prophetic powers, having some kind of influence over the weather, or communing with the spirits. It is easy to see that when people live very close to the natural world, and are not distracted by modern gadgetry and 'clever' people expressing doubt, that an understanding of the world of the spirit is much easier to acquire. The rain forest jungles are an ideal milieu for such a culture, even so, Shamanism is not confined to such areas. The word Shaman itself comes from the 'primitive' people of Siberia, the Tungus. When we use the word Primitive, that in itself indicates a kind of superiority of our culture to theirs. We must remember that the Shaman, witch-doctor, or whatever he is called, is very much valued by his people, and his prognostications are known to be reliable, and have an immense influence on the people of that society. The shaman is just as likely to be a woman. It is not a matter of training, although novices may need a little guidance at the start of their careers. Often a trance is induced by the use of some kind of drug, but not always. The shaman is the one who can commune with the spirits of the (1) unseen world and give guidance to the local people. Shamanism does not simply take one form; there are as many variations on it as there are shamans. If it were to be thought that shamanism is confined to so-called primitive societies, this would be misleading. There are many modern variants on it in modern western culture. The medium who is the key to the spiritualist churches. Also there are spiritual healers. Many of our priests and ministers are regarded as very close to the world of the spirit. Also there are various grades of Satanism active in modern society.

How does this relate to religion, particularly Christianity? In the Bible we see various (2) examples of shamanism in the Old Testament. The witch of Endor is an example. The prophet Elijah was seen as imbued with extraordinary spiritual power and awareness. If one were understood to be a prophet, one would be assumed to psychic; hence when they blindfolded Jesus and struck him, he was ordered to identify the assailant. What this means is that religious faith is dealing with matters which are very largely beyond the remit of scientific investigation. If science is concerned with factual matters which can be observed down a microscope or through a telescope, for instance, enquiries into spiritual matters are not quantifiable in the same way. It is an entirely different level of reality. It is no use the atheists trying to allege that this is all imagination. Space will be given to how Psychical research is attempting to probe these matters on a scientific basis. How far they succeed will be interesting to discover. (3)

Another essential factor that the anthropologists encountered was the element of organisation of society. There is almost always some form of leadership in whatever culture one may encounter. This includes modern 'developed' societies, where a monarch, president, dictator or some other version of 'top of the pyramid' is in charge. But the same is true in virtually every other group, tribal or otherwise. In some cases, the shaman is the chief adviser, but more often there is some form of king or headman ruling the population. That person is very often seen as imbued with spiritual authority, not necessarily in the same way as a shaman, but as someone who is an intermediary with the unseen world of the spirit. It may be necessary to justify one's claim on the throne, in which case one may encounter an interesting myth about how one was mysteriously appointed by the spirits, thus giving one the political authority to reign. A classic example of this would be how Henry 7th managed to trace his ancestry back to King Arthur, but this is by no means the only example. Many of the African kingdoms have some kind of reference to the ancestors to justify the reign of a certain king. Another classic example is how the Japanese Emperor justifies his authority by claiming to be descended from Amaterasu, the Sun goddess. (4)

Given the importance of leadership both on a political and spiritual level, we can see how Jesus was understood to be the ultimate shaman and also king. We notice that the Bible stresses the importance of Jesus being descended from King David, and also from the great patriarchs such as Abraham and Jacob, who also could be seen as spiritually close to God. Also he is seen as psychic, a healer, in control of the weather, able to overwhelm evil spirits. All this indicates a spiritual power not normally seen in human beings. Many of the findings of anthropology simply serve to underpin what is recorded in the Gospels about Jesus, and also the prophets in the Old Testament. This explains why many 'primitive' people instantly relate to and understand material recorded in the Bible. These are aspects that are very largely lost on modern materialistic mankind, but not entirely, since the basic instincts going back to primeval times are still there in our make-up, what Freud would call, the 'id'.

For the benefit of republicans, when we talk about Jesus being a 'king', it is clearly (5) metaphoric. This was the mistake made by the Jews and the Romans, to assume that Jesus was literally a political figure expecting to commandeer an empire. He stated plainly that his kingdom was not of this world. When we apply the term 'king' to Jesus, it implies leadership of the church, and also his status as the ultimate authoritative intermediary between God and mankind. To call Jesus the ultimate shaman is slightly misleading, since the shaman does not converse with the one true God; Jesus did, however. One might term him a 'super-shaman'. Certainly he was dubbed as a prophet, on the same level as Elijah, and a priest, who again is another variant on being an intermediary between God and mankind.

One of the interesting aspects of anthropology is what is termed 'ethnology'. This means the actual process of describing different cultures in their own setting. An example of this would be going to live with a tribe in the jungle and recording their mode of life. It would be fair to say that many such tribes are still living in the 'stone age'. In one sense this is true, in that they do not have iron or steel to work with, unless they are offered such materials from First World peoples. But just doing without modern equipment or gadgetry does not have to mean that these people are mentally or culturally in the stone age. What they are, is, that they are all well-adapted to the conditions under which they live. If they were not well-adapted, they would not survive, or be compelled to migrate in search of better conditions.

There used to be some sort of assumption that there were 'primitive' peoples in the world, in other words, very different from modern, urban, industrialised, Western peoples. It was assumed that these 'primitive' peoples had not evolved to something more sophisticated. We notice the evolutionary assumption in this, which may seem somewhat shaky. When we come to grips with the language situation, the picture looks entirely different. We have to admit that no one knows what sort of language stone age people spoke. The humanoid remains we have so far discovered do not give us any indication of what sounds they could make. But to assume that some people in the world are still speaking like stone age people is a very shaky idea. It would seem that language across the world is so varied and variant in complexity, that one marvels at how they must have occurred. There are some languages which are comparatively simple, such as Italian and French, but also much harder, such as Russian. When we look at some tribal languages, we find also that some are not too difficult to learn, such as Tikopia (New Guinea), but others, such as Nookta (Amerindian)(1) is fiendishly hard. Also, looking at the alphabetic aspect of things, some of them are comparatively easy, such as the Latin alphabet, but others, much more complex, such as Chinese, Japanese and ancient Persian. What this indicates is that high intelligence is not confined to modern 'civilised' humanity. When coming to translate from one language to another, this too is never straightforward. Every language has its own cultural backdrop, which influences its vocabulary. Every language has its own collection of pejorative words, and convenience phrases. Also, every language moves along according to circumstances, with new words being coined, and other words going into obsolescence. It is fair to say that there are no 'primitive' languages in the world. They are all up-to-date, but vary greatly in complexity and mentality.

One wonders why humans speak a vast array of languages. We all know that languages go by groups. One example is how Latin became the basis of French, Italian, Spanish, Portuguese, Romanian, and to some extent, English. We can also see how they mutate from an ancestor language. A classic case of this is how English is drifting away from basic English, to something in America, Canada, Australia and a dozen other countries. But this does not explain how isolated languages, completely different, occur, such as Magyar and Basque, and Finnish, in the same area. If we are to talk of evolution, then we have to admit that the whole thing is far more complicated than we realise. Why is it, for instance, that the Far Eastern languages are completely different from European ones? Does this mean that these peoples have been separated for a very long time? Or does it mean that there is something seriously wrong with the common assumption about Evolution?

Looking at the Biblical approach to the question of languages, we can look at that enigmatic passage in Genesis 11:1-9, the account of the Tower of Babel. It claims that at one time, the whole earth had one language, even if it were 'few words'. That would make sense if it is true that the (7) human race came from one area, originally, in Central Africa. Of course, the writer of Genesis may not have known about different strains of humanity, such as the Neanderthals and the Denisovans.(8) But the passage points out that because people began to become far too clever for their own good, God confused their language and scattered them all over the world. In one sense there is a lot of truth in this, in that given that 'Babel' is ancient Babylon, its language developed into various semitic languages in that area, plus Egyptian, Hittite and Persian. One might even add, Greek. One wonders if, in our day and age, we are not becoming far too clever for our own good, as we delve into matters microscopic, with genes, atoms and photons, and also macroscopic, with adventures into outer space. Are we to expect all this to collapse in disarray one day?

However, the Bible does have its own answer to this question of language. If we look at Acts 2:1-13, we see the disciples receiving the Holy Spirit and being enabled to speak all kinds of languages. This phenomenon is known as 'glossolalia' and is a well-authenticated feature of certain Christian churches in the modern world. What it is saying, in effect, is that even if we all have different languages, there is a basic unity in humanity, in spite of superficial differences.

Each language, or language group, has its own peculiarities in vocabulary, grammar structure and mentality. If we take Hebrew, for instance, there are few adjectives and adverbs, and hardly any abstract nouns. There are only two verb tenses; the past, and the present combined with future. This may sound all very simple, except that it is more complicated in other ways. Verbs come in three modes; ordinary, intensive and causative. To take a simple example, the root DBR means to talk. If we double the B, it intensifies the meaning, so DBBR means to chatter, natter, jabber. If we put an H in front, so HDBR, that means to cause to talk, ie, extract information from. In other words, the complications and subtleties are found in a different mode from English.

Now we look at Classical Greek, which was current at the same time in history. Here we see so many subtleties. There is a whole array of verb tenses, with all the permutations we know of in English. I talk, I was talking, I do talk, I will talk, I would talk, I would have been talking etc. Also, Greek goes in for abstract words and plenty of adjectives. Does this suggest that the Greeks were more intelligent than the Hebrews? No; it just means that they thought on different lines with very different assumptions about God, life and eternity. What we can say is that the classical Greeks must have been every bit as intelligent as us with modern English, if not more so. What we do see is the constant debasement of language in the modern world, with slang, sloppy pronunciation and misuse of vocabulary. One wonders if this is happening to all languages, or is it just us in England and America that are sliding downhill? This would tend to argue in favour of a complete rethink on the matter of evolution, at least, social evolution, which has been a common assumption in anthropology until recent times.

One of the major issues with regard to Anthropology is the question of what do we mean by 'normal'? We, in the modern western world routinely assume that our way of life, expectations and urges are the normal thing, and that others, with a different approach to life, are wrong. It would be difficult to make a list of the 'normal' things in common for all of human nature, but I would venture at least to make a tentative start.

1. A mother's love for her child, and vice versa, the child's love for his mother.
2. The drive to provide food and shelter for oneself and one's dependants.
3. The need to explain the origin of all things, and also where things are heading.
4. The need for some form of security in an unpredictable world.
5. The awareness of deity, the world of the spirit, however one wishes to phrase this.
6. The need to assess one's relationship to other features in the world, such as flora, fauna, history and other communities.
7. Coming to terms with death, funerals, fear and mourning associated with it.

The list could be expanded, but there is enough here to show that we all have basic needs. Our methods for coping with these matters vary greatly from one part of the world to another. But these ideas are enough to explain why humanity constructs so many elaborate myths about Creation, the origins of human kind, and also eschatology. Some of these mythical ideas have a lot in common, but some function on a different basis. Even so, the symbolism employed in mythical thought is much the same the world over. If one were to think that myth is something pertaining to past ages, one would be seriously wrong. Just let us remind ourselves of how modern western thinking has indulged in speculation on such matters as Star Wars, Star Trek, investigations into outer space which are supposed to find interesting other peoples on distant planets. No; us in the 'modern' world are just as fixated on myth as we ever were, and to compound it we have such ideas as Dr. Who and Harry Potter. (9)

Even in such areas as the Sahara Desert, where the climate is much the same all year round, life is still unpredictable. There is the need for security and to assure oneself that one will survive to see another day. This explains why, in the ancient world, sacrifice was accepted as the normal thing. This was supposed to persuade the deity (whose identity would be a matter of opinion) to safeguard one's future. We notice that this presupposes belief in a deity or multiple deities. This mentality is still active in some parts of the world, and is assumed to be normal behaviour, to kill an animal and burn it. That sort of behaviour is now seen as seriously abnormal in modern society. What happens instead is that we pay vast sums of money to insurance companies, hoard up vast sums of money in savings, and most horrific of all, we have a world war in which millions have to be killed. All this is to do with feeling safe. Human nature does not change; it just finds a different permutation on the same theme.

It would be fair to say that every culture has its own ideas on normality. There are some peoples who are very friendly, accepting, helpful, and anyone who is different from that is regarded as abnormal. There are other peoples where it is the opposite; violence, aggressive attitude and an argumentative approach is the norm, and anyone displaying peace, reconciliation and love is regarded as abnormal. We, in our world, have increasingly encouraged such factors as love, consideration, mutual understanding, mercy, giving, caring respect for life, and cheerfulness. This is because of the heavy influence of Christianity, stemming from the New Testament. It would be misleading to say this was unique in world affairs. The Buddhists, with their adherence to the teachings of Siddhartha, have also maintained an attitude to life which is very similar, though not totally the same.

One of the problems with ethnological studies, is that fact that, despite the thorough descriptions made of differing cultures, it is not at all easy to get inside the thinking of other peoples. Obviously, a head-hunter in the South Seas will have very different assumptions in his head as compared with a Cockney living in East London. That of course, is an extreme example. But it must be fair to say that the nationality, community, climate, and other conditions clearly become one's basic assumptions in life, and someone coming from outside, will have difficulties in assessing it. Even so, those seven suggestions offered above, must be ruling factors for all peoples, regardless of circumstances.

How do we settle on something called 'normal'? If one is a Christian (which I aspire to be), then one has to accept the guidance found in the Scriptures. Firstly, there is the norm offered by the Ten Commandments (Exodus 20). The basics of this can be seen underpinning virtually every society in the world, including the atheistic ones that try to ignore the spiritual aspect of human nature. Then we come to the teachings of Jesus, notably in the Sermon on the Mount (Matthew 5ff) and other places. This is a basis of normality for all peoples, regardless of what variant beliefs they have. This is a firm basis for saying that cruelty, bloodshed, nastiness, selfishness and dishonesty are wrong. Such behaviour is abnormal.

It is interesting that while we can subject other cultures to anthropological studies, we can also do the same with the Bible. In the Bible, we see so many fascinating stories stemming from Iron Age Palestine and also the eastern Roman Empire. These accounts, however, are not the (10) normal course of events. Very little of normal life in biblical times is seen in the Scriptures. Why is that? It is because, space being at a premium, the writers concentrated on the unusual and spectacular events. What would be the point of recording humdrum day-to-day matters? For them, that would have been a waste of papyrus. We are seeing the dramatic events such as the Passover, the Sinai encounter, Elijah and Elisha and the Fall of Jerusalem. In the New Testament we are seeing the antics of the Herods and the Roman Procurators, and the early martyrdoms. To discover what 'normality' meant in Biblical times, we have to consult the archaeologists. This will explain why my next chapter is on that very matter. (11)

To take one example from the Bible. We see the appearance of John the Baptist. He was not normal, by anyone's canons of thought. He may have functioned under the tradition of people like Elijah, but such people were very unusual. Then we have Jesus himself, who cannot be regarded as normal, even if one discounts the miracles. What does this tell us? It means that the abnormal has its part to play in the workings of society as much as the normal. It is unfortunately true that people are intolerant of abnormal people, and find them disturbing and threatening. Even so, if there were no such people, we would never learn anything new and life would go on in the same way with no change, excitement or learning process.

The same goes for such people as Siddhartha, Confucius, Mohammed and Lao Tzu. These were religious leaders who made a deep impression on people's thinking, then and now. I am not trying to say that such people were equal, or superior to Jesus, but they did exert a major influence on culture and the future of the world. What anthropology must face up to is, that variety in human nature cannot be avoided, abnormality is not a nuisance and must be balanced against something called normality. Major figures in history and at the present are not just a factor to be coped with, but these are the people that condition the future of mankind.

**Footnotes**

1. An excellent example of Shamanism is found in the Huichol culture of western Mexico, described in chapter14 in Myth, Legend and Symbolism.
2. The witch of Endor, whom Saul consulted with, I Samuel 28:7. This was strictly speaking illegal under Mosaic Law
3. See chapter 17 on Life after Death.
4. Several examples can be seen in Myth, Legend and Symbolism.
5. John 18:36.
6. Nookta, a Wakashan language spoken on an Island off Vancouver.
7. The account of the Tower of Babel is clearly located in Mesopotamia, but so far, no mythical story like it has been found in that area.
8. The Neaderthals lived in Germany and France and are now extinct. The Denisovans lived in central Asia and possibly America; now extinct.
9. Modern mythology is discussed in Myth, Legend and Symbolism.
10. The prophets in the Old Testament, particularly Elijah, strike a chord with shamanistic cultures.
11. See chapter 16 on Archaeology.

# 16

## *Religion and Archaeology*

This field of knowledge can be called the Anthropology of the past. Just as anthropologists investigate the life-styles of peoples in the present day, the archaeologist is probing into the cultures of peoples in the past. This can extend back to the very beginnings of civilisation, but is now extending into recent times, such as the First and Second World Wars. Whereas the Bible and many ancient texts concern themselves with the outstanding events and personalities of the ancient world, archaeology gives us an insight into the less spectacular aspects of ancient life. What was it like to live in a Mediaeval House, or a mud brick house in Egypt? Archeaology is noted for discovering some of the most headline-grabbing finds, such as Tutankhamen's tomb, the Terracotta Army and the Staffordshire Hoard (to name but a few), but such matters tend to obscure the more fascinating aspects of life in the past. What was going on in the hearth and home of ordinary people? In some ways, that is every bit as important as digging up something like a Saxon burial at Sutton Hoo.

It is also worth mentioning that many of the matters referred to in ancient texts, have found corroboration in recent archaeology finds. The classic example of this is the excavation of ancient Hisarlik, now identified as ancient Troy, but there are many others, some of which substantiate (1) matters mentioned in the Bible. An example of that would be the Pool of Bethesda, as described in St.John's gospel. It has now been found, forty feet below ground level in Jerusalem. This goes to (2)show that those who were sceptical about claims made in ancient texts, should be more cautious.

As a discipline, archaeology began as some kind of crude treasure-seeking exploit, which meant that places like Pompeii were just ransacked on the assumption that gold and other valuable artefacts could be found. Since the 18<sup>th</sup> century, a more systematic approach has been developed, which means that more artefacts from the past have been unearthed, and more importantly, information about how people lived and their beliefs have been found. It is now at the point where highly sophisticated technological methods are being employed to assess matters which, years ago, would never have been dreamt of. Also, there is a long way to go. There are archaeological sites that are deliberately being kept undisturbed and secret, pending the development of even more technological advances. It is for this reason that we can now call archaeology a Science. Moreover, it has much relevance to religion; not quite as much as anthropology, but almost. I would say that the chief shortcoming with archaeology is the inability to interpret finds in the light of religious belief, and this is a result of the materialistic mentality of the present. We see things through materialistic-tinted spectacles. Also, we see things through evolution-tinted spectacles.

Another shortcoming with archaeology, though not quite so serious, is the usual mistake made by scientists, namely that of generalising from the specific. It is unusual for a site to be completely excavated. This is because time and money are always at a premium. Normally, a trench is dug, on the assumption that this will reveal a representative sample of the rest of the site. There is a certain amount of validity in this notion, which means that, for instance, if we find a bronze axe in the trench, that the rest of the site can be assumed to be Bronze Age. But the assumption might be completely wrong. Supposing that axe got there by another means, such as an Iron Age man discarding it because it was less useful than an iron axe? There are all kinds of assumptions at work in archaeology, some fairer than others. But the question of interpretation is an important one.

It is one thing to dig down into a spot which is suspected of containing something interesting. Then we find something such as a piece of pottery. The styles in pottery have been a key factor in dating sites and other artefacts. This is less true now, but is still an important indicator. Say the pot is a Greek urn, and appears to be Mycenaean. How do we interpret that? Was it made on the site or was it imported? Does this mean that this site is of the Mycenaean age? Or did that pot arrive later and was just dumped on a rubbish heap because someone did not like it? Or was there a potter that fancied the idea of imitating Mycenaean ware, but in a much later age? Much depends on the context of the find, and also how much the site has been interfered with or corrupted by previous bounty-hunters. To take a recent example; the Staffordshire hoard. This collection of gold and other Saxon ware was found in a field (which must not be disclosed for obvious reasons). One is amazed at the craftsmanship involved. Does this mean it was the property of a king, perhaps a Mercian king? Or had a thief stolen it and buried it to avoid discovery? We can construct all kinds of theories, but since it was found in an open field, with no obvious context, it is anyone's guess as to its significance. What it could indicate is that the Saxons were far richer and artistically advanced than we had ever guessed before. However, the religious significance of it is more difficult to assess. There was one artefact that included a golden cross. Does that imply that the king (?) was a Christian, or that he had stolen it from a king (?) or a bishop (?). The fact that the cross was screwed up might imply something. Was the thief a pagan who despised Christianity? Or was it just a convenient way of compressing the hoard in order to hide it? In general terms, it fits in with our understanding of how the Saxon world was teetering in the brink of forsaking paganism and embracing Christianity. But the implications in it could be manifold. It is all a matter of how one interprets these things.

The most puzzling matter circulates around Stonehenge. Theories abound as to how it was constructed, and why, and at what age. There is no certainty in any of it, except to say that in common with many other stone circles, they have some relevance to observing the heavenly bodies. Archaeological investigation has turned up all kinds of pointers as to the use of Stonehenge, but (3) since they are not able, or allowed to dig up the entire area, generalising about it is always liable to be shaky. We still do not know for certain how the stones were fetched and erected, in spite of all kinds of experiments done to indicate some sort of solution. Stonehenge, along with so many other Neolithic structures, will remain an enigma, unless something turns up to give us more clues. But there is little doubt that such structures were an essential part of religious belief and practice in ancient times. What we lack, is the spiritual insight that ancient people had, that motivated them to produce such amazing structures. They still are in use for religious purposes, since Druidic ceremonies regularly take place at such sites.

One of the big mistakes that has been made in archaeology is to formulate a theory in one's mind and then try to prove it by archaeology. What this means is that whatever one finds, can so easily be interpreted in such a way as to agree with one's preconceived idea. One of the most crass examples of that was when the Third Reich (inspired by Heinrich Himmler) sent out teams of archaeologists to central Asia with the express purpose of 'proving' the validity of their racist doctrines. Also it was pre-digested thought that the Japanese were actually Aryans but the Chinese were not!! This annual mission went on from the mid 1930's right into the War, but needless to say, they were disappointed. This approach does not always have to be wrong. We now have the example of King Richard 3$^{rd}$'s skeleton being found in a Leicester car park. What this does indicate is that common assumptions, and the dramatic claims in Shakespeare, might be taken more seriously than before; Richard did have scoliosis (a crooked back!)

What this means, is that we ought to be careful about easy dogmatisms when dealing with archaeological finds. We should always be open to fresh evidence as it emerges. It is worth pointing out that the recent finds in a cave in South Africa, have discovered two different strains of early (4) humanity, not known before, and the implications of this may take some time to unravel. At the least, it is admitted that many of the dogmatic statements made in textbooks will have to be thought out afresh. We must always maintain an open mind when dealing with finds from the past.

One of the most salient advances in recent years concerns dating methods. Time schemes used to be based largely on pottery styles and also stratigraphy. The latter works on the basis that each era of occupation leaves behind a layer of rubbish, and this builds up like a liquorice allsort, so that the most recent material is at the top and the oldest material next to the bedrock. Even with this, there was no total certainty about absolute dating. There is much guesswork and assumption. Since the 1950's we have seen the advent of radiocarbon 14 dating, which admittedly has been refined up to the present day, but it will only work on bone, wood, fibre, seeds and shell, and will only extend so far back into prehistory. It can of course be subject to fallacies. We take the case of the Turin Shroud, which when tested by carbon 14, resulted in a date in the Middle Ages. But this is almost certainly an illusion; we know that parts of the shroud were repaired by the nuns in the Middle Ages, which means that the testing was done on a later 'patch'. (5)

Along with carbon 14, there are also some highly sophisticated methods now available. There is the radiometric method which will only work on igneous rocks. Also the thermoluminescence method and the optically stimulated luminescence method, which work on burnt flint, ceramics and sediments exposed to sunlight. Also there is the electron spin resonance method which works on tooth enamel, and the uranium series dating method which works on stalagmites and stalactites. All of these ideas are highly ingenious but also have their limitations, not just in terms of calculating times in the past, but also assumptions about the purity of the samples analysed. Even so, it has become much easier to make up a time scheme for ancient civilisations such as Egypt, Mesopotamia, China, the Incas and the Mayans, for instance. At one time, we were heavily dependent on calculating the reigns of kings, such as the Israelite ones and the Pharaohs, but now all this is much clearer.

Another aspect of technological cleverness concerns bone and teeth analysis. It is now possible to calculate what sort of diet a person ate, and also what part of the world he was raised in. One of the most fascinating factors has been to discover that in the ancient world there was far more interchange between peoples who were previously thought to have been isolated. So, for instance, international trade in the Roman Empire was far more extensive than had previously been imagined. This is something that we could have guessed at before, since Herodotus, a Greek historian makes a passing reference to 'the tin islands', in other words, Britain. (6)

Since we now have ways of isolating pollen, in its varieties, it is also possible to identify where an artefact originated, not just geographically but historically. Noteworthy is the fact that pollen relevant to first century Israel has been found on the Turin Shroud. This must go a long way to establishing its authenticity, but also it must make us cautious about the results of Carbon 14. (7)

The future must hold much promise for such dating and locating methods. Doubtless there will be fresh techniques developed in times to come. It may be that many of our preconceived ideas about the ancient world will be turned upside down. It is unwise to cling to dogmatisms in archaeology, that might have to be modified and indeed scrapped altogether.

A prime example of this concerns the discovery of the Neolithic settlement (9 to 8 thousand years ago) in central Turkey, a place called Catalhöyük. The findings there astonished everyone. (8) There were wall paintings and plaster reliefs, sculptures in stone and clay, advanced technology in weaving, woodwork, metallurgy, and obsidian. There were also ideas on architecture and planning, agriculture and stockbreeding, and evidence of trade and import of raw materials. Most notably, there were numerous sanctuaries with evidence of advanced religion, symbolism and mythology. What it indicated was that the new stone age people were (potentially) much more sophisticated and skilled than we had ever imagined before. When we compare this with artefacts from the (9)ancient world, that appear to be beyond explanation, it all seems to appear in a different light. The ancients were not as stupid as some people have imagined. Moreover, I would suggest that in some respects they were cleverer than we are, in proportion to the level of knowledge that they had. In respect of religious faith, it looks very much as though they were more spiritually sensitive than we are now. This is certainly the impression one gains from reading the Bible and other quasi-scriptural materials from the past. It is also the impression that one gains from archaeology; that mythology and religious belief were a much more dominant element in their lives. As a rider to this, it is a fact that the ancient Egyptians did not have a word for 'religion'. This was because there was no distinction between sacred and profane in their way of life. Faith and theology were endemic in all aspects of life. The same would almost certainly be true for ancient peoples all around the world.

One of the most important aspects of archaeology is the unearthing of burials. The most spectacular one in recent years has been the tomb of Tutankhamen. We were all stunned by the magnificence of the grave goods which demonstrated the sophistication of the artistry. This has only recently been matched by the discovery of the Terracotta Army in China, which still has much to show us as excavations continue. The same is true for Pompeii and Herculaneum. What we have to appreciate is that the next world was very real to people. The Egyptians imagined that the next life would be just like this one, which entailed leaving supplies of food and other useful things in the tomb. The effort that went into tomb and pyramid construction gives us an indication of how seriously they took this world and the next. Also, it indicates how much they associated their kings with the gods. Sacral kingship was a dominant factor in the Ancient World, and continued to be so right into the modern world. An example of this would be the Japanese Emperor being descended from Amaterasu, the sun goddess. But in general terms, the coming of Christianity has done much to defuse this idea; the idea that Jesus Christ is the ultimate king, and that all earthly rulers only hold power as an offspin from him has put a limit on the extremes of sacral kingship.

In a way, we need to be glad that the pagans took burial rituals so seriously with their elaborate tombs and grave goods. Because of this, we can learn so much about life in the ancient world. This concerns not just kings and Pharaohs, but also people lower down the social scale. This concerns not just their luxury items, like gold and jewels, but also every-day objects like weapons, clothing, food, and skills in artistry and artisanry. It was the Christians who indicated that such elaborate funeral rites were unnecessary, and that the next world was not just a repetition of this world. The Christians orientated their burials towards the east, feet first, unless one were a priest, in which case, it would be head first.

The relationship between archaeology and religion is at its most acute when we consider the archaeology of Palestine. Clearly, this has a strong relationship with matters mentioned in the Bible; not just the Old Testament historical material, but also the New Testament. It is a fair comment to make, that extensive excavations in that area have unearthed all kinds of material which relate to the religion of the Jewish and early Christian faiths. Nothing has been found which directly contradicts the written material of those times, whether it be of the Bible, or of ancient authors such as Josephus and Herodotus. I shall take a few interesting examples, but there is a wealth of literature available written by such people as Kathleen Kenyon and William Albright.

Although there is direct evidence of Israelite activity in Palestine as they invaded and took possession of the land, much questioning has gone on about the account in Joshua as to how the walls of Jericho fell down. Successive excavations have revealed the great age of Jericho, and its (10) continuing importance down to the time of Jesus. However, the period in question, which is claimed to be the Middle Bronze Age, circa 1500 BC, appears to have disappeared. This can be explained by the Biblical account describing how the town was destroyed and left unoccupied for some time. (11) Practically all the evidence of that period has been eroded away. Even so, collapsed walls have been found at Jericho, but of a different age. How do we interpret this? Does this mean that the Biblical writer was slightly confused about his time sequence? Or does it mean that Kenyon got her dating wrong somehow? At the very least, it indicates that city walls were liable to collapse, and this is understandable, since the accumulation of debris building up behind the walls, would exert a massive pressure on the structure, and anything like an earth tremor would easily push the walls over.

Another important piece of evidence is the Black Obelisk of Shalmaneser 3rd, an Assyrian (12) king contemporary to the monarchy of the Northern Kingdom of Israel. On it, is a graphic depiction of Jehu, the king of Israel, grovelling before Shalmaneser and offering tribute. King Jehu is known to us in the second book of Kings, chapters 10-12, as the fiery but devious reformer who went in for massacres and the destruction of the Baal religion. The Bible makes no mention of his dealings with the Assyrian king. However, gaining support from Assyria is fully consistent with how things worked at that time. With the kingdom of Aram (Syria) causing so much trouble for the northern kingdom, it was normal to make trouble for Aram by appealing to Assyria. The historian, The Deuteronomist, may not have known about Jehu's dealings with Shalmaneser, or possibly did not wish to admit to it. Looking at the Black Obelisk, one wonders how to evaluate this scene. It is not impossible that Jehu enlisted the help of Shalmaneser, but did he really grovel? Is this a piece of exaggeration? Did Jehu really go in person to the king's palace, or is it purely symbolic? Is it propaganda to flatter the Assyrian's ego? Was Shalmaneser like Goebbels, incapable of being accurate with the truth?! We know from other records, that the Assyrians were given to grandiose boasting, which may have been some way off the mark. As with so much in archaeological findings, it is a matter of how one interprets it, and to allow it to become some sort of dogmatism is not very wise. But the importance of this scene from the Black Obelisk, is that this is the first indisputable evidence of the Israelite monarchy and the dating that flows from it.

Another fascinating matter concerns the Pool of Siloam which is mentioned in the second book of Kings and also in the Gospels. This relates to the time of king Hezekiah, when there was the need to bring the water supply into Jerusalem because of the impending siege. Inside the tunnel, there is a complete description, in archaic Hebrew, of how the tunnel was constructed. It was a (13) marvel of civil engineering, since it was carved out from both ends at once, did not go straight, but still met up in the middle. One is amazed at the engineering skill involved! One can visit the tunnel today but entry to it is not recommended. What this means is that matters recorded in the Bible can be taken more seriously than some people have been wont to do.

Coming down to the time of Jesus, there is a wealth of material relevant to Herod the Great. There was a time when people even doubted the existence of that king, but that is all history now. (14) Herod was a prolific builder, and his structures are still to be seen in many places in Palestine. These are mainly palaces, such as Herodium (at Bethlehem) and Masada, but also parts of the Temple that still survive. His masonry can be identified as a particularly cleverly constructed rustica work, so finely fitted together as to avoid the use of mortar, and so close that a pin cannot be inserted into the joints. In addition to this, following advice from ancient documents, archaeologists have recovered fragments of a tomb at Herodium, which they are fairly certain belong to Herod. The coffin, now broken in pieces, has flower designs that were normally reserved for a king. Does this actually prove anything? Not really; again, it is a matter of how one interprets these things. But the balance of probability is in favour of Herod the great builder who held sway just before the life and times of Jesus.

HERODIAN MASONRY                                                    THE BASILINDA

With regard to Jesus himself, it would be difficult to find an archaeological artefact that could be undeniably related to him. However, in the Via Dolorosa, the path we assume Jesus took on the way to the crucifixion, forty feet down below ground level, they have found the limestone floor of the Roman fort (the Antonia) where assumedly Jesus was tormented by the soldiers. On one of the stone seats is inscribed a game called the Basilinda, the game of the king, a sort of board game like Snakes and Ladders. This game is evidenced from other parts of the Roman Empire, as it involved taking a slave, probably an unruly one, tossing a dice and subjecting him to rough-house and even hanging. Does this help us to see the tormenting of Jesus after the trial, in a slightly different light? Does this explain why they dressed him up in purple, like a king? It is all a matter of interpretation, but not certainty. In the final analysis, religion is a matter of faith, as opposed to certainty.

Archaeological findings go a long way to supporting and helping to explain matters appearing in the Bible. There are so many ways that Archaeology casts a slightly different light on many of the matters occurring in the Bible. It helps to explain all sorts of things. The word 'proof' is not really appropriate here, but there is enough in it to make the doubters stop and think. The Bible may be a lot nearer to real history than many people like to assume. In general terms, though, archaeology, as a science, has been highly supportive of religion. This applies very largely to the Bible, but not entirely. We think of the Terracotta Army in China, only recently discovered. What it indicates is the reverence given to the first Chinese Emperor, and also the way in which the human emperor was seen as an earthly copy of the Jade Emperor who was understood to be their equivalent of God Almighty.

One of the fascinating aspects of archaeology in the Middle East in recent years, has been the discovery of many cuneiform texts written on clay tablets and found in various locations in Mesopotamia. Many of these texts contain the creation myths of these ancient Semitic peoples. There is no need to describe them all in detail, since I have discussed them in my previous works, Myth, Legend and Symbolism, and also The Theology of Truth. It would be so convenient if we could say that the writer of early Genesis copied these ideas, but it might just be the other way round. 'Moses' or someone else in the early Hebrew tradition might have provided the inspiration for the Babylonian and Assyrian Myths. The main biblical texts involved are the Creation in Genesis 1, the Garden of Eden in Genesis 2, Noah's Flood in Genesis 6 to 9. What we are seeing is the difference between a polytheistic view of creation and a monotheistic view of it, as well as the appearance of the human race. As with many other artefacts found in Mesopotamia, dating them is always an interesting matter for debate. It is one thing to pin a particular clay tablet down to a date, but that does not really tell us the real age of the story written upon it. It may have been in circulation as folk legend, orally transmitted, for many generations before. What it does tell us is that the early material in the Old Testament fits comfortably with what people in the semitic world were thinking, with their mythological assumptions.

Genesis chapter 1 relates to the myth of Enuma Elish, often called the Babylonian Creation Epic, in which Marduk, the champion god defeats Tiamat, a monster of the deep. The Creation myth from Sippar is a much shorter version. Another myth from Ashur relates to Tiglath Pileser 1st, a contemporary of King David, and may have been written long after the early parts of Genesis had been formulated. In these accounts we see gods depicted in very crude anthropomorphic terms, something that Genesis avoids doing. The Hebrews clearly had a much more spiritual understanding of God.

Genesis chapter 2, The Garden of Eden story is also matched with various pagan texts. The Epic of Sippar relates to this chapter, but more poignantly, the Epic of Gilgamesh. Also the Epic of Atrahasis relates to this. Even if the stories do vary a great deal, the underlying theme is consistently the same. It is the question of life and death, and why we have to die. (15)

Even more famously, the account of Noah's Flood is matched by the Epic of Gilgamesh and to a lesser extent by the Epic of Atrahasis. There are so many details in these accounts that match up with the account in Genesis, that one is forced to wonder if there was direct borrowing between 'Moses' and the Mesopotamian writers. Even so, we have to accept that not all the details match up, and to be fair, the Biblical description is far more real, and probably nearer to the actual events. There is no doubt that Mesopotamia was (and still is) subject to severe flooding, and this again is evidenced from archaeological explorations in that area.

If one were to assume that these early accounts in the Bible are completely mythical, this might be a faulty idea. These accounts do contain actual place names, and names of rivers. Examples of these are, Pishon, Gihon, Euphrates, Tigris, the land of Havilah and the mountains of Ararat. This has encouraged explorers to attempt to locate the Garden of Eden and the remains of Noah's Ark on the mountain. It would seem that in spite of Pishon and Gihon not being known today, the Garden of Eden must have been located somewhere in what we now call Iraq or Saudi Arabia. Mount Ararat is still known to this day, in northern Iraq, but extensive digs have failed to locate anything that would resemble the Ark.

As with all these matters, the word 'proof' is not applicable. What we are looking at is the way in which archaeology casts a slightly different light on material found in the Bible. It is not a matter of deciding who is right or who is wrong. What we are seeing is that the early parts of Genesis fit with the ethos of the second millennium BC in Mesopotamia. It does not matter who wrote which text. The same assumptions and basic elements of faith are patent in all the texts. Also the relationship between the Hebrew and the pagan texts show us how the early impetus for monotheism can be compared with the polytheistic assumptions of their neighbours.

For this reason, it is fair to say that Archaeology has in so many ways helped to substantiate, reinterpret and cast a different light on matters of faith in the Jewish tradition and the Christian too. It is a good example of how science has underpinned religious belief, and has all the appearance of continuing to enrich our understanding of the scriptures. I am quite sure that much more is waiting to be found. It would be possible to fill an entire book with archaeological material which is relevant to the Bible, and there is a wealth of literature on the subject. I have selected just a few examples in order to be economical with space in this book.

The other obvious comment one should make is that new finds are constantly being made not just in this country but anywhere in the world. One can never tell what light it will throw on religion, practice of faith and theology. An open mind on these matters is essential.

**Footnotes**

1. See Ekrem Akurgal, *Ancient Civilizations and Ruins in Turkey.*
2. The Pool of Bethesda, John 5:1ff.
3. A. Thom has made a thorough survey of stone circles and advances all kinds of suggestions about how they are orientated to stars etc. The latest development is the discovery of the same type of stone found in the Marlborough Woods only 14 miles to the north. This means that all the clever theories about how monoliths could have been fetched from the Prescelly Mountains now fall into ashes.
4. The Rising Star cave in South Africa. Naledi, 335,000 years old, allegedly; Sediba 2 million years old, fossil, allegedly.
5. There was a fire in the monastery and the Shroud was damaged. The nuns did a high quality repair, and the carbon 14 test may have actually tested the patchwork as opposed to the original material.
6. Herodotus; Loeb Classical Library.
7. See; Ian Wilson, *The Turin Shroud.*
8. An Introduction to Archaeology.
9. Von Daniken, the Chariots of the Gods, thinks that men from outer space gave early mankind all kinds of ideas.
10. Kathleen Kenyon, *The Archaeology in the Holy Land.*
11. The Book of Joshua describes how the Israelites completely destroyed towns such as Jericho and Ai, and they were left uninhabited for a long time.
12. See Winton Thomas, *Documents from Old Testament Times.*
13. Circa 701 BC. The tunnel was constructed by Hezekiah. 2 Kings 20:20; John 9:7.
14. See Michael Grant, *Herod the Great.*
15. These early epic accounts are discussed in *Myth, Legend and Symbolism.*

# 17

## *Life beyond the grave and Science*

This is an area where belief or disbelief are at their most acute, when dealing with the matter of life after death. Practically every religion in the world has included this aspect in its system of thought. The exception to this would be the Communists and the Humanists, but these are a form of secular, ethical and political faith which tries to eliminate the reality of God. This remains unconvincing to most people, as does the denial of the spiritual aspect of human nature. If we look back into history, it is obvious from the way that tombs and burial customs were carried out, that practically everyone assumed that there was life after death. A study of the Egyptian Book of the Dead shows just how elaborate beliefs and procedures could be on this subject, but the (1) Egyptians were not the only ones to take matters to extremes. The essential question arises; how can this belief have any relationship to science? Can the process of death be subjected to scientific investigation? Or is the world of the spirit above and beyond materialistic analysis? This matter has attracted much attention in the twentieth century, and I would refer the reader to Ian Wilson's book, The After Death Experience. He makes a thorough study of these matters with abundant evidence. He is not the sort of person who would be carried away by every spurious claim. He examines these matters carefully and rationally, and the conclusion is that we cannot avoid the reality that something of us does continue into the next world. I shall not attempt to repeat all of his case studies; a careful selection will be enough. Anyone wishing to go into this matter in more detail, can contact the Society for Psychical Research, which has groups in this country, America and also Russia.(!)(2)

First, we begin with the matter of people seeing ghosts. This is something which has been attested from all parts of the world and going back in history. It would seem that not everyone is capable of seeing a ghost. The reason for this is not clear, but it may be that some people are more spiritually sensitive than others. Of course, this matter raises the emotions greatly, and is a favourite theme for dramatists and novelists. A good example of this would be in Shakespeare's MacBeth, in which the Ghost of Banquo comes to stir up MacBeth's conscience over the murder of Duncan. Clearly this issue finds its target deep in the instincts of mankind, regardless of whether one actually believes in it or not.

The encounter with a ghost, or ghosts, may be in various modes. 84% of them involve the phantom being seen; 37% involve some kind of noise or speech; 18% involve the sensation of a change in temperature; 15% involve being touched in some way, or some kind of 'presence'. It has been recorded that two or more people have seen a ghost at the same time. Other people in the vicinity might not see or hear anything. Many ghosts appear solid as opposed to transparent. Usually, they are wearing clothes, which is helpful for identification and location in history. A ghost might not appear at floor level. He might be standing on a level that was appropriate for him in times past. Sometimes, it might be a whole group of phantoms.

A materialist might attempt to argue against this kind of experience. What if it is just a (3) holographic time-imprint etched into the fabric of the buildings? This is the opinion of Henry Price. He thought that there is was a sort of 'psychic ether' permeating all matter and space. There may be an element of truth in this, since we know that many phantoms have been associated with some kind of tragedy or catastrophic end to their lives. Such a phantom might appear regularly and frighten people in the present day. There are specially trained priests who perform exorcisms to release the tortured soul and clear the site of the haunting.

Personally, I find no difficulty in accepting the reality of ghosts. I used to see a man from the Civil War on my patio, often on a Friday afternoon. I was aware that there had been a minor battle of the Civil War just up the road. When my father came to stay, we both saw the Cavalier together at the same time. I had not told my father about his haunting, and he was not the sort of person to be carried away by this sort of thing. I am quite prepared to accept the reality of ghosts. Seeing is believing, as many a scientist might admit.

Attempts have been made to take a photograph of a ghost. Unfortunately, there are people who have fraudulently managed to obtain such an impression by the trick of double exposure. This sort of prank simply confuses the issue. As far as I know, no convincing picture of a ghost has ever been produced.

One wonders what would be the purpose of an apparition appearing to someone. It may be that the ghost is intending to convey some kind of message or warning to the subject. In my case, the ghost on my patio meant nothing to me whatsoever. I am not aware of any of my ancestors being in the Cavalier Army, or of being involved in a battle next to Bromsgrove. But there seems to be a common theme, in the cases quoted by Wilson, of bereaved people receiving comfort from the unexpected appearance of a dead relative. In other words, the phantom is telling the subject that death is not really death at all; there is life beyond the grave.

The next avenue for discussion concerns the activities of mediums who claim to contact the dead, often in some kind of séance. We assume that this business of raising the dead spirits is related to the matter of ghosts, but it might be a separate issue. This is a case of trying to induce the ghost to make an appearance on some kind of human schedule. This activity clearly relates to Shamanism, as discussed before, and is specifically forbidden in the laws of Moses. Even so, one of the earliest known cases of consulting the dead, comes in the Book of Samuel, where King Saul (4) consults the witch of Endor in the hopes of raising the spirit of the prophet Samuel. A kind of parallel to this is found in the Iliad, where the dead hero Patrocles appears to his friend Achilles, and informs him that he cannot pass into Hades unless his funeral rites are properly enacted.

Since it is only a few select persons who have the ability to raise spirits, or indeed have that spiritual sensitivity to cope with these matters, the whole matter is wide open to fraud and theatrical manipulation. It may be true that certain mediums have succeeded in persuading spirits to come into contact with them, perhaps in the a séance or elsewhere, but can this always be manipulated according to human timetabling? It has become apparent that many séances have been carefully rigged to make it appear that a spirit has arrived, or that the medium knows information about people, making it seem that they are psychic. But does this mean that the whole business is a sham?

The modern version of 'spiritualism' can be traced back to the late 1840's in the small community of Hydesville, New York State. So it hails from America; are we surprised?! The Fox family, in a small, clapboard cottage, became aware of a ghost, and decided to devise a method of communicating with it, by a series of knocks, a kind of code. From this humble beginning, a (5) complete craze swept America and Europe, as séances and spiritual encounters became all the rage. This was in total contradiction of the laws of Moses. But we can see it as a reaction to the materialistic, atheistic mentality engendered by the Evolutionists. Many 'white crows' or 'spirit guides' or 'controls' appeared, too many to list here. But we can briefly cite one, a certain Doris Stokes, of Grantham, Lincolnshire. Because of her remarkable public appearances, on stage, television and radio, she became world famous for her mediumship. Many people were convinced by it. It would seem that she did not need the normal trappings of darkened rooms, fancy (6) paraphernalia and funny noises; she appeared to be perfectly natural. She claimed to have had 'after death' experiences. There may well have been a basic core of genuineness in her psychic utterances, but of course, if one is hoping to convince an audience 'on tap', there is always the temptation to organise things in advance. This was very cleverly done, so as to convince doubters, but it became apparent (to Wilson), that Doris was 'salting' the audience. By this, I mean, that she was offering free tickets for the front row to people from whom she had elicited information in advance.

What do we make of people like Doris Stokes? It may be that there is, or was, a genuine element at the basis of it all, by which I mean, they genuinely can come into contact with the spirits of the dead. However, can this be done predictably, as per some kind of timetable? What if the spirits will not oblige at the right moment? This is where the temptation to fraud is at its most acute. It may be that the medium's prognostications have brought solace to many people who have been bereaved. However, if it is known, or suspected that this is done by some kind of theatrical swindle, it simply throws the whole matter of spiritualism into confusion. All it does is to obscure what might be the genuine core of the matter, namely that it is possible for people in this world to contact those in the next world. Now we see the sense in that law of Moses which prohibits spiritualism.

One seminal incident reported by Doris Stokes in her book, Voices in my Ear, concerns a woman dying in hospital. Stokes observed a wisp of mist coming from the woman's head, and then her spiritual body appearing, face down, above the physical body. As the spiritual body rose higher, it could be seen to be attached by a silver chord, analogous to an umbilical chord. Stokes watched as the spiritual body rose higher and higher and the chord was stretched, and then broke. That was the moment of death. The woman was talking to her husband, Henry, already deceased. The doctor in attendance did not see the chord or the spiritual body. This simply indicates that some people are more spiritually sensitive than others.

There is no reason to deny Stokes' experience in this case. An awareness of this kind of thing was known in Ancient Egypt, as recorded in the Egyptian Book of the Dead. There is an artist's impression of the BA (one's spiritual body) floating above the body of the deceased. The silver chord is not shown, but there have been many instances of people seeing the chord, whether it is a (7) bystander or the deceased himself in the process of dying. If the chord breaks, the soul floats away, but if it does not, the soul comes back into the body and the patient is revived. There are many instances of this recorded in Wilson's book.

One might attempt to explain all this away as some kind of hallucination, but there is more to it than this. Very often the patient is aware of dead relatives in the room and speaks to them. Often, the patient revives and shows knowledge of matters that he could not have known otherwise. A good example of that would be of a woman having an operation. She was face down on the table, but she was floating up in the air to the ceiling. She watched the surgeons working on her back and removing a disk from her spine. Also she noticed the dust on the top of the light fittings. This could not be seen from floor level. (Wilson page 119). Many other such examples have been recorded by Dr. Sabom, one of the chief investigators into this phenomenon. This 'floating above' claim is so consistent and well-attested that there is no reason to deny it. What it indicates is that what is called 'the out-of-the-body' experience is not just an idle tale, but a reality. The silver chord is seen sometimes, but not always.

It becomes even more intriguing. Many have recorded that out of the body, they found themselves in a dark tunnel, leading to a beautiful light. An aura of great peace, joy, happiness was felt. There was a beautiful garden, and a presence. One example was an old man who later was identified as someone's great grandfather. Otherwise, one might encounter a person all in white. One could move at massive speed, go through walls, visit other places and countries and hear beautiful music. All this happens not according to earthly timings but instantly. Then comes the return to the body and a recollection of a fantastic experience which one never forgets.

"When the light appeared, the first thing he said to me was 'what do

you have to show me that you have done with your life?'" Then came
a review of one's life, recalling scenes from early childhood. (Page
143, Wilson).

All this ties in with traditional teachings about heaven and the afterlife. One
could ask, what about Hell? That too is on record, that some, in an out-of-the-
body experience have experienced torment or terrors. This is nowhere near
as common, but is on record. Instead of a heavenly encounter, one plunges
into a totally black void, with a sense of overwhelming proximity of forces of
evil. (Page 161, Wilson). With these reports of heaven and hell, there seems
to be no comment on the subject of good or bad conduct, or merits. One
wonders how or why one encounters the one or the other.

It is interesting that the Koran describes heaven as a beautiful garden. It
also goes into lurid descriptions of hell. These do not seem to surface in the
spiritual experiences so far quoted. A (8) quotation from St. Bede, an Anglo-
Saxon monk who had this kind of encounter.

"I was most reluctant to return to my body, for I was entranced by
the pleasantness and beauty of the place I could see and the company
I saw there. But I did not dare to question my guide." (Wilson, page
150).

How do we evaluate such experiences? Can they just be dismissed as pure
hallucination? If so, how do we explain the patients coming back with
information which they could not otherwise have gleaned? Does this mean
that we are genuinely gaining a glimpse of the next world and the life of the
spirit? Those of a materialistic mentality will find all this most strange and
there is the temptation to laugh it off. I would say that just as there are people
who are tone deaf, and others who have a highly acute sense of musical pitch,
the same is true for spiritual sensitivity. There are those who are capable
of having an awareness of spirits, the after-life, however one terms it. Also
there are those who have no such quality and find the whole matter beyond
their comprehension. The same is true with eyesight; some have highly acute
eyesight, and others are totally blind. I suggest that those who are spiritually
'deaf' or 'blind' need not be quite so critical of those who do have highly
attuned faculties.

Taking this into account, I think we have to admit that something of ourselves does survive death; but exactly what? That is the problem; how to define it. Broadly speaking there are two theories. There is the mechanistic or monist theory. This means that we are merely self-contained machines, which function on physical and chemical processes. Our minds are just finite prisoners of the machine into which they have been placed. Also, there is the interactionist or dualist theory. This proposes that the mind and the body are separate, interacting elements. The 'mind' , the nature of which is not yet determined, is not necessarily contained in the body, and can survive it. The First theory (mechanistic) is the main assumption in scientific circles in our times. It has been the basis of the behaviourist approach to psychology, with such people as Skinner and Watson. This approach assumes that only that which is measurable and observable is to be taken seriously. We notice that the same assumption was held by Heisenberg, the physicist. This idea may satisfy many who are not so acute spiritually, but it does not explain everything. What about these reports of those who have had out-of-the-body experiences and returned to consciousness with information they could not have received from anywhere else? A neuro-surgeon called Penfield, has managed to demonstrate that we all have a stored memory of everything in our past lives. This reminds us of the saying that when someone is in acute fear of death, their whole lives 'flash before them'. What this indicates is that something of our mind can function regardless of our physical state, and it is not conditioned by some sort of time regime. Some of them can come back from a lengthy coma, but recite all kinds of encounters that (from our earthly point of view) would have taken much greater time. Are we seeing the paradoxical relationship between history and eternity?

The implications in this are various. One of them is of acute relevance to the factor of prophecy. If one can store memories of the past in one's mind, why not store memories of the future? (If it is true that past and future have no meaning in eternity?) Once one begins to take the phenomenon of prophecy seriously, it then involves taking predestination as a reality. That, of course, is going against modern liberalistic assumptions. Free will is very much the doctrine of today, but is it enough?

Another aspect of 'mind' being a separate, possibly free, element of our make-up, is the question of reincarnation. If we are to take these out-of-the-body experiences seriously, what about taking the claims made by some Hindus that they can recall factors from a previous life? This does not have to mean that everybody goes from one life to another in an endless series, but it might (9) suggest that there is an element of truth in the doctrine of 'karma'. At least, one cannot just dismiss the matter just because it cannot be subjected to independent analysis in a laboratory.

One can fairly say that this whole matter does not fit comfortably with the rationality of this world. This is an elevated way of saying that science cannot really cope with spiritual matters. But science is really dealing with the logic of this world. We have already seen that at the quantum level, there is some other system of rationality in operation. All those tiny entities do not function in ways which we can comfortably predict. The same may be true of matters out in deep space; in all appearance, there may be another system of logic at work. What this means is that we need a certain degree of humility when encountering these matters. Easy dogmatisms are not appropriate, and it is best just to accept what evidence has been found, and be economical with clever theories which attempt to cope with these matters.

The suggestion that science cannot really cope with these matters comes out strongly with regard to experiments done on the subject of ESP (extra sensory perception). This is an area which, unlike dealing with ghosts and out-of-the-body experiences, could, in theory be quantified with (10) experimentation under controlled conditions. The history of this goes back about a century, with the work of Joseph Rhine, who in 1922 devised an experiment using five different cards, each with a different design on them. Those involved in the experiment were supposed to inform each other, by 'thought-transference', which card had been selected. He claimed the results provided very strong evidence for ESP. Unfortunately, even if Rhine himself was sincere, some of his co-workers were found not to be of such quality; in other words, there was some cheating going on. In addition to that, his method was seen to involve various methodological faults. Other researchers were not able to replicate his results; that is an important aspect of science, that of any experiment being capable of obtaining the same result by someone else using the same method.

However, in 1994 a new initiative in ESP research came on the stage with the experiments done by Chuck Honorton. The key difference in his approach was to have the subjects in a totally relaxed state. Honorton devised the 'ganzfeld' procedure which entailed the removal of all (11) distractions, and via headphones is given the sound of the sea in his ears. This does not entail guessing at cards; it is a video of something, in fact, anything, and the subject is completely free to offer guesses as to what it was. This method seemed at first to be promising. It was claimed that the method showed strong evidence in favour of ESP. But like all these schemes, it was heavily criticised and seen as not conclusive. One interesting factor that Honorton found was that a subject who was artistically creative, or who had done ESP experiments before, or who had practiced methods of meditation, did better than others.

Various experiments continue to be tried, but it has to be admitted that the results are sometimes encouraging and sometimes not. It is by no means proven, by psychoanalytic tests, that ESP is a reality. It may be in the future, but as yet, there is no indisputable evidence in favour of it. Even if ESP is a reality, its relationship to ghosts, and out-of-the-body experiences is not obvious. It may be a quality of the human mind which is entirely normal but as yet not clarified or quantified. It does not tell us whether there is life after death or not. At the moment we see that clever people, sometimes genuine and sometimes fraudulent, are capable of making it into fascinating theatre and clever stunts, but nothing more.

Another issue which has become entangled with the paranormal, is the matter of UFO's. I am not quite sure why this has to be connected with life after death or the world of the spirit, but I sense that many people seem to confuse the two issues. The history of UFO's goes back at the very least to the early 1940's, when British and American bomber crews over Germany caught sight of what they called 'foo-fighters'. There seemed to be no rational explanation for them. Theories (12) abound as to how the Germans had managed to produce this effect, and it is strongly suspected that the technique (whatever it was) went to America along with all that expertise with rockets. Since the War, during the late 20th century, there have been numerous claimed sightings of such things as flying saucers and strange lights in the night sky. I do not propose to delve into these matters too deeply, since I think that, firstly, they have nothing to do with the world of the spirit, and secondly, they are terrestrial, in that they are some sort of gadget being tested by the military. They certainly have nothing to do with aliens from far away planets; if they are, why have the men in the space stations not seen them coming in?

Much research has been done on this subject in the last few decades, and all manner of theories have been dreamt up, both psychological and 'factual'. Unfortunately, when such alleged encounters occur, there is no scientific team on hand to subject the matter to independent rationality. All this is not helped by such films as E.T., in which a funny little man arrived from a distant planet and was hidden by three children. There are people who will take this sort of thing as the literal truth, and that does confuse the issue. It is wonderful entertainment and as some sort of analysis of human nature, highly instructive; but nothing more. If there were such things as these aliens, they would be just as physical as we ourselves. No one is suggesting they are angels, or gods or even less, devils! But the interesting thing about this craze for aliens, is that it is assumed that they are at a higher level of evolution compared with us earthlings. I do find that interesting that evolution has managed to work its way into this sort of fantasy, along with so many other things.

Returning to the factor of 'thought travel' or ESP, it is easy to conclude that this is not supported by scientific testing, but there may still be some element of truth in it. It might not be quite the same as the mind leaving the body, but might be of some relevance to the matter. Why is it that two individuals can have the same thought at the same time, but be many miles apart? Why is it that identical twins, reared apart, and not knowing of each other's existence, can be so similar in thoughts and behaviour? Dr. Tom Bouchard has assembled much in the way of case histories of separated twins, how they had so many characteristics in common. This is not just facial similarity, but all manner of other aspects in their make-up. We would now say this was related to their DNA being virtually the same, but it goes further than that. Wilson terms it as some kind of 'radio-type transmission' between two people. This is what the early experiments on ESP were trying to establish, but not very successfully. This does not have to be twins or two people related in some other way. To quote; (Wilson, page 179).

"It seems to indicate, that what we call ourselves, or 'us' really is something rather more than just the finite assemblage of physics, chemistry and genetics that the mechanists would have us believe.... something that arguably survives beyond physical death."

This is dealing with matters which are, at present, beyond the reach of science as we know it today. However, Penfield says, to quote, (Wilson, page 82).

"When the nature of the energy that activates the mind is discovered... the time may yet come when scientists will be able to make a valid approach to a study of the nature of a spirit other than that of man."

This must raise the question of the physics of the non-physical. Does that sound like a contradiction in terms? But we have come across strange paradoxes before, and this may be yet another one.

What happens when a machine, such as a clock, responds to the passing of its owner? Various examples have been noted of someone's clock stopping or doing something strange at the moment of death of its owner. This is not confined to clocks. Technical failures or malfunctionings in other types of machinery have been noted. This phenomenon is termed 'psychokenesis'. It reminds us of the antics of one Yuri Geller who made quite an impression on the public some years ago. It may indicate some kind of unknown force of the mind that can influence physical machines. In our own times, such matters are only just beginning to be taken seriously. It puts a large question mark against the materialistic and atheistic assumptions of twentieth century science.

I conclude with a personal comment on these matters. In my experience I have had a taste of nearly all of these phenomena listed above. I have to be honest with myself; I have no doubt that there is life beyond the grave and another, glorious existence waiting for (most of) us. How this works, the relationship between the physical and the spiritual, is beyond me, and anyone else to quantify, at least at the moment. It may be that in future times, scientific methods will improve to such an extent that the spiritual may be assessed with proper observation, but we have not reached that point as yet. It is rather like trying to prove the existence of God. Proof is not really the right word; intuition, yes, certainty, no, at least, not yet.

However, it is possible to say that this area of reality is, or should be, giving the materialists something to think about. If the scientists, mostly psychologists, can embark on experimentation in these matters, it indicates that somewhere in the scientific kingdom, there are questions being asked. One day, we might find some interesting answers to these matters.

### Footnotes

1. The Egyptian Book of the Dead is reviewed in *The Theology of Truth*.
2. Kensington.
3. Mentioned in Ian Wilson, *The After Death Experience*.
4. Exodus 22:18, Leviticus 20:27.
5. As described in Ian Wilson, *The After Death Experience*.
6. Wilson goes into some detail about Doris Stokes.
7. The silver chord is attested by many who have had this kind of experience.

8.  The Koran goes into much detail about heaven and hell.
9.  The Hindu doctrine of Karma is about reincarnation; one goes from one life to another, hoping to gain 'promotion'.
10. Sometimes such stunts as thought transference appear on the television; one is left wondering whether it was nothing more than a stunt.
11. 'Ganzfeld' literally means 'complete field.'
12. The whole matter of UFO's and flying saucers is discussed in *Myth, Legend and Symbolism*, page 267.

# 18

## *Pseudo Science and Pseudo Religion*

Both areas of knowledge are quite liable to be encumbered with mistaken ideas, hoaxes and downright lies. For many of us, it is not easy to tell the genuine from the nonsense, or indeed something that holds a partial truth but with elements in it that are mistaken. A few simple examples will elucidate these remarks.

In 1797 a creature called a duckbill platypus was discovered in Australia. Because it was so weird it was assumed, in this country, to be a hoax. But of course, with more sightings of them and more witnesses, it had to be admitted that the creature was real.

In 1832 someone called Barnum presented us with a creature called the Fiji mermaid. It had the head of a monkey and the tail of a fish. Eventually it was found to be a hoax, but people were taken in by it at the start.

In 1702 someone called Charlton claimed to have found a new variety of butterfly, which he called a brimstone. Eventually it was shown to be a fake.

The most famous fraud in science has been the Piltdown Man, which was 'discovered' by Charles Dawson and Martin Hinton. It was a human skull with an ape jaw, which was supposed to be an example of the transition between monkeys and humans, according to the evolutionary scheme. This was in 1912, but it took 40 years for someone to test the specimen and realise that it was a fraud. This was not the only swindle that Dawson perpetrated.

Another famous and emotive question surrounds the Loch Ness Monster. There have been numerous 'sightings' of this alleged creature, and so-called photographic evidence. There is the strong suspicion that this is just another hoax; however, there is no absolute certainty about it. The real certainty is that it is helpful for the tourist trade in Scotland.

222

Photographic evidence might not always be quite what it seems. In 1835, John Herschel showed pictures of the moon, with bisons, unicorns, trees, oceans all to be found there. We do not know how many people were taken in by this, but it is thought he did it just for fun. In the end, we discovered for certain that this was just a hoax.

In 1957, Richard Dimbleby did a programme showing how the spaghetti grew on trees in Italy. It all sounded so convincing, until one took a glance at the calendar; it was April 1st! Another April Fool's trick was played by Patrick Moore on Radio 2. He alleged that all the planets were going to be in alignment and this would cancel out the gravity of the earth, and produce weightlessness. This may seem all very amusing, but can also cause trouble. In 1938, Orson Wells produced a radio programme called War of the Worlds, in which it was alleged that there would be a gas attack raid from Mars. It caused panic in the USA. I think the British saw the thing in more moderate terms.

Of course, the most famous trick with a camera has been the Cottingley Fairies. Elsie Wright and Frances Griffiths, in the 1920's claimed to have taken pictures of fairies in their garden. Many years later, in their old age, they admitted that they had contrived the pictures by the trick of double exposure. However, they still maintained that the first picture, which actually does look slightly different from the others, was not a hoax.

One could evince many other hoaxes or non-hoaxes of this type. One wonders what the motive could have been to attempt to deceive people. Various motives have been suggested. One, could be just to be mischievous and tease people. That would take care of the spaghetti hoax. Another could be to get money out of people. Another could be for revenge. Another could be to convince people of some kind of theory that one had convinced oneself was absolutely true; that would account for the Piltdown swindle. What it means is that we have to be very careful about stunning claims made by what appears to be clever people. These claims ought to be tested and the motive behind them given some assessment.

These examples can be matched from the world of religion. In New Testament times, (1) someone called Simon Magus set out to 'prove' to the public that he was some kind of divinity. He had a tower built and a mechanism which required a slave to turn a handle. Simon dressed up as an angel, put on a harness, swung himself out over the edge of the tower, and as the slave turned the handle it gave all the appearance of an angel flapping his wings and flying round the tower. It was all very impressive and doubtless many people were deceived by it. Unfortunately one day, the mechanism got stuck and he was left jerking about in mid-air. This just goes to show that stunts may work for a time but eventually come unstuck.

Another stunt man was Bar Kochba in 135 AD, who started the last Jewish revolt against the Romans. There had been various uprisings brought about by false Messiahs, and in fact, they still keep appearing to this day. Bar Kochba used to put straw in his mouth and set light to it, giving the impression that he was breathing fire. "With the breath of his mouth he will slay the wicked" was probably the underlying thought here. But it all went wrong when the Romans overwhelmed his band of hope. (2)

Another 'Messiah' appeared in 1844, a Mahdi relevant to the Moslem Faith. This was Sayyid Ali Muhammad Shirazi, who claimed to be in receipt of divine revelations. He was followed by (3) Baha'u'llah, which means 'the Glory of God'. His real name was Mirza Husayn 'Ali Nuri, and he was the true founder of the Baha'i faith. In spite of all these elaborate claims, it remained unconvincing to other religionists, as well as the Moslems themselves. The Baha'is continue as a sort of offshoot from Islam, but have not made the impression on world religions that they thought they ought to have. In general terms, we should treat with extreme caution any magnificent claims made by would-be Messiahs. Almost always they turn out to be frauds of one kind or another.

Another example of trickery concerns the production of the Book of Mormon. Joseph Smith claimed that brass, (or was it golden), sheets came down from heaven, inscribed in a strange (4) language, and he was the only person who could translate them, since he was given a special pair of spectacles. No one else was allowed to examine the sheets or analyse the language inscribed on them. The sheets went back up into heaven. An examination of the Book of Mormon reveals that Joseph (or was it the angel) could not have been very intelligent, since there are numerous anachronisms in the text. Clearly it is a forgery, at least as far as I am concerned. The Mormons, however, regard it as sacred scripture on the same level as the Bible. This is not to say that the Book of Mormon is worthless in theological terms. It does contain a few worthwhile factors. However, one is concerned at the racial prejudice included in the book, which is clearly Joseph Smith's personal bias, and is clearly contrary to the spirit of the Christian Gospels.

One of the most prevalent swindles perpetrated in the Christian era is over the matter of indulgences. In the late mediaeval times, it was common for pardoners and others to sell bits of paper which were alleged to remit one's time spent in purgatory. How many people were taken in by this would be difficult to say, but it all came to a head when Martin Luther had the courage to speak out against the various abuses in the western church, one of which was the idea that one could buy one's way out trouble in the next world. This confrontation precipitated the 16th century Reformation, which is only now, in our times, coming to a conclusion. (5)

Looking at the Hindu frame of thought, they had (and still do have) a system of caste, which meant that social stratification of society was rigidly enforced. If one were an outcaste, one had no hope of improving one's lot. The way to achieve social mobility was to accrue so much merit that one would be reborn into a higher caste, and eventually, after trying very hard, one would arrive at the top and possibly reach Nirvana. It was the influence of Christianity that led to the abolition of the outcaste status, and other cruelties such as the practice of suttee. (6)

But the most disgraceful and hypocritical manipulation of people's religious impulses must be the theatrical séances produced by so-called mediums. I will cite one or two examples, but the matter has already been discussed in chapter 17. There was a certain Mr. William Eglinton who claimed to receive 'spirit' messages on a special slate. He was exposed and it was shown to be merely a clever conjuring trick. There was a Mr. G.H.Moss who claimed to be able to make 'spirit' photographs of people who had died, and appeared in a ghostly fashion with living relatives. He was exposed when someone showed how Moss had doctored the photographic plates. A Mr. William Roy managed to produce 'spirit voices' of the dead. He was caught out when it was found that he had an accomplice who rifled peoples' coat pockets before the show and then relayed the (7) information via a tiny radio receiver into Roy's ear. This all goes to show that any spiritualistic session of this kind ought to be treated with extreme caution. I am not saying that there are no genuine mediums; people who are particularly sensitive to the world of the spirit. But to falsify this matter is inexcusable. According to the Laws of Moses, no one ought to be indulging in this kind of behaviour, and any responsible minister of religion, belonging to the mainstream churches, will strongly advise against it.

We now come to consider aspects of science that are not a deliberate attempt at deceiving the public. This may be, for instance, a trend in science which is genuinely and sincerely believed in, and yet, in the course of more research, turns out to be a big mistake. We are now on the ground of grey areas, by which I mean, that there may be an element of truth in the theory, but in general terms it might be a big mistake. The use of medicinal leeches, which has been going on for centuries, and is now out of favour, is a case in point. One wonders if there was some benefit in the procedure, otherwise doctors would have given up on it back in Roman times. But to overdo it and assume it will cure every problem, is a fallacy. A case in point is Princess Charlotte who might have acceded to the throne of Britain if she had not been virtually bled to death. Even so, I understand that medicinal leeching is now being tried again for certain ailments. (8)

Many people may not have heard of Phrenology. This theory, devised by Francis Gall, was all the rage in the 19th century. It meant that one's personality and tendencies could be determined by studying the bumps on one's skull. This may seem absurd by today's standards, but the idea was (9) actually used on the developing field of criminology. This idea is now discounted by all scientists as nonsense, but we must realise that in its day, it was regarded as cutting-edge science, and in America it was regarded as the truth. Is there a lesson here for us to learn; that the latest clever idea coming from an expert might actually be total rubbish?! But there was no doubting the sincerity of these experts, and also no doubting the unfairness for people who were dubbed as having criminal tendencies.

Following on from this, we consider the theory of Eugenics. This was begun by Francis Galton, and involved the identification of those who are deemed as 'unfit' to breed. It was an idea that swept America in the early 20th century, and had a strong influence in Europe, not forgetting Britain. This was mainly an attempt at reducing the number of 'imbeciles' by segregating them from society into special institutions. Sterilization was also used, sometimes without the consent of the patient. It was a theory which found much favour with the Nazi's, who took the matter further and simply murdered anyone who was not deemed fit to live. This, in time, included the Jews and any other minority group that did not fit in with the Nordic/Aryan ideal. The methods of diagnosis were (from our point of view) truly bizarre. Measuring the distance between one's eyes and assessing the shape of one's nose were among the methods. It has now been dubbed as 'science's greatest scandal', but at the time, it was thought to be plain common sense and the rational thing to do. There are still countries that work on this idea, although not going to the extremes that were seen in the early 20th century.

An earlier craze would be Mesmerism, a method of healing devised by Franz Mesmer. He believed that we all, including fauna and flora, have some kind of magnetic fluid in us, and this can be used to induce a kind of hypnotic state. It is not done by words, but by gestures and staring, with the mesmeriser inducing an unconscious state in the patient. This idea must have had some merit, since it was claimed to relieve pain in some patients. It was a precursor of hypnotism, a technique which does not involve animal magnetism, but is effective in rendering a patient unconscious. Needless to say, such methods may have beneficial effects on certain patients that are highly suggestible. Such techniques can also be abused quite seriously. It is interesting to note that hypnotism is just beginning to come back into favour, though mesmerism, in its original form, is quite out of favour. (10)

All this goes to show that strange ideas come into favour and fall from favour. When we look at the methods in use nowadays, and the scientific theories that are current, how are we to know whether it is not some cranky idea, or a sound theory? Doubtless we shall be told that a certain idea has evidence to support it, but what do you mean by evidence? Doubtless all these strange ideas were taken as the cutting-edge of science in their day. A recent one must be the electric shock treatment that was popular in mental hospitals late in the 20th century. One could allow that it was beneficial for some patients, but that does not have to mean that everyone with mental problems would have to be cured by this technique. Thankfully, electric shock treatment is largely out of favour, and I understand it is seldom used nowadays.

A system of thought which attempts to splice religion in with science is the movement called 'Christian Science', a late 19th century craze instigated by Mary Baker Eddy in the USA. Baker claimed that all medicines and doctors are a lot of nonsense. I have gone into details about this movement in The Theology of Truth. At one time it was hailed as a fantastic new idea for coping with illness; one simply had to ignore it and it would go away! Now of course, there is just a sliver of truth in this, that mind over matter does actually work in some cases. But to imagine that some serious infection like smallpox or corona virus, or indeed a broken limb, can be controlled by just pretending it is non-existent, is absurd. If it means that a serious infection can be allowed to go out of control, that is wicked. Christian Science has been dubbed as neither Christian nor scientific. Even so, it still persists in small groups to this day. (11)

It would be easy to list many pseudo-scientific claims and also pseudo-religious claims, but this is not necessary. It is more to the point to offer some pointers as to how to avoid being carried away by some religious or scientific idea which has all the appearance of being a wonderful new idea. We can start with the essentials of sound scientific thought.

Science is principally concerned with the physical world and attempting to explain, analyse and discover laws of nature. As Heisenberg rightly stated, we should be concerned with observable matters, rather than just speculating and applying guesswork. Any experiment which results in an interesting finding, ought to be repeatable by someone else, and moreover, every experiment ought to be compared with the results from a control experiment. If this is not done, the results might be meaningless. When it goes further than this and scientists begin to draw ethical and political implications from their work, then is the time to apply great caution. It is inevitable that science, which is operating on one level of truth, somehow gets involved in other areas of truth, such as philosophy, ethics and theology. All areas of knowledge are interlinked and interrelated in many interesting ways. But to confuse science with other areas of knowledge is not very wise, and has, in the past resulted in all kinds of confusion and misuse. I would say that there has to be a limit on scientific experimentation. Anything that involves cruelty to either humans or animals should only be done under the closest of scrutiny, if at all. Anything that involves consequences over which we are likely to lose control, making problems for future generations, ought also be heavily controlled and scrutinised. Ethics and religious principles must have their say.

Religion, which is backed up by theology, works on an entirely different level of reality. It is not about experimenting in order to discover the laws of Nature. It is more likely just assuming that there are laws of Nature as given, and as reflected in the many ethical law codes in use. Whether one's religion is based on one God, many gods, or no God at all, we need a few basic pointers as to the validity of any given creed. Any doctrine that advocates violence, cruelty, exploitation, racial discrimination, destruction of property, murder, family break-up and intolerance ought to be viewed with the greatest of suspicion. Obviously, there is a time and place for everything, according to circumstances, but in general, the vast majority of people in this world are desperately hoping to achieve world peace and cooperation between nations. This cuts across all religions and secular faiths, and one would hope involves the scientific community. We would all like to have freedom of religion; after all, that was one of the reasons for fighting the Second World War, but again, as with Science, there has to be an ethical limit on religious practices.

It is a regrettable fact that most ISMs have gone through some sort of violent phase at some point in their history. It is easy to pass judgement on these matters based on our circumstances today. But I would refer everyone to the carpenter from Nazareth, who made a point of helping people, healing them, feeding them and giving himself entirely for the benefit of the human race. He refused to become involved in violence, even if the temptation was strong to do so. He refused to grasp at political power and proclaimed himself as a 'servant' as opposed to a master. I am not trying to say that other religions do not have such a policy; many believers of different traditions would agree with this, even if they baulk at actually making a commitment to Christianity. But I would say that those who are genuinely the children of God, have this mentality of humility and service in their hearts. Moreover, there is a basis of unity and purpose between all those who espouse these values.

I shall doubtless be criticised for being biased in favour of Christianity. I make no apology for this; at least, I am open with the readership, in that I am telling you my bias. That does not mean I am opposed to people of other faiths; I am on good terms with people of many different faiths, and have found that I can work with them, on the ethical basis as outlined above. Fundamentally, this ethical basis rests on the Ten Commandments, and the way in which Jesus, in the Sermon on the Mount, brings them all to fulfilment.

There will be many who would claim to respect this ethical basis of life, but not necessarily believe in gods, or one God. I would say that this is not enough. Any law code or ethical standpoint has to have some form of backing, or authority behind it. That backing might be a collection of laws enacted by one's government, but as we know, governments have their failings too. Far more effective is the understanding that justice, decent behaviour and caring are supported by a spiritual authority, whatever god it is that one assumes to rule the situation, or by whatever name one calls one's god. I am now assuming that God does not have any failings; there has to be some kind of benchmark of perfection somewhere otherwise life becomes meaningless. (12)

## Footnotes

1.  Simon Magus, described in J. Stevenson, *A New Eusebius*.
2.  Bar Kochba, is described in Yigael Yadin, *Bar Kochba*, It is Jerome who claims that Bar Kochba stuck lighted straws in his mouth.
3.  The Kitab-i-Aqdas the holy book of the Baha'is is described in *The Theology of Truth*; the beliefs of the Baha'is.
4.  The Book of Mormon is described in *The Theology of Truth*.
5.  Martin Luther's Ninety five theses are described in James Atkinson, *Martin Luther and the Birth of Protestantism*.
6.  Suttee was when a widow was expected to climb on to her husband's funeral pyre.
7.  Ian Wilson, *The After Death Experience*.
8.  Lytton Strachey, in Queen Victoria describes this in chapter 1.
9.  Phrenology is described in Kaufman and Kaufman, *Pseudoscience*.
10. Mesmerism is also described in Kaufman and Kaufman.
11. Mary Baker Eddy's ideas are reviewed in *The Theology of Truth*.
12. This brings us back to the Moral Theory for the existence of God, as discussed in chapter 12.

# 19

## *Miracles and Science*

Anyone of an atheistic mind, or rational or inclined to doubt, will find the matter of miracles a problem. The matter is confused nowadays by the careless use of the word 'miracle'. Every time a baby is born, people see it as a miracle. The experience of the Dunkirk evacuation has been dubbed a miracle. The Germans had a similar experience when the Russians were poised to drive across the river Oder in January 1945; the river unfroze just at the right moment. In this discussion, when we talk of a miracle, we are talking about the things described in the four Gospels, first and foremost, and going on from there, in the Acts of the Apostles and the Apocryphal Gospels. These are mainly of two kinds; the healing miracles and the natural world miracles. All of them appear, at least on the surface to go against what we normally expect in day to day living, and indeed the scientific approach to life.

Is it possible to accept the miracles as described in the Gospels and yet take a rational view of life? I believe it is; I know many people cannot cope with it, but I have reason to accept what the Gospels say. I know there are people who will accept bits of the Gospels which happen to suit their preconceived ideas, but that is not good enough. Either you accept the witness of the Gospels, which has all the appearance of eye-witness material, or you fail to accept it.

Taking a look at the way the miracles of Jesus are recorded, we see two distinct methods at work. The Synoptic Gospels have queues of people chasing Jesus around, in the hopes of being curing of their ailments, and he becomes massively tired and has to escape to lonely places to recover his strength. With St. John, however, he has selected five highly significant miracles that he describes as 'signs'. He does not have endless queues of people waiting to be healed. This gives us the indication that the miracles are being performed for a purpose; not just to relieve people of their illnesses, but also to show us the true nature of Jesus. Let us briefly look at each one.

The first one is the changing of the water into wine, John 2:1-12. This has traditionally been interpreted as the contrast between the Old and the New Testament. God has reserved the best 'wine', ie. the higher quality covenant for later. It indicates that the Old Covenant of Moses has been superseded. The comment from St. John is 'and his disciples believed in him.' The steward of the feast was baffled; the servants were not. This is typical of Jesus, in that he did not make a grand spectacle of his miracles, but it was covert, recondite and not in the public gaze. This can be called a natural world miracle, as opposed to a healing miracle.

The second one is the paralytic at the Pool of Bethesda. We notice that this is related to a feast day and also the Sabbath. The result was that the Jewish strict legalists were infuriated that it had been done on the Sabbath. Also the paralytic at first did not even realise that this was Jesus; only later did he come to realise it. We can see the agenda here; that the strict legalism of Judaism is not to be taken so seriously. The New Testament is about healing, freedom and celebration.

The third one is the Feeding of the Five Thousand in John 6:1-14, this time associated with the Feast of the Passover. This is highly appropriate, as the suggestion is that Jesus brings in the new Passover; just as the Old Covenant was a result of the Passover in Exodus, so the New Covenant is associated with the coming of the Messiah. We notice that there were 5000 men in attendance, which reminds us of the Pentateuch, the old Laws of Moses. Also twelve baskets of food were left over, which reminds us of the twelve tribes of Israel. It is highly significant that this miracle, which can be call a natural world miracle, is recorded in all four Gospels, and in fact five times over, since St. Mark has two accounts very much the same. This is the only miracle that is in common for all four Gospels. Why is this? It is surely their way of giving heavy emphasis to this event. St. John goes on to unravel the significance of it. Jesus is 'the bread of life' (6:35). The implication in this is that he is the one who sustains the whole of life, not just for the people of Israel, but for all people. This ties in with the LOGOS doctrine in Chapter 1, where we see that it is Jesus, the Word of God, that brings everything into existence, and sustains everything.

The fourth one concerns the blind man who was also healed on a Sabbath. This ties in with the saying 'I am the light of the world' (8:1). Again, the first stirrings of Creation are brought to mind, as in Genesis 1 God created the light, which was not the same as the Sun and the Moon. We could call it 'enlightenment' or 'discernment' or 'true understanding', and it raises up the issue of whether one believes or not (9:37).

The fifth one is the Raising of Lazarus from the dead in John 11:17-44. Again, the connection with a Jewish feast, this time, the Passover again, is blatant (11:55). But that iconic claim by Jesus goes with the miracle, 'I am the Resurrection and the Life.' (11:25). This indicates that Jesus is not just the life that sustains the whole world, but also the new life which means that death is just a mere detail; that he has provided another more wonderful life for us all at the end of this life. This ties in with what we have said in Chapter 17.

We stop at five significant miracles. The opportunity to make it six is left out by John. As Peter cuts of Malchus' ear (18:10), there is no attempt from Jesus at healing this injury. See Luke 22:51. The symbolism of the Five miracles, or signs seems important, as reflecting the Five books of the Laws of Moses. Always, we have the theme of belief in contrast to the denial and failure of belief; a theme which dominates St. John's Gospel. This issue is just as decisive nowadays as it was then. Jesus attracts those who place their trust in him; also he repels those who cannot make any sense of it.

Up to this point, a doubter or rationalist will still be saying, "why should I believe in miracles?" A fair question, but if we take a look at some of those miracles described in the Synoptics, more light can be shone on this issue. What we must remember is that St. John's Gospel is first and foremost a theological document and is in no way any attempt at a scientific analysis. He is talking on a completely different level of truth as compared with Science.

I shall not attempt to discuss all of the miracles in Matthew, Mark and Luke. Many of them are a repeat scenario, since we understand that Mark was copied by the other two.

St. Mark does what St. John appears not to do; he has Jesus casting out demons. This reflects the age-old belief that sickness is the result of some kind of evil spirit invading one. In this we see that Jesus is also a child of his age, in that he assumes the same idea, and 'casts out' the demons. In 1:21-34, we have the contrast between someone who is mentally deranged in the synagogue and Peter's mother-in-law, who is sick with a fever, both being

233

healed. This indicates that Jesus has authority over physical matters in this world, and also spiritual problems in the other world. This is given heavier emphasis at the stilling of the storm in 4:35-41. The disciples conclude 'who is this that even the wind and the sea obey him?' Heavier emphasis is given to Jesus' authority over the world of the spirits, when we see the Healing of the Gerasene Demoniac in 5:1-20. Here we have someone who in our times, would have been classed as severely schizophrenic and consigned to a padded cell. As Jesus casts out the evil spirit, people are deeply frightened and totally amazed.

An indication of how this works comes in Mark 5: 25-43. A woman with a hemorrhage sneaks up to him in the crowd and touches his garment. Immediately she realises that she is healed. Jesus senses that the power has gone out of him and wants to know who touched him. This miracle is tied in with the raising of Jairus' daughter. The indication is that Jesus possessed some kind of numinous spiritual power which is not normally seen in most people. Clearly, this kind of ability is not the sort of thing that can be subjected to scientific analysis. It is not as if one can observe it, quantify it and analyse it by peering down a test tube. But there is no reason to be sceptical about this factor.

The essential element of faith is emphasised in the epileptic boy in Mark 9:14-22. The disciples try to heal him but fail. Jesus does heal him, and comes out with the seminal remark, 'all things are possible to him who believes.' It is noted that Jesus did not succeed in healing some people in Nazareth, his home town, because his own people did not accept him. 'He marvelled at their unbelief' is Mark's comment. We can marvel at their unbelief now. My comment is that if this carpenter from Nazareth really is the full and complete representative of the Eternal God, one would expect him to do something quite out of the ordinary. Many of the miracles are not just purely and simply done to heal people; they are done to epitomise the spiritual power that Jesus had. Also they indicate his acceptance of Samaritans and Gentiles, again something which annoyed the strict Jews exceedingly.

More information about the miracles of Jesus can be found in the Apocryphal Gospels. These were not included in the New Testament, and on reading them, we can guess why. They are not taken very seriously nowadays, any more than they were in the days of the early Church. Here we see an element of exaggeration, almost to the point of the ridiculous. For instance, Jesus is described as working in the carpenters' shop, and on finding a piece of wood that was too short, pulled on it and made it longer. As a child, he made birds out of clay, and then ordered them to fly away. Admittedly we know very little of the childhood and adolescence of Jesus, but these gospels make an attempt at filling in some details. How reliable these claims are, is open to debate, but they have never been, and never will be, accepted as canonical.

We can see how the Gospel writers are at pains to give us the truth about Jesus of Nazareth. St. Luke begins his gospel thus; '...those who from the beginning were eyewitnesses... to write an orderly account, that you may know the truth.....' (Luke 1:1-3). Also whoever gave us the postscript to the Fourth Gospel tries to impress on us the truth of his record. 'This is the disciple who is bearing witness to these things, and who has written these things; and we know that his testimony is true." (John 21:24). Why do we have to disagree with this? How else would they have managed to impress on us the truth about Jesus of Nazareth?

What we need to appreciate is that the element of symbolism is at work, especially in St. John, but not absent from the Synoptics. This is particularly noteworthy with the blasting of the fig tree recorded in Matthew 21:19. In this context, the fig tree withers away 'at once'. However, in the same situation in Mark 11:11-20, the fig tree is seen to have withered rather more gradually, possibly overnight. In Luke 13:6, the incident is turned into a parable which reflects the three year ministry of Jesus. The fig tree is symbolic of the Jewish people, who are refusing to accept his ministry, and therefore, they are doomed to destruction. The incident also has its mythological overtones. The world tree is a constant theme in world mythology, and the fig tree is not just a symbol for the Jewish race, but also for the connection between heaven, earth and the underworld. The suggestion is that as the tree withers, Jesus himself becomes the genuine and eternal connection between the three zones of the universe.

What this means is that with many, if not all, of the miracles, there is the symbolic element and also the overtones from mythological truth. They are speaking to us on a theological and mythological level. Science does not really come into it, except to say that the 'rationalists' will try to deny that these miracles ever happened. They are likely to say that the miraculous goes against the Laws of Nature. But do we know all the Laws of Nature? Constantly we are discovering more of the Laws of Nature. One important finding, with regard to the Quantum world, is that there are areas that function on a different system of logic compared with our own. It is arrogant to claim that everything has to conform to what we know about life at the obvious, day-to-day level.

With regard to miracles in today's world, there is much that can be said about spiritual healing. I have already mentioned such people as Harry Edwards, Christopher Woodward and Russell Parker. There are probably many more who do not appear as sensationalised in the media. Why is that? I would suggest that this materialistic society finds it very difficult to cope with such matters, since it goes against all their preconceived ideas about rationality. This is in spite of such phenomena as Lourdes in Southern France, where healings are regularly recorded in conjunction with the spa waters in the grotto.

One notable example which appeared in the late 1960's was the case of Linda Martel. No less a person than Charles Graves went to a lot of time and care to research this matter. It was a little girl born in Guernsey. She was a spina bifida case and was not expected to survive for long. However, it became apparent that she had powers of spiritual healing and also diagnostic abilities. She had visions of the Virgin Mary and of Jesus. It would be easy to be scornful and say that she was being raised as a Roman Catholic, but that was not true. I have yet to find a doubter who can talk his way out of this example. The book, by Charles Graves, The Legend of Linda Martel, gives us details of people being healed. This can hardly be called a 'legend'; more likely well authenticated facts.

In addition to this, on a personal level, I can say that I myself have had experience of spiritual healing, and of such healers. I have no doubt that it is a reality, and those who pour scorn on it are not facing up to the evidence. It is all very well to talk of rationality, but we should be aware that human rationality is only one system of logic available. This system works well with scientific investigation, but even then, it does not always quite work. Obviously faith, and numinous spiritual energy have much to do with it, but these are matters that are not quantifiable in the terms of science at the moment. It may be that in the future, we may devise ways of finding an explanation for such things, but as yet, our science falls short of such analysis. Also attempts are rationalising the miracles are seen to be clumsy, inept and in some cases, plain wrong.

One could maintain that the healing miracles stand to reason, as described in the Gospels, and also with Linda Martel. Why stop at that?

If someone with massive spiritual power can cure what may seem to be incurable conditions, why can he not perform natural world wonders? This does not mean that I am antagonistic towards Science; far from it. I believe we should be investigating the natural world in order to make improvements in our lives. But I have little time for the hardened doubter who will not even give the slightest consideration to the reality of the world of the spirit, and that certain people, probably a very few, are gifted with numinous spiritual power.

## Footnotes

1. Simon Magus, described in J.Stevenson, *A New Eusebius*. It is Jerome who claims that Bar Kochba stuck lighted straws in his mouth.
2. Bar Kochba, is described in Yigael Yadin, *Bar Kochba*.
3. The Kitab-i-Aqdas is described in detail in *The Theology of Truth*; the beliefs of the Baha'is.
4. The Book of Mormon is analysed in The Theology of Truth.
5. Martin Luther's Ninety five theses are described in James Atkinson, *Martin Luther and the birth of Protestantism*.
6. Suttee was when a widow was expected to climb on to her husband's funeral pyre.
7. Ian Wilson, *The After Death Experience*.
8. Lytton Strachey in Queen Victoria describes this in chapter 1.
9. Phrenology is described in Kaufman and Kaufman, Pseudoscience.
10. Mesmerism is also described in Kaufman and Kaufmanl
11. Mary Baker Eddy's ideas are reviewed in *The Theology of Truth*.

# 20

## *Pandemics and Covid-19*

Only this year we have been confronted with a new challenge to medical science and our whole way of life. In a sense, it is new, in that Covid-19 is a virus not seen before and has taken everyone completely by surprise. On the other hand, it is not new, in the sense that pandemics have occurred before and will doubtless confront us again in the future. We think immediately of the Black Death, the Plague in London (1660's) and more recently the Spanish Flu pandemic of 1918. How or why these infections appear as if out of nowhere, is at the moment beyond us to explain; but they do suddenly appear and then seem to wear themselves out and subside. We all hope that will happen with Covid-19, but how long it will take is anyone's guess.

I will tentatively make a few remarks on the matter of pandemics, but anything that I may say on the subject of the Corona virus may easily be completely out of date in a few day's time. We are all on a steep learning curve with this one and easy answers and dogmatisms are not at all wise. I think the main difference today is that we have a much more sophisticated understanding of contagion and how to control it, than was so in 1918. That having been said, it would seem that we still have lot to learn, as this pandemic appears to be much more virulent and one might go so far as to say 'crafty'.

This Corona Virus is not the only one; it may be some kind of mutation from Corona SARS-CoV2. We have had experience of similar things over the last decade. The Sars epidemic of 2003 (Severe Asian Respiratory Syndrome); also the Mers epidemic of 2012 (Middle East Respiratory Syndrome). Both of these seem to be of short duration. Singapore, having been the worst affected by Sars, was well prepared for Covid-19, and the result has been that they have managed to cope with it more successfully than many other countries.

How is it spread? We do not know exactly how it started in Wuhan, China, but it is thought that it began in a wet market. Even that has been challenged. Having started, it spread rapidly through people being in close contact with each other. Coughing, sneezing, touching, being jostled together in a crowd, just breathing; it would seem that the virus can fly around on the vapour coming from people's breath. It can also survive for two or three days in confined spaces, and also survive on various types of surface such as door knobs, paper, and plastic for up to three days. One can carry the infection without realising it; having no symptoms is no guarantee of being clear of the matter. One carrier could infect hundreds of people without realising it. Also an animal, such as a pet cat or dog could be a carrier and not necessarily exhibit any symptoms (or so it is claimed).

How did it arrive in Britain? It is thought that the virus had arrived at a certain ski resort in Austria, Ischgl, with its Kitzloch Bar. From there it reached Britain, Germany and Denmark. However, with so many jet planes circulating the world, with their air-conditioning systems, this too could account for the virus spreading so rapidly. After all, if the virus can survive on tiny droplets of moisture in the air, a whole planeload of people could be at risk. It has become quite clear that isolation is the most effective way of avoiding the infection. Wearing gloves and face-masks are basic precautions, but the best way is to keep one's distance.

What are the symptoms? The symptoms are fever, breathlessness, sore throat, cough, mouth ulcers, nausea, lack of taste or smell. Some of these might be very mild and mistaken for just a common cold or ordinary flu. Those infected in the same household might have different symptoms. One might have the infection and hardly show any signs of it, thus becoming a carrier. On this basis, even with all our precautions, it must be very difficult to avoid catching the virus. For most people in good health, it poses no real threat. However, it is clear that those who have some kind of serious health problem already, the virus does pose a serious threat. In that category are those over 70, or with diabetes, bronchitis, hepatitis, heart disease, Parkinsons, kidney disease, sickle cell anaemia, HIV and on chemotherapy. It has recently been noted that Covid 19 has some kind of relationship to diabetes, and that in turn may have implications for diet. Further research may clarify this.Those with blood group A appear to be more susceptible to the virus, but we have no idea why that should be. Such persons with health problems may not automatically die, but the risk is much greater. Having said that, we are now seeing youngsters with no apparent health problems, dying, but the risk is much less. It would seem that if one's immune system is weak, this leaves one open to serious problems. It is still not clear whether having had Covid-19, one will retain a partial or complete immunity, thus making it unlikely one will contract it again. The immune system in the human body is only partially understood; there is so much more to learn, and it is exceedingly complex. In addition to this, we still have to discover whether Covid-19 is seasonal, by which we mean, does the warmer weather and longer daylight hours diminish it, as with other types of flu?

Finding a cure for Covid-19 is a long way off. All we are doing (as with many other conditions) is just coping with symptoms. Many sufferers are helped by application of oxygen, but that may not be available for every case. One ray of hope can be learned from the Pandemic of 1918. They discovered that if the blood of a recovered patient is injected into a sufferer, it has the effect of boosting the immune system; the antibodies are encouraged. We are a long way off developing a vaccine for Covid-19, although there have been promises of a vaccine by October 2020. Other flu viruses have a habit of mutating, so that they reappear later in another permutation which can sidestep the vaccine; so far, this does not seem to apply to Covid 19. At the moment (Summer 2020) the Oxford scientists are working frantically to devise a vaccine, and trying out various drugs which are used for severe asthma, pulmonary disease, inflammation (of lungs), antimalarial drugs. Even if a successful drug is developed, it may take some time to make it widely available.

What all this means is that we are all at risk to some extent and should all take precautions. For all our advanced ideas in health care and medical expertise, we have been taken by surprise by this new monster and it is a race against time to devise preventive measures.

The positive side to all this is that we are now discovering or learning more about contagion and how to take preventive measures. We are seeing just how persistent and virulent a virus can be. Taking account of the recent outbreak of Foot and Mouth coming from South Africa, it became clear that the infection could actually blow on the wind, which meant that not only had ones own cattle to be slaughtered, but ones neighbours' on the next farm. Clearly, we cannot employ methods like that to stop Covid-19; we cannot just shoot humans to stamp out the infection! But drastic measures may still have to come into force, such as more thorough lock-downs.

Another positive aspect of this is that people are being seen to be far more neighbourly than before. Old people stranded at home have neighbours doing shopping for them. This mood has been seen right across the world, with many countries cooperating with each other in the fight against the virus. It would be wonderful if this policy of cooperation could continue into the future! Sadly, however, a crisis like this also brings out the worst in some people. There are those who ignore government instructions, resort to violence and vandalism, and attacks on the police. In addition, there are the inevitable collection of 'experts' who are wise after the event; this is a particularly childish approach.

Yet another positive factor to be noticed is that during the lockdown, with the severe reduction in road and air traffic, there is much less atmospheric pollution. We may expect that this could have implications for global warming, or rather, conversely, global cooling, an issue which is of acute concern at the moment.

What are the theological aspects of this situation? In the Bible, especially the Old Testament, we regularly see the three major fears that terrified people; the threat of war, famine and plague. This is heavily emphasised in Jeremiah,(14:12 et al), and Ezekiel adds a fourth element, that of wild beasts. (Ezekiel 14:19) We do not have to worry too much about wild beasts, unless one lives in lion country in Africa. Mind you, there is some fear that the Corona found on some animals (for instance, bats) could transfer itself to humans. But the threat of war nowadays does have everyone terrified, given the weaponry now available. The lesson we learnt in 1945 was that all-out world conflicts between major Empires was total folly. Admittedly there have been minor outbreaks of violence in specific parts of the world, but in general terms, with the United Nations, the mood is heavily in favour of world peace. Long may it last.

As far as famine is concerned, we do have this problem in many third world countries, and it is thought to stem from global warming. In response to this, we now have many countries adopting policies to reduce wastage, emission of greenhouse gases and careful usage of resources. In addition, there are many strategies for international aid for those starving in countries where the climate has ruined the productivity of the land.

As far as pandemics are concerned, whether one calls it a 'plague' or a 'pestilence', the causes, on a physical level, are less obvious. Even if we can see that Covid-19 has developed out of another Corona virus, we still do not know why, or what was the reason for it originating in Wuhan (if that is the truth). Suddenly, like the Assyrian army outside Jerusalem in 701 BC, we are confronted with a monster that takes all our ingenuity to cope with. What is this telling us? That it is no use being complacent about life; we survive by the grace of God. Like skating on thin ice, our cosy, self-satisfied life can suddenly all crash in disarray. The fragility of life is something we should all bear in mind; it has been said that this pandemic is likely to change life completely. Scientific analysis can only go so far in explaining these matters; the underlying reason must be sought at the theological level.

So often in the Bible, War, Famine and Plague are understood to originate from God who is punishing some kind of wickedness. The Plagues of Egypt (in Exodus) are a case in point. But the lesson to be learnt from that is that they need never have happened if Pharaoh had been prepared to listen to the message from God as given by Moses and Aaron. It was Pharaoh's obstinacy that precipitated these disasters. The same is seen to be largely true in other situations where disasters overtook people. It is not a comfortable thought, to assume that God is punishing us with these disasters, but it is far more palatable to see that we bring these disasters upon ourselves through our own stupidity.

As far as warfare is concerned, God is telling us to grow up and stop behaving like hooligans. There is no need for any armed conflict. As Churchill said, 'it is better to jaw-jaw than to war-war'. In other words, all these political disagreements can and should be settled up peacefully with a sensible conversation. As far as famine is concerned, this too can be ameliorated by policies of cooperation, international aid, and improved methods of farming. All the resources to achieve this are with us; it is only laziness and selfishness that cause delays, while people starve on the streets.

As far as plague is concerned we are up against forces which are not so obviously under our control. We could begin by thinking in terms of improved hygiene and avoidance of contagion. An example of that would be the cholera epidemic in London; this need never have happened if there had been a policy of clean water in force. But there is more to it than that, and I would say there is a spiritual side to this.

We can take into account the book of Job in the Bible. Here was someone who was very virtuous and did not deserve to have anything go wrong in his life. But in the spiritual realms there was God and also a fallen angel called Satan. We notice that they are in collusion with each other in spite of the one being good and the other being bad. They agree that Job should be tested; is his loyalty to God purely on the surface and if things go wrong, will he turn into an atheist? We notice that Job's losses are not deserved in any way. None of this is some kind of punishment, which is the alternative understanding from the idea that disasters are God's punishment. But we also notice that the plagues which hit him were not purely of a physical origin; it was of a spiritual source, the powers of evil. As it turned out, he did not succumb to the temptation of cursing God, but remained faithful. In the end he was rewarded for his constancy.

I am aware that in the modern world people have difficulties over the reality of the powers of evil; some have difficulties over the powers of good, ie, God. But I would point out that it is one thing to explain these disasters on a purely physical level combined with the stupidity of the human race, but it is another thing to see these matters on a spiritual level. Let us ask ourselves a few important questions.

Firstly, what is God telling us through these disasters? One might say, why does he not send in a prophet to tell us plainly, someone like Moses or Elijah? But we can see how much notice people take of such a person; they sneer and accuse him of being a dinosauric crank! I would say that God is telling us , through Covid-19, that we can all be far more neighbourly, cooperative and caring, if we just put our minds to it.

Secondly, God is telling us to value life much more than before. We all do value life, but so often we take it for granted. Now is the time to see life as a valuable gift, but a fragile one. It can all fly apart just by the intervention of a tiny little fragment of life called a virus. If we can value life, we can also be thankful for it. So many people have lost the habit of being thankful, on the assumption that nothing can possibly go wrong.

Thirdly, God is saying to us all, but especially the medical scientists, you think you know it all, but you do not. You have a long way to go, and it is urgent that you keep on trying so that the quality of life, especially with regard to health, is improved. If we can learn just one factor from Jesus; he was the great healer, and enemy of bad health and of any evil influences that might be involved. God wants us to have good health, both physical and mental. That can be achieved by hard work, dedication and commitment to improving the human situation.

Fourthly, God is making us wonder what actually is going on at microscopic level, and subatomic level. If it is true that a tiny entity like a photon can have a degree of rationality, or however one terms it, why cannot a virus also have some kind of 'thought'? As we saw with Einstein and the experiments with light, the light quanta or photons did appear to have some kind of logic at work in them. It is a teasing thought that a virus or even a bacterium could also make decisions about whom to attack and how severe the attack might be. This might go some way to explaining why some patients have very mild symptoms (if at all) and yet others are critically ill. Again, it tells us we have still a lot to learn about contagion and immunity.

Fifthly, this period of time called the 'lock-down' reminds me of something axiomatic in the Bible; the element of Sabbath. So far, June 2020, we have had 12 weeks of economic standstill. There is the threat of further lock-downs if there is a 'spike'. To put it another way, the economy, right across the world, has managed to gain a breather. Unfortunately, this breather does not apply to everyone, since we have medical scientists and some manufacturers working flat out to find preventive measures for the pandemic. But in general terms, with the hectic way that life proceeds now in the modern world, the idea of a shut-down is far from people's minds. But the advice from the Bible is different; we should take a breather, and if we do not, God will organise one in spite of everything. After all, as Jeremiah pointed out, the Exile of the Judean Kingdom was God's way of allowing the land to have its Sabbaths, namely seventy years. This is a purely personal thought, but I would suggest, not a trivial one.

These remarks are clearly the way in which I see things. Others may see it differently. One lesson we learn from the chapter on Psychology, is that perception can vary enormously from one person to another. A lot depends on our basic assumptions in life. I personally am heavily influenced by the Bible, and the pattern of thought which involves warfare, famine and plague. I am not completely happy with the thought that God's wrath brings these things about. That is because I have been raised in a liberalistic atmosphere which finds difficulties with God as being angry. But there is no doubt the stupidities of human nature have a lot to do with these three factors that go wrong. Whether that is the total picture, I have my doubts. I am left with the creeping feeling that disasters do have something to do with the world of the spirit, something which is clearly seen in the book of Job. But it may not be God; it may be the unseen powers of evil, something of which I do have an awareness. That is my perception of the matter; yours may be different.

In conclusion, looking at the political aspects of the matter, it is now clear that a sea-change has occurred in the government of the country. This may not yet be seen in some countries, but some, such as Italy and Spain, have been forced into this. It would seem that the Prime Minister has had to assume the role of dictator. Just as the acute crisis of June 1940 required Churchill to assume that role, the same, though in a different mode, has occurred in the early months of 2020. In 1940, it resulted in a National Government, with full cooperation between the ruling party and the opposition. Mr. Attlee was the Deputy Prime Minister for the duration of the War. It looks very much as though something similar will emerge now, with the leader of the opposition giving full support to the government. It would be senseless if the opposition were to attempt to interfere with every instruction given to the public; it would simply confuse matters and destroy their own credibility. In effect, we have a dictatorship, but one which can hardly be avoided when quick and decisive decisions have to be made. We all hope that when normality is resumed (if it ever can) we can return to the normalities of democracy.

It is interesting to see that for all that the Prime Minister is issuing diktats in our best interests, he is not really calling the trumps. It is the scientists who are in fact issuing instructions. It may be dubbed as 'advice' but that is hardly the point. In effect, it is the scientists, mostly of the medical kind, who are ruling us at present. The wisdom of that may be seen in times to come, but we all hope that their 'advice', which is based on somewhat scanty facts, will turn out to be sound. But it has had the effect of closing all the churches (along with just about everything else) and forcing the religionists to see the plethora of church buildings as very largely unnecessary. In short, they can worship together by electronic gadgetry, which is one of the latest developments offered to us by the scientists.

We seem now to be at a sort of crossroads with Covid 19. Will it wear itself out or will there be another outburst as we enter the Winter season? The Daily Telegraph for 30th July, 2020, makes an assessment of how the Pandemic has changed everyone's lives over the last five months; changes which may be with us for a long time. It is interesting that it admits that the scientists are not unanimous in their analysis of the situation, and in fact arguments still rage over it. Another factor, (in that article) which I see as indicative of the modern failure to cope with spiritual matters, is the absence of any comment on a theological level. The nearest we come to it would be the realisation that life is fragile and there are no certainties about the future. The optimism which seems to accompany materialism is now being seen as yet another illusion. There is no mention of God or of the powers of evil; I suppose that would be seen as politically incorrect! Nevertheless, that is the kind of thought that will go through people's minds, inevitably.

As I remarked elsewhere, the relationship between religion and science is a curious one, with all kinds of subtleties and interesting permutations.

# 21

## *Concluding remarks*

Clearly there are many more aspects of Science and Religion that could be explored, but we would probably find that the same picture would emerge. There is no way that Science and Religion are contradictory to one another. In so many ways, they are complementary, interwoven and mutually supportive. This is in spite of the fact that they are talking on two completely different levels of truth. The mistake occurs when the religionists start refusing to face up to the evidence that the scientists have found; vice versa, it is another mistake when the scientists try to tell us that there is no world of the spirit, and that everything is purely a matter of physical realities. There is no need for this kind of disagreement. This brings me to the first major conclusion that I have reached based on the discussion in this book.

My first important conclusion is that we ought to be somewhat less inclined to heavy dogmatisms, whether it be of Science or of Religion. We have just lived through a century in which there have been too many voices taking on an authoritative tone , and telling us all what to think. This includes the great dictators, as well as the lesser dogmatists in religion and science. If we can learn anything from history, it would be that the idea that was all the rage in at one time, suddenly goes out of fashion, only to be replaced by another clever idea. Clearly, there would have been a smattering of truth in whatever doctrine was being forced on people, but to allow it to become the whole truth, and dominate just about every other aspect of life, requires caution. Doubtless I shall be dubbed as a complete crank, but I apply this dictum to the theory of Evolution. I would say that the vast majority of scientists and many religionists now take Evolution as a certainty, and if one tries to argue against it, one is regarded as deranged. There are, however, a small minority of scientists and many religionists who think differently. But let us just remember, that many of the dogmatisms of the past have turned out to be some kind of illusion, or even self-delusion. How do we know that Evolution is not some kind of illusion? I know that the evidence can be offered in such away as to make it appear to be quite convincing, but then the same was true when most people assumed that the earth was flat and was the centre of the universe.

I conclude; let us not be quite so eager to fasten on to some kind of dominating doctrine, or at least, if we do, be prepared to give some thought at least, if an alternative theory should emerge.

My second important conclusion on doing research for this book, has been that it is apparent that circularity is a dominating factor in just about every aspect of life. This applies to the mega-picture of outer space, with planets and stars behaving like gyroscopes, through to earthbound matters such as the water cycle and others, down to the atomic level and even the subatomic level. So many factors are behaving like roundabouts. Is there a reason for this? Is it something to do with maintaining stability? Everything is alive in some respect, from far away galaxies down to tiny protons and photons. This ties in with the Hindu-Buddhist theology, that everything is circular, including human life. It also ties in with Taoist theology, which says that everything in the world is moving, and if it were not, it would be a dead world. How does this relate to Judaeo-Christian thinking, which assumes that history proceeds in a straight line? In a sense, it does, but what we also see in the scriptures is that just as everything has a beginning, so too it has an end, which means that everything comes full circle. The Garden of Eden is restored when we come to the garden in Revelation.

Following on from this, is the factor of balance. In so many ways, we can see that life is some sort of balancing act. It emerges in the health of the human body, which is a constant tussle between health and the invasion of harmful factors. Every atom is alleged to be balanced within itself. Every living thing is thought to have an opposite factor, a sort of mirror image of itself, which results in another kind of balancing act. The Solar System is in balance with itself, with opposing forces of gravity keeping the whole thing operating smoothly. Even the human mind has instinctively an impression of balance, which comes out in such things as justice, fair play, righting of wrongs. We assume that God is the source of all justice, equity and balance. I cannot see how this factor of balance between opposing forces could have installed itself. It requires a superior spiritual force which is not dependent on anything else, to produce a universe which functions fundamentally on the basis of balance. Taking this to its logical conclusion, there has to be an opposing factor to God himself. For the polytheists, there are evil spirits and devils that oppose the good gods. For the Christians, there is Satan, who ultimately was a product of God, but is essential for producing a balanced situation in human life. So the whole of human life is a tug-of-war between good and bad, righteous behaviour and wickedness. It was the Zoroastrians who gave this theology a lot of emphasis. Attempts at saying there is no evil or wrong, remain unconvincing. The whole of life is a balancing act between plus and minus, in so many permutations. If this were not so, say for instance everything were to be plus, there would be no life at all, no progress, no new ideas, no scientific theories, and no theological theories either. It would be like electricity; if there is no minus, then plus has no meaning or force. Both are needed, and the whole of life is sustained by this balancing act; it makes no sense to say that it just installed itself; it has to have been installed by something or someone superior.

The factor of balance comes out in all sorts of ways that we do not always realise. One may have noticed that if one is deficient in one factor in life, something else comes in as compensation. So, for instance, a blind person finds that his other senses, such as touch, hearing and other sensitivities become more acute. This is another aspect of balance. Another example comes from the contrast between the rich and the poor. It may seem unfair that some people are vastly well endowed with money and the power that goes with it, and the poor have to struggle. But the compensation is that the rich have the responsibility, whereas the poor can hardly be held responsible for anything that goes wrong. Often the compensation is not seen in this life. That reminds us of that parable that Jesus told us, about Dives and Lazarus. For all those who are having an easy time of it in this world, the question arises, what will become of them in the next world? The rectification of all inequalities is in God's hands, and the poor, having had a tough time of it in this world, are in line for an easy time in the next world. The factor of balance may also be seen in the concern over global warming. It may be true that the earth is warming up, but is this just another factor in the gyroscopic behaviour of the world? We swing from one ice age to another; one warm spell to another. Is this all a matter of balance and compensation in world climate?

There is nothing wrong with scientific enquiry. It is an instinctive response in human nature, to attempt to explain, in rational observational terms, the world around us. Clearly, a lot of progress has been made in the last few centuries, and I am sure that any honest scientist will admit that there is much more waiting to be discovered in times to come. We may see another Einstein appear, and throw all our theories up in the air and think of something else. It may be that methods may be devised for quantifying the numinous or spiritual aspect of life. The technology that has flowed from science has been put to much good use, making life a lot easier for all of us. However, we all know that destructive and frightening use has been made of certain scientific developments. It is like a hammer; it can be used for a positive purpose, such as driving in nails; it can be used for a destructive purpose, such as committing murder. The key to the situation is the responsible use of everything for the benefit of the human race, rather than causing problems.

This is something that science shares with religion. It too can be used for the benefit of the human race. I am not talking about just one religion. Any religion which encourages love, caring, unity, freedom and a happy relationship with one's god, should be commended. Sadly, history has shown us that religious faith has not always worked in this way. Gross cruelties, hatreds and constriction of the conscience have been perpetrated. Some people would go so far as to say that religion is the primary impulse behind all wars. There is some truth in this, in that each side in any given war has usually claimed that they are on God's side, or rather that God is on their side. This is a convenient way of easing one's conscience over the aggression and loss of life involved. However, I would offer the thought that wars are usually fought with the acquisition of territory and the wealth that goes with it. Religion is drawn into the picture to justify the aggression. It just goes to show that, like the hammer, religion can be used to good purpose, but also can be misused to cause much harm. I maintain that the way to moderate religion (as with science) is to take seriously the life and teachings of Jesus of Nazareth, and that can hold true regardless of any elaborate beliefs or non-beliefs that one may hold.

There are so many ways in which religion and science can interrelate and complement each other. To take just a few examples, all those findings in the field of quantum mechanics simply show us how complex, wonderful and amazing the building blocks of life can be. I find it very difficult to see how these tiny structures could have just occurred all by themselves. Then there is the intriguing way that the natural world functions, with its amazing varieties of flora and fauna, interrelating and supporting each other in so many ways. How could all this come about unless there was a superior spiritual force that devised the whole thing? It brings us back to the issue of proofs for the existence of God; not that these are proofs in the normal sense of the word. However, they will not go away, and persist in reappearing repeatedly albeit in different guises and phraseology. I believe that the reality of God is inescapable, and science needs that assumption, namely the reality of laws of Nature, otherwise it becomes meaningless.

There is still, however a problem. If we assume that science and religion are talking on two different levels or reality, there is no problem. Just describing the workings of the physical world does not have to affect one's religious belief. Unfortunately, history has shown us that religious dogmatists have attempted to interfere with the workings of science, and vice versa the scientists have tried to interfere with people's faith. As we can see above, it is inevitable that the two matters do interrelate, and both have implications for each other. But we should remember that all levels of truth or knowledge interrelate with each other; it cannot be avoided. Music with mathematics, sculpture with geology or metallurgy, history with literature, linguistics with ethics; these are just a few examples. It is artificial to attempt to separate them into isolated boxes. It is absurd to assume that science and religion can just carry on with no reference the one to the other.

The crux of the matter seems to come over those first two chapters in Genesis. There are people who will take those passages totally at face value; you do not have to be a fundamentalist to allow those passages to have a massive influence on one's outlook on life. But we are not looking at a scientific document, still less a sociological analysis or a biological assessment. We are looking at a theological document, and whoever wrote them must have been a theological genius, which has had a massive influence on the faith of Judaism and Christianity, not to say various other belief systems. Those passages are 'real' in the sense that they speak to the very deepest impulses in human nature; wonder, fear, relationship between humans and animals, and the sexes, guilt, work ethic and also hope for the future. It is foolish to allow these passages to be taken as a biological or geological textbook, but unfortunately people do assume something like this. But this, unfortunately has become the crux of the standoff between religion and science in the last century or so.

I maintain that there is no need for this standoff. We can allow the scientists to speculate on geological ages stretching back millions of years. I see no reason to disagree with them on that matter. We can allow them to speculate on evolution, for there are certain aspects of it that hold true, without allowing it to become an all-out fundamentalism of a different kind. I maintain that there are problems with evolution, just as there are with just about every other scientific theory, and that the appearance of life on this earth is nowhere near as straightforward as some would have us believe. But whatever theory one espouses, makes no difference to belief in God the Creator. Whatever methods he used, we still have the same result on our hands nowadays, and the same problems. If we can introduce just one strand of thought from Genesis, which holds true regardless of anybody's theory, it would be this. That God created all things as 'very good' at the start, but sadly, along came the human race, interfered with this wonderful work, and so everything is a lot less than 'very good'. Let's just look ourselves in the mirror before we try to make out that God is careless, unjust, cruel or even disinterested.

It would be fair to say that everyone has to have some kind of 'sky-hook'. It is very unusual to find someone who has absolutely no theory of life and its meaning; that would be the true atheism. Nearly everyone has some kind of ISM at the back of their minds, or more likely, at the front of their minds. But that ISM, whatever it may consist of, has to have some kind of justification, rationale, 'proof'. The 'sky-hook' is the thing that we attach our ISMs on to. But what is the sky-hook attached to? It is something out of sight, but real enough for those who wish it to be real. Every theory of life, whether it be theological, or political, or just plain secular, has to find some kind of reasoning; if it did not it would hardly be any use as a theory of life. For the Monotheists, the sky-hook is the One God; for the polytheists, it is the god that one believes is helpful to one; for the Chinese, it would be the Jade Emperor (it was Chairman Mao at one time, but he seems to have slipped a little); for the Japanese it would be the Mikado, descended from Amaterasu; for the Nazis it would be those fascinating Nordic myths, plus a few racist additives; for the Italian Fascists, it would be that wonderful old Roman Empire; for the Communists, it would be some kind of Garden of Eden, even if one could not actually call it that; for the logical-positivists it would be human logic, even if that can turn out to be faulty; for the Capitalists, money can become a complete mania in itself, even if we all know it is some kind of illusion; for the Scientists, it would be some kind of logico-observationist approach, with a strong influence from the theory of Evolution. In fact, Evolution has managed to infiltrate virtually every ISM one could find and become a sky-hook for so many people. What a shame it has various problems with it! Nevertheless, we all need some kind of guiding light in our lives; some kind of reasoning which is essentially unprovable and yet is essential for life to have any purpose. If one's sky-hook is attached to something out of sight (in the sky) then it can hardly be shot down, or to put it another way, it cannot be disproved. The human mind needs something to hold on to, some kind of certainty in an uncertain world.

I would maintain, (and this is my parting shot) that the Christians, regardless of whatever permutation they have on traditional doctrines, are at an advantage in respect of all these other ISMs. They not only have a sky-hook, namely God the Father, but also an 'earth-hook', namely Jesus of Nazareth. The two hooks are inseparable; the one divine, the other human. One can fasten on to Jesus as a real, historical figure and form one's life on what he came to show us. I am quite aware that some would say he never existed, but I feel that that idea is not good enough. We have plenty of evidence in the New Testament and in the Early Church that such a stunning person did appear and made a massive impact on the course of human history. In the end it comes down to a matter of faith. All these other ISMs require some kind of faith in that 'sky-hook'; some would go further and talk of certainty. But in a world where so many things are far from being a certainty and there are so many contrary opinions circulating, in the end it comes down to making a choice which is going to cause the least amount of problems for us all. I maintain that the life and message of Jesus of Nazareth is the message we all need to take on board, regardless of how real he is historically, or not, as the case may be, and also regardless of whatever other ISM one might attach oneself to. If life is about love, caring, giving, helping, then that is the core of values that we all need.

Science has its place; so too does religion. It is folly to assume that they are a contradiction of each other. They can both cooperate with each other; in many ways they are intertwined and inseparable. In spite of all the dogmatisms that press down on us, let us always keep an element of open-mindedness which allows us to consider all the evidence and all the factors in the picture. A closed mind is a dead mind. Let us open up to all those new findings in Science, but also open up to God, the ultimate criterion of all things.

# Index

# Bibliography.

Akurgal, E. Ancient civilizations and ruins in Turkey.

Atkinson, J. Martin Luther and the birth of Protestantism.

Bettenson, Documents of the Christian Church.

Carey, N. Hacking the code of life.

Cheatham, J. Nostradamus.

Chown, M. The Ascent of Gravity.

Collins, F. The language of God.

Coogan, M. Ancient Near Eastern Texts.

Darwin, C. The origin of species.

Doudna, J. and Sternberg, A crack in creation.

Easwaran, E. Bhagavad Gita.

Eysenk and Law, The Paranormal.

Hames and Hooper, Biochemistry.

Hard, R. Constellation Myths.

Hawking, S. A brief history of Time.

Herodotus, The Loeb Library

Hick, J. Proofs for the existence of God.

Holy Kojiki, Cosimo.

Hua-Ching Ni, Complete works of Lao Tzu.

Inyat and Babbit, The Jataka Stories.

Kaufman and Kaufman, Pseudo Science.

Kenyon, K. Archaeology in the Holy Land.

Mead, G.R.S. Corpus Hermeticum.

Moneta, G.B. Positive Psychology.

Montesquieu, C. Spirit of the laws.

Moorey, T. Understand Chinese mythology.

Ramakrishnan, V. The gene machine.

Richards, E.G. Mapping Time.

Ridpath, I. Astronomy.

Rogers, B. Perception.

Spenser, E. The Fairie Queen.

Stevenson, J. New Eusebius.

Strachey, L. Queen Victoria.

Sumner, W.A. The Theology of paradox.

Sumner, W.A. The Theology of Truth.

Sumner, W.A. Myth, Legend and Symbolism.

Thomas, W. Documents from Old Testament times.

Thorogood, C. Weird Plants.

Von Daniken, The chariots of the Gods.

Weatherall, D. The quiet art.

Wilson, I. The after death experience.

Wilson, The Turin shroud.

Yadin, Y. Bar Kochba.